Encounters for Change

Encounters for Change

Interreligious Cooperation in the Care of Individuals and Communities

DAGMAR GREFE

WIPF & STOCK · Eugene, Oregon

ENCOUNTERS FOR CHANGE
Interreligious Cooperation in the Care of Individuals and Communities

Wipf & Stock
An Imprint of Wipf and Stock Publishers
199 W. 8th Ave., Suite 3
Eugene, OR 97401
www.wipfandstock.com

ISBN 13: 978-1-60899-521-9

Manufactured in the U.S.A.

To Julie C. Porter

Contents

List of Tables and Figures

Foreword

A MAJOR THEME IN any analysis of the cultural and religious landscape of contemporary America is the dramatic growth in religious
diversity since the Immigration and Nationality Act of 1965. There is
no doubt that this has led to increased contact and cooperation among
people of different faiths; but, as sociologist Robert Wuthnow points out,
even many of those who give lip service to the value of religious diversity
still regard religions other than their own as somewhat backward, close-
minded, and conducive to violence. Still others have reacted to this new
diversity with fear, asserting their own religious identity over against
these neighbors of another faith (especially, in this era, Muslims) and
perpetuating stereotypes about them.

At the National Council of Churches, where I serve as general secretary, much of our agenda involves interfaith partners. For one thing,
the issues of the day—poverty and unemployment, lingering racism, destruction of the environment, widespread warfare—are too big for any
one religious community. If it is God's mission (not just the church's) to
heal such brokenness, then surely it is appropriate to engage in it with
like-minded partners from other religions. For another, the command-
ment to love the neighbor calls us, to take the most obvious example,
to stand with Muslims at a time when some in this country threaten to
burn the Qur'an, oppose the building of mosques, or associate the label
"terrorist" with the entire Muslim community. It is Christian faith, as
well as concern for the common good, that lead us to undertake dialogues with persons whose faith is unlike our own.

The problem, however, is that much of this work doesn't reach local
congregations; and the dialogues are generally carried out by "experts"—
national religious leaders—whose theological background means that
they approach dialogue primarily as an encounter of beliefs.

And that is why this book by Dagmar Grefe is so timely and important. Grefe begins from the premise that when persons of different faiths

meet in local settings, sometimes in moments of personal crisis, they bring not only their beliefs but their cultural heritage, their histories, their anxieties, their religiously shaped identity and sense of belonging. And in order to understand this complexity better, she invites us to look at interfaith engagement not only theologically but through the lens of social psychology.

Unlike much literature on this subject, this book is highly practical. Grefe argues that religious communities—local ones—are well positioned to set up small contact groups, and then she shows us why and how such groups can build relationship, even friendship, promote cooperation, and "unmake prejudice." Her approach helps us recognize that interfaith relations involve emotional and behavioral dimensions of our lives, not just cognitive ones. She draws on recent research in social psychology to show how minds get changed and perceptions altered as we develop personalized knowledge of the other, come to appreciate similarities and differences, and begin to see ourselves as part of the same larger group. To put it another way, education about the other, while important, is not enough. It is not just that changed thinking leads to changed behavior; changed behavior can alter the way we think about ourselves and our neighbors.

Throughout the book, Dr. Grefe uses examples from her rich personal experience, but especially so in the two chapters that speak directly to chaplains, counselors, and clinical pastoral education supervisors. She argues that crisis intervention must include connecting people to the resources and practices of their own religious communities—and gives guidance on how his might be done.

There is real wisdom in the practicality—and modesty—of Grefe's argument. Intergroup contact theory, she insists, can be an important, and previously overlooked, tool for fostering interreligious relations—but it should be seen as one tool among many. Cooperative action, because it doesn't threaten one's religious identity, can be a valuable entry point for persons who have been wary of interfaith engagement—but there is much to discover beyond cooperation. There are places where her argument may seem like good, old common sense! But even there, Grefe defines terms and frames the discussion in very useful ways.

At the end of the book, I found that I was left with several difficult questions. Grefe emphasizes the importance of appreciating differences; but aren't there some religious teachings and practices that should not be affirmed? After all, as she points out, religion can foster prejudice and conflict as well as counter them. How do we determine when to say no to the words and actions of neighbors of another faith precisely for the sake of interfaith relations? In the same way, Grefe has a wonderful, infectious confidence that familiarity with the other will breed respect; but is this always the case? Aren't there times when small groups and attempts at cooperation can drive people apart?

Such questions, however, are but the sign of a provocative book— one that should be a great value to people of faith in various local settings.

Rev. Michael Kinnamon, PhD, general secretary
National Council of the Churches of Christ in the USA

Acknowledgments

I AM GRATEFUL TO many persons whom I have encountered in my pastoral work as a chaplain, pastor, and supervisor of the Association of Clinical Pastoral Education, Inc.: patients, families, members of interdisciplinary health-care teams, parishioners, students, and colleagues. They have allowed me to share important moments in their lives, taught me, given me new insights and challenged me to learn and grow. My experiences in working with them have inspired this book and are captured in vignettes and case examples throughout the text. I have changed names, circumstances, and details about the situations I describe in order to protect the privacy of the persons involved.

Among the many who deserve public thanks, I mention a few: Alexei Smith, Mark Diamond, and Jeffrey Utter have shared their rich experiences in interreligious work and have allowed me to include my interviews with them in chapter 5. Thank you to Alex Lau for contributing his reflections on a learning project in medical school. A special thank you to Jackson Kytle for cheering me on and giving me constructive feedback of my work in this book, to Ulrike Guthrie for her encouragement, coaching, and editing, and to Kristin Firth for carefully editing the final manuscript. A number of colleagues have read drafts and provided feedback. Thank you to Jim Corrigan, Christie Mossman, Janie Ito, Bryan Ferry, Tina Gauthier, and Sarah Badran. Thank you to Rolando Gomez for assistance in formatting illustrations, to Suzanne Taylor for support and flexibility, and to the staff at Wipf and Stock. I am appreciative of the following organizations who have provided a stimulating learning environment and assistance: Children's Hospital of Los Angeles, Healthcare Chaplaincy in New York, the Templeton Foundation, Claremont School of Theology, and the Association of Clinical Pastoral Education, Inc. I am deeply grateful to Julie Porter for her patience and support.

Introduction

IN HIS BOOK *BEYOND Tolerance* religion reporter and professor for religion and media Gustav Niebuhr tells a powerful story: A few months after 9/11 some adolescents set fire to a Sikh house of worship in upstate New York. Because Sikh males wear a turban to bind their hair the young people thought they were Muslims, and the local Sikh community found itself caught up in the post-9/11 backlash against the Muslim community. The story does not end here. Mark Lichtenstein, the local school board president of the town where the Sikh house of worship was located, not only facilitated connections between the schools and the Sikh community leaders and was there when they forgave the arsonists, he also educated the community about the Sikh faith, and he traveled to India to offer an apology to the partner community for what had happened in his town.

Niebuhr comments: "It's easy to find labels for the arson incident. It might be called a hate crime, or at the very least, an act of intolerance, of a particular virulent kind. But how do we label its spiritual opposite—the work of deliberately constructive relations between groups?"[1]

This book seeks to spell out the spiritual practice of developing relationships between communities and individuals of different religious groups. I believe that cooperation is a pathway to such constructive relationships. The main idea of this book is that cooperation between people and communities of different faiths is much needed and is possible if approached intentionally. When people of different faiths work together, they not only care for the larger community and each other, they also heal their distant and strained relationships. The following chapters paint a picture of what interreligious cooperation might look like—in local communities and in the care of individuals in crisis.

The book is primarily written for religious and community leaders of different faiths, for chaplains, pastoral counselors, spiritual directors,

---

1. Niebuhr, *Beyond Tolerance*, 36–38.

theological educators, as well as community members and lay people. One of the lessons I have learned from working with people from diverse social, cultural, and religious backgrounds is that each of us speaks from a particular context. I am writing as a female minister, ordained in the United Church of Christ, born and raised in Germany, and living in the United States. My pastoral experiences in Germany and the United States, in congregational ministry, as a chaplain and supervisor with the Association of Clinical Pastoral Education, Inc., have motivated me to write the book. Cooperating across cultural and religious diversity has been the norm in my pastoral work, as it is increasingly the norm for those who work as congregational clergy, community leaders, chaplains, counselors, and educators. Whether taking first steps in developing a partnership with a local mosque, or supporting a Buddhist family whose loved one was dying, or teaching a group of interfaith clergy in hospital ministry, the encounters have been complex and provided much food for reflection.

At first glance one may think that what keeps religious communities apart from each other are differences in beliefs and religious practices. I have found that these differences only tell part of the story. When people of different religious traditions meet as neighbors, co-workers, or in hospital rooms, they bring their beliefs, but also their cultural heritage, their histories, their perceptions of each other, their interest in the other, and their fears with them. In other words, it is not belief systems but people who encounter each other. For example, as a German, the history of anti-Semitism and the Holocaust make up part of my heritage. I cannot leave that history and the complex feelings connected with it behind when I visit Jewish patients or supervise rabbinical students. It cannot but influence me. This painful history is also a driving force motivating me to search for ways that bring people of different religious communities together and provide an alternative vision to voices of bigotry and isolation. Like interfaith leaders whose voices will be heard in chapter 5, I can say that my encounters with people of other faiths have not only provided questions and challenges. More than that, I have received many gifts. The connections and friendships that I enjoy with colleagues of different religious traditions have been incredibly enriching and encouraging, showing me possibilities of interreligious connections.

German practical theologian Ernst Lange's ideas have inspired my approach to investigating the nature of and possibilities of interreligious encounters. About forty years ago, he wrote about the ecumenical movement, which faced not so much differences of diverse religions but of diverse cultural, geographical, and social contexts. He felt that it was not just theological factors but also nontheological factors that were at play in the relationships of churches: group dynamics, anxiety in intercultural and international discussions, and prejudice, to name only a few. He proposed that ecumenical theology needed to be an interdisciplinary exercise, addressing theological and nontheological factors and involving the human and social sciences.[2] His assessment rings true for interreligious work as well. The majority of intentional interreligious work is done at the level of academia and religious leadership. It has yet to become more relevant at the community level, helping our local communities, institutions, and individuals to constructively engage the religious diversity of our society. To engage in interfaith work at a grass roots level we need to understand not just different beliefs but also the social and relational dynamics between people of different religious communities. To facilitate interreligious connections, we need to prepare the ground and be intentional about how to support these encounters.

This book is an interdisciplinary exploration of contact between people of different faiths. I weave together theological considerations and insights from social psychology, especially from the field of intergroup relations. Social psychology provides us with analytical tools to understand the complicated, conflict-laden, and, yes, also often enjoyable and enriching relationships between people of different cultures and faiths. For decades the field of social psychology has developed and tested approaches that bring diverse people together and, in that process, reduce stereotypes and conflict. I tap into this rich resource, developing tools for use by interfaith clergy, community leaders, counselors, institutional chaplains, and educators who meet diverse people and who want to be proactive in bringing them together. There is much promise in applying theories of intergroup relations to religious conflict and the reduction of bias. This book is a first step in raising these themes, exploring them in conversation, and experimenting with them in community religious work, spiritual care, and clinical supervision.

Chapter 1 portrays the context of religious pluralism. Concepts from sociology and cultural anthropology help clarify the role of religion in the global village. Because different religious and cultural groups are

2. Lange, "And Yet It Moves," 125f.

closer than ever and because together we face difficult political, social, and environmental problems, it is urgent for religious communities to work together to care for the local and global community.

To help ourselves and our communities engage the religiously other, we need to start where we are. Chapter 2 explores what keeps people of different religious traditions apart. Theories of social identity, bias, stereotypes, and fears aid in understanding why it is difficult for people to reach across borders and where we have to begin our work.

Chapter 3 examines the relationship of religion and prejudice. Introducing intergroup contact theory, it delineates under which conditions the contact between different groups can result in the reduction of bias. Bringing different religious groups together to cooperate in service to the community approaches interreligious relationships implicitly rather than explicitly. In the process of extended, cooperative, and informal contact, people of different groups get to know each other as persons. This approach seems particularly appropriate for interreligious contact at a grassroots level. In intergroup contact, our categories and perceptions of the other change.

Chapter 4 lays out concrete strategies and tools that can be used in encounters of religiously diverse groups, in cooperative service projects or contexts of interreligious learning. I explore how contact between different religious groups can transform the way we think, feel, and behave toward the other.

Chapter 5 connects the concepts of the previous chapters with interfaith cooperation that is already underway. The chapter gives voice to interfaith activists. I have interviewed interfaith leaders in Los Angeles and report several examples from the growing literature on interfaith encounters across the United States. I extract common themes and summarize what can be learned from these different experiences.

Chapter 6 explores the interpersonal and intercultural dynamics at work in the care for individuals. The work of chaplains and counselors in public settings, such as hospitals, prisons, and college campuses reaches across cultures, denominations, and faiths. The chapter articulates issues and opportunities of interreligious spiritual care.

Just as the work of spiritual care and counseling is increasingly interreligious in nature, so is its preparation and supervision. Chapter 7 describes the clinical supervision of pastoral work as a setting for interreligious learning. It delineates considerations for supervisors and educators when designing a curriculum, establishing a working alliance, and facilitating a supervision group in an interfaith context.

In the opening paragraph of this introduction, leaning on Niebuhr's statement, I called developing constructive relationships between different religious groups a spiritual practice. Chapter 8 explains why I see interreligious cooperation as a practice of my Christian faith. In this chapter I look at interreligious encounters through a theological lens. I can only do that from my own Christian faith tradition. After a brief overview of how Christians have understood their relationships with people of other religious paths, I propose my own relational-ethical approach to interreligious dialogue and cooperation. While my own perspective as a Christian minister clearly shapes the book, I believe that chapters 1 through 7 can be useful for religious leaders and community members of diverse faiths. As we bring our own tradition to the table when we meet each other as people of different faiths, it would be impossible and unhelpful to try to leave my Christian faith outside this book. I hope my reflections encourage readers of the Christian and non-Christian traditions to articulate their own theological or spiritual approach to cooperative relationships between people of different faiths.

1

"I See Your Mosque from my Church Steeple"

Religion in the Global Village

T HE BOARD OF AN inner city Protestant congregation in Germany is discussing a proposal from some church members to raise funds to place a large cross on the outside wall of their church building. The board members feel that the modern design provides a low profile and a cross on the outside wall would identify the building more clearly as a church. Other board members prefer raising funds for programming rather than for a costly, large symbol. A heated discussion begins. The proponents of the new cross report that numerous church members are bothered by the recently initiated Arabic language public call to prayer, "athan," at the local mosque a block away from the church. Church members feel as if foreigners are infiltrating their neighborhood. Sounds of a strange language from a different culture that are signs of devotion to another religion practiced right down the street seem so much louder to their ears than the bells of their church steeple. In response, some board members feel the need to express their own faith identification more assertively. They see the placement of a large cross on the wall next to the main street as a step in that direction.

The congregation is located in a relatively poor urban neighborhood inhabited by German and migrant families from different parts of Europe, North Africa, and Turkey. Integration has been difficult and, for the most part, German citizens and migrants live in the same part of town but do not know much about each other. Aside from German citizens moving out of the neighborhood, secularization has also contributed to a steep decline in church membership.

On the surface, the discussion about a new cross seems to be one of different beliefs and practices and their symbolic expressions. A different religious tradition has made its presence known through the call to prayer. The church feels compelled to express its presence outwardly through a religious symbol that identifies it clearly. Is the need to assert one's own identity in the face of these changes a sign of fear of losing that identity? The coexistence of different religious traditions in close proximity can cause feelings of insecurity; it points out that the belief system of the predominant culture is no longer the only existing and valid one.

Consider a second pastoral situation, this time in a public health-care setting in the United States. A large, secular urban medical center is undergoing renovation. The executive leadership has recognized the need to accommodate spiritual needs of patients and families in times of crises and has approved space for an interfaith meditation room. The spiritual care advisory board, comprised of interdisciplinary staff and community members, has the task of developing a space that meets the needs of its diverse population. Here is part of the discussion:

Chaplain: With the new building I think we should move away from the concept of the traditional chapel we have currently. A space with pews and stained glass has too many Christian connotations. It just does not reflect the diversity of patients and staff we have in our institution.

Social Worker: I have seen a number of hospitals creating their meditation rooms as a neutral space. They use nature scenery as art and sometimes put a water fountain in the center. It's just a quiet space.

Nurse: Could we offer our weekly mass in such a space?

Roman Catholic priest: We could get portable religious symbols and chairs that we get out for Sunday Mass. However, I think a space without specific symbols would be pretty meaningless for our many Latino Catholic patients. The image of our Lady of Guadalupe is so important and comforting to them.

Interpreter: For some of our Buddhist patients Quan Yin, the Goddess of Mercy, is a helpful identification figure as well.

Physician: Many of my fellow Muslims might be uncomfortable praying in a space with icons.

Rabbi (community representative): Jews, too, might have trouble in a space with specific symbols such as Mary or the cross.

Roman Catholic priest: I understand. I'm just saying that all the Catholic patients who come to the chapel now will not come if there is no symbol. It would be meaningless to them. How about building a chapel and a neutral meditation room?

Hospital Administrator: You mean you can't get all the religions under one roof? For heaven's sake! I can tell you right now, space is an expensive commodity in this city. We can be glad that a new meditation room has been approved. We can't build two, that's for sure.

Chaplain: It looks like we're faced with the difficulty of creating a space that will meet very different needs of very different people. In a crisis, people need to be able to connect with something familiar, which means images for some, no images for others. The space also needs to indicate directions for prayer toward Mecca and Jerusalem and provide a simple quiet space for different groups of people. I wonder if we can come up with a design that incorporates the particular needs and still is a common place for all people. I think we should talk to a designer and try. What do you think?

Hospital Administrator: Fine with me, as long as you stick with one room.

Some board members feel that the diverse spiritual needs of patients, families, and staff can be best addressed by a generic design based on a common denominator among different religious traditions. Others think that a neutral space cannot really accommodate the various spiritual needs of the population. The difficulty of designing an inclusive religious space of meditation and reflection in a diverse urban setting is indicative of larger questions. Religions express particular beliefs that are different from each other. Are religious traditions so different that there is no or little common ground? Is there a way to address universal and particular expressions of faith?

Both scenarios raise the question of how religious communities and leaders can relate to the growing religious diversity in our society. Not only in large urban areas but also in midsize towns throughout the United States, the cityscape has become multicultural. Storefront signs in different languages, restaurants and grocery stores with ethnic specialty foods mark diverse cultural influences in urban neighborhoods. Next to churches are synagogues, mosques, Hindu temples, and meditation centers for practitioners of Eastern religions. New waves of immigration have brought more adherents of non-Christian religions to the United States. Europe has experienced increased immigration from former colonies, North Africa, and the Middle East. In this chapter I explore religious diversity in the larger context of globalization. I describe some main features of the global village and how we experience it in our local communities. Then I take a closer look at how we can understand and engage the cultural and religious diversity in our pastoral work.

THE GLOBAL VILLAGE

With a click of my computer mouse I can go to places far away. I type my destination, let's say Nairobi, into Google Earth. The globe on my computer screen turns slowly and brings the city into focus. I can zoom in as if I were flying over the city. I can see the local landscape, streets, rows of houses, and landmarks. I can change perspectives as if I were standing right in the city. Granted, this virtual trip does not allow me to walk the streets, smell the smells, hear the sounds, or talk with people living there. But it does bring the world closer to my fingertips. Social networking and video-conferencing allow us to stay in touch with family and friends far away. Electronic trading enables business transactions to occur instantly and around the clock. Events from anywhere in the world make it onto our home TV and computer screens within minutes of happening. Information and communication technologies have revolutionized how we experience the world. This large planet with an ever expanding population of seven billion–plus people is shrinking in the sense that we speak of the world as a global village. Information and communication technology, international travel and trade are the main drivers of globalization, but it has more dimensions. There is no consensus as to how exactly to define it or when it began.[1] In the following section I briefly address a few aspects of the global village.

The word "globalization" brings to mind economic development. Since the fall of socialist systems in the late 1980s, free market capitalism has been the prevailing economic system in the world. International trade has grown quickly with a focus on export and consumption. Capital

---

1. Nederveen Pieterse, *Globalization and Culture*, 8, 17f.

moves freely, and the production and trade of goods are handled more flexibly, supported by trends of economic deregulation.[2] Globally, wealth and income is distributed extremely unequally. The economic benefits of globalization are concentrated in North America, Europe, and Asia. In the southern hemisphere as well as within individual societies divisions are widening and the gap between the rich and the poor is growing.[3]

In the face of financial crises governments have reduced spending. The role of states in the global economy is changing.[4] The configuration of states is also undergoing change. Nation states have formed larger regional alliances, such as the European Union. The cold war geopolitical model of "First World" (capitalist West), "Second World" (communist-socialist East), and "Third World" (developing countries in Africa, Asia, Latin America) is outdated. The world is multipolar with centers from the West moving increasingly to East Asia and Southeast Asia.

The word "globalization" thus describes the "empirical process of increased economic and political connectivity"; subjectively, we are also more aware of global interdependence.[5] For example, the ecological crisis has made us more mindful of the reliance of all on the earth. The growth of the world population and the emphasis of the global economy on consumerism push the world to the limit of its resources. Climate change and global warming have awakened us to the fact that the fate of the global community is one and the actions of one part of the world impact the whole. Increasingly, small communities and individual citizens expand their personal ethics code, consider their carbon footprint, and opt for sustainable life styles.

Technological innovations have hastened intercultural connections of people, goods, and information. Foods from different parts of the world are readily available in supermarkets. Air travel, information technology, as well as "cultural" goods, such as fashion, foods, music, and films create a large cultural context. Migration to Europe and the United States has brought people of different cultures, traditions, and customs more closely together. For our purposes it suffices to note that globalization shapes much of our experience with multiple technologi-

2. Schreiter, *New Catholicity*, 7; Nederveen Pieterse, *Globalization and Culture*, 9–10.

3. Schreiter, *New Catholicity*, 7; Nederveen Pieterse, *Globalization and Culture*, 13.

4. Nederveen Pieterse, *Globalization and Culture*, 11.

5. Ibid., 16; See also Robertson, *Globalization*, 8.

cal, economic, ecological, sociopolitical, and cultural dimensions. Some sociologists date the beginning of globalization to the second half of the twentieth century. Others see its beginning in the birth of modernity in the fifteenth century when in Europe the theory of the sun as the center of the universe caught on, and an expanded geography and the spread of the Gregorian calendar formed a unified way for understanding the world.[6] The cultural anthropologist Jan Nederveen Pieterse considers the widely made equation of globalization and modernity to be Eurocentric and instead describes globalization as a deep historical process. He reminds us that while intercultural contact is accelerated in today's world, ancient populations centuries ago wandered, traded across cultures, and spread world religions such as Buddhism, Hinduism, Christianity, and Islam in ways that allowed them to mutually influence each other. Nederveen Pieterse thus understands the globalization we experience today as an acceleration of a long existing phenomenon. People have been fundamentally connected across time and space all along.[7]

In summary, the terms "global village," "global neighborhood," "complex connectivity," and "compressed single space" capture the developments that have linked parts all over the world closer in time and space.[8] We experience globalization as deeply ambivalent. We enjoy its opportunities and increased access to cultures and places around the world. At the same time we can feel overwhelmed and powerless in the face of global problems. The prevailing market system is driven by a consumerist ethos, which endangers the sustainability of resources and widens the gap between the rich and the poor. The increased close contact between cultures is full of opportunities and offers an enriching diversity. At the same time, it increases the potential for conflict, a daunting prospect considering heightened armament throughout the world. As the UN report *Our Global Neighborhood* states, "Never before have so many people had so much in common, but never before have the things that divide them been so obvious."[9] After reviewing several aspects of globalization I will ask how this global context shapes our understanding of cultural diversity.

6. Robertson, *Globalization*, 58f.

7. Nederveen Pieterse, *Globalization and Culture*, 25f.

8. Tomlinson, *Globalization and Culture*, 2f.; Commission on Global Governance, *Our Global Neighbourhood*, 41.

9. Commission on Global Governance, *Our Global Neighbourhood*, 41.

CULTURES IN CLOSE CONTACT

Culture and place are closely connected. The landscape, weather, the food grown in a particular place, its languages, and customs shape our cultural identity. Through globalization people, cultural goods, and products are more mobile, which changes our relationship to the local place. Sociologists describe this development with the term "deterritorialization," facets of which John Tomlinson describes in detail in *Globalization and Culture.*[10] Compare the experience of shopping in a local community with small stores and a farmer's market with going to a shopping mall that looks the same anywhere in the country. While local stores and markets are unique and its merchants familiar, the mall consists of chain stores controlled by corporate headquarters elsewhere.[11]

Many of our activities and experiences are less dependent on the physical local place than they were in the past. Through Internet and media we access the world virtually. Food as a part of cultural identity also has undergone transformations.[12] In the northwestern hemisphere, foods from all over the world are available all year round. We consume them without knowing much about their local origin or how they have been grown and harvested. Most consumers in the North West buying a cup of coffee on their way to work are unaware of the worker who harvests the coffee beans for too few wages, unable to provide even a small percentage of our food consumption to his or her family. Tourists visiting a beach resort in Sri Lanka will hardly get a sense of the life of the country's citizens.

Migrants experience deterritorialization when they have to leave their home in the countryside in order to seek work in the city. Many people leave their home countries for economic or political reasons and have to establish a new life in a foreign nation. Working-class members of communities in the United States and Europe may experience the displacing effects of globalization when they become unemployed because the manufacturing of products is outsourced to another country with low wages and taxes.[13] Or they experience the transformation of familiar place when their neighborhood slowly changes into a multiethnic envi-

10. Tomlinson, *Globalization and Culture*, 106f. Other terms emphasizing different aspects are delocalization and displacement.

11. Tomlinson, *Globalization and Culture*, 106–8.

12. See Ibid., 121ff.

13. Tomlinson, *Globalization and Culture*, 133.

ronment.[14] The first scenario of this chapter illustrates this point. Many of those German church members have seen their neighborhood change drastically in the last decades. New stores address the needs of migrant families, and schools struggle with German language instruction. The church members have difficulty adjusting to this new situation and feel as if foreign influences are taking over the part of town they have lived in for decades.

These different developments of deterritorialization do not mean an end to local culture, but the relationship to the local sphere is transformed and more complex.[15] Cultural identity is less dependent on the locale. As familiarity is no longer drawn from the immediate physical space, many people experience a sense of cultural uncertainty and fragmentation. The global changes the local, and some communities meet that challenge by retreating and tying themselves even more closely to their particular identities of nation, ethnicity, or religion.

How we engage cultural and religious diversity depends largely on how we perceive it. Nederveen Pieterse introduces three different models of how the interaction of culture is understood: cultures clash (cultural differentialism), cultures merge (cultural convergence), and cultures mix (hybridization).

The first model emphasizes the differences between cultures. It understands cultures as civilizations that see the world differently. They are separate entities distinguished through language and territory. The idea of a cultural interaction is that of a mosaic consisting of fixed pieces. A multicultural society is imagined along the lines of closure and separation.[16] Cultural differentialism may assert local "authentic" culture in defense of globalizing forces.[17] One pronounced and increasingly influential position in the political discussion is Samuel Huntington's concept of the clash of civilizations according to which cultural differences are seen as generating conflict and rivalry.[18] He predicts that conflict between different civilizations will be more frequent, more sustained, and more violent.[19] He states that the "paramount axis of world politics will

14. Ibid.

15. Ibid., 149.

16. Nederveen Pieterse, *Globalization and Culture*, 55f.

17. Ibid., 45–47f.

18. Ibid., 42, 47f.

19. Huntington, *Clash of Civilizations*, 48.

be the relations between 'the West and the Rest'" and sees the conflict as playing out particularly with Islam.[20] Cultural differentialism is concerned with boundaries, with national and cultural purity.[21]

The second model sees cultures merging in the context of globalization. In terms of a multicultural society and a culturally diverse world, the concept of cultural convergence is related to the idea of assimilation with the dominant group at the center.[22] Those who see culture merge in the global village are concerned about a single global monoculture. Because of the dominance of the English language, Western cultural goods and global capitalism, this notion of a capitalist monoculture has been called "Coca-Colonization" or "McDonaldization."[23] Sociologist George Ritzer coined the term "McDonaldization" to describe the process by which the fast-food restaurant's business principles of efficiency, calculability, control, and predictability increasingly have shaped American culture—from education, entertainment, and health care to politics.[24] A number of sociologists see the global culture as an expression of Western modern culture overwhelming and threatening less powerful traditional cultures. Others find that this notion does not do justice to the complex processes of cultural interactions.[25] They point out that in order to be successful companies like McDonald's have adjusted not only menus but also business practices to match the local customs and needs in other countries.[26] Other cultures incorporate cultural goods from the West, transform them, and give them their own twist. In addition, the West has been and continues to be influenced and shaped by Asian, Latin American, and African cultures as well. Scandinavians drink the most coffee in the world, thereby consuming a plant that is hardly cultivated there. The potato is considered such a staple of a traditional German meal that it seems it always has been part of that country's diet. Yet, even after its introduction to Europe from South America, it took until the middle of the nineteenth century for it to become popular. The popularity of Eastern meditation and yoga in the West illustrates that cultural

20. Ibid., 31–32, 48.

21. Nederveen Pieterse, *Globalization and Culture*, 56.

22. Ibid.

23. Tomlinson, *Globalization and Culture*, 83.

24. Ritzer, *McDonaldization*, 14–22.

25. Tomlinson, *Globalization and Culture*, 94.

26. Nederveen Pieterse, *Globalization and Culture*, 50.

interaction is not a one-way street. The dominance of the West in global capitalism is declining. Therefore, the notion of the hegemony of the West over the rest of the world may be too one-sided. Even so, many sociologists agree that globalization is a deeply uneven process. Some benefit from it, others lose out. Some regional and corporate entities have more power than others to shape culture.[27]

In contrast to models that see cultural interaction as a clash or a merger in the global village, a third approach understands it as a mixing. The term hybridization is applied from biology to culture and describes the crossover and syncretism that occurs in intercultural connections. According to this view, cultures have mixed throughout history as ancient populations migrated, traded with, and influenced each other. Culture is not confined to territorial boundaries, is always changing, and never remains in a pure, original state. According to Nederveen Pieterse, hybridization is a model that acknowledges the existence of the mixed breed, the many persons who crossed borders or combine multiracial and multiethnic backgrounds in their DNA.[28] Hybridization emphasizes the fluidity and connections of cultures, not their separateness. Because culture is not primarily understood as bound to a certain place but as "human software," people can claim multiple identities, and different cultures are compatible.[29] For example, a multicultural urban area in Los Angeles in numerous regards may have more similarities with London, Paris, or Buenos Aires than with a smaller homogeneous U.S. city. The understanding of culture as fluid and permeable seems to be most appropriate for the context of globalization. Culture understood as "human software" is not without a space but is outward looking, and it refers to commonality as well as diversity.[30]

The enthusiastic endorsement of hybridization does not account for the cultural uncertainty many contemporaries feel. Perhaps Huntington's idea of the "clash of civilizations" has become popular because it captures—and reinforces—fears of the messiness of a multicultural society. An attempt to help persons to embrace cultural and religious diversity of their environment must take seriously the fears that keep them from doing so.

27. Tomlinson, *Globalization and Culture*, 94, 97.
28. Nederveen Pieterse, *Globalization and Culture*, 52f.
29. Ibid., 78.
30. Ibid., 78, 46.

As local places become less important for cultural identity, ethnic or religious boundaries may emerge in their place. The theologian Robert Schreiter points out that today boundaries are not so much boundaries of territory as boundaries of difference.[31] In order to gain a sense of cultural belonging and certainty, people may rely increasingly on identification with their particular ethnic or religious group.

In the next chapter I will address in more detail how important membership in social groups is for the sense of self. Here, suffice it to say that belonging to social groups bestows a sense of identity. This identity is often asserted over and against other groups. The psychological pressures of deterritorialization and the experience of diversity can reinforce the tendency to emphasize group boundaries. In other words, the belonging to a particular religious group can be a powerful source of identity in a social context marked by fragmentation and an overwhelming plurality of ways of life. Religion can be used to defend against fears of losing one's identity.

Still, the model of hybridization opens a way of understanding culture that can help contemporaries embrace the diversity they experience in their daily lives. Seeing culture as hybrid all along, not as static or bound to territory and nation but with permeable boundaries, normalizes the diversity in our society. The model of hybridization also helps us to conceptualize the relationships of different religions in less static terms. A further concept that helps us articulate our place in the global village is "glocalization," the notion that global and local mutually influence each other.

GLOBAL PLUS LOCAL EQUALS GLOCAL

As we become more aware of the globe as a single space, we begin to pay increased attention to the local space. As we begin to appreciate particular cultures, we begin to respect diversity worldwide. The momentum of technology and the global market has sparked reactions by social movements, grassroots associations, and nongovernmental organizations that seek to counter threats to local cultures.[32] Earlier, we compared a local community with corner shops and a farmers' market to a shopping mall with chain stores. In numerous cities the downtown areas are being revitalized and farmers' markets are being reintroduced to provide alter-

---

31. Schreiter, *New Catholicity*, 26.

32. Richard Falk, *Religion and Human Global Governance*, 120.

natives to the suburban mall. The concern for empowering indigenous and native cultures in global organizations illustrates the reassertion of the particular and the local in the face of the global.[33] Other forces that reassert the local in reaction to globalization are fair-trade movements found particularly in churches and local farming networks.

In order to find a terminology that appropriately expresses the relationship of the global and the local, the particular and universal, sociologist Roland Robertson appropriated the term "glocalization" from the economic arena and applied it to sociological and cultural discourse. It is a translation of the Japanese word *dochakuka* that describes a micro-marketing strategy. In order to be successful in selling products globally, strategies of tailoring and advertising products to particular and local markets need to be adapted.[34] The market becomes more diversified, and capitalism brings about hybrid products. The term "glocalization" expresses that global and local often go hand in hand. Some sociologists find the term to be too optimistic in the face of larger homogenizing tendencies that overwhelm and overpower local forces.[35] Still, the concept of glocalization is widely seen as adequate to describe the relationship between the global and the local, the universal and particular.[36] Moreover, the notion of glocalization can be a helpful tool for individuals and communities to understand their place in the global neighborhood.

Tomlinson introduces the idea of "ethical glocalism," a stance that allows people to "to live in both the global and the local at the same time." Ethical glocalism describes an attitude that allows persons to affirm their own cultural commitments while cultivating a sense of connection with other human beings.[37] In his concept of ethical glocalism, the universal and particular, our commonalities and differences as human beings, are held in a creative tension. I will return to the concept of ethical glocalism from a religious perspective shortly. Before doing that I consider different ways in which religious communities engage the global village.

33. See Robertson, *Globalization*, 171.

34. Robertson, *Globalization*, 173; Nederveen Pieterse, *Globalization and Culture*, 50.

35. Ritzer introduced the concept of "grobalization," according to which global forces with their interest in "seeing their power, influence, and in some cases profits grow (hence the term *grobalization*) throughout the world," have the power to shape culture in various local and geographical regions. Ritzer, 170.

36. Nederveen Pieterse, *Globalization and Culture*, 53.

37. Tomlinson, *Globalization and Culture*, 194f.

RELIGION IN THE GLOBAL VILLAGE

While secularism has spread in the Western world, religion still plays an important role in the life of many. Nine out of ten Americans say they believe in God, and how citizens vote in Western countries is still influenced as much by their religious identity as it is by their social class, location, or profession.[38] In recent decades, religion has resurged and new religious movements have sprung up, not only in Asia, Africa, and Latin America, but also in Western societies. The global religious landscape today includes New Age spirituality in North America and Europe, Pentecostalism in North and Latin America as well as Africa, new religious sects in Buddhism as well as fundamentalism in Judaism, Christianity, Islam, and Hinduism. In the global village people of diverse cultural and religious traditions are in closer contact than ever before. Not only is information about different religious traditions available through the media and Internet, many Americans also encounter people of other faiths as next-door neighbors, as co-workers and fellow students. Religions engage in meaning making through particular and often very different symbols, spiritual practices, beliefs, and customs. In a shrinking global village these differences become more visible and tangible.

While some find the diversity enriching, others feel their own belief system challenged by the presence of another house of worship in the same neighborhood. One's own values no longer hold the self-evident position and role they once had. Like the church board members who want to raise funds for a large cross, some people feel a need to assert and preserve their particular religious identity over traditions that have recently moved into the neighborhood. The social scientist Robert Wuthnow conducted the Religion and Diversity Survey, a three-year national survey with hundreds of in-depth interviews, to study the views of Americans about religious diversity. In his assessment pluralism functions best in our legal system. While numerous American Muslims, Buddhists, and Hindus report that they have experienced unfair treatment because of their membership in a minority religion, they also note that U.S. laws and customs provide them with religious freedom.[39] When it comes to cultural pluralism, cultural minority groups still struggle with loss of identity through assimilation and stereotype due to misinforma-

38. Prothero, *God Is Not One*, 7f.; Grew, "Cultural Context of Fundamentalism," 20.

39. Wuthnow, Challenges of Religious Diversity, 63.

tion. Engaging religious pluralism presents the toughest challenge.[40] In the United States as well as in Europe, Christianity is the established religion. While many Americans appreciate and embrace diversity theoretically, the general population seems to be ignorant about basic beliefs and practices of minority religions. Many Christian churches deal with increasing diversity by ignoring it or keeping contact with other religions to a minimum.[41] The need to develop understanding through religious literacy is great.[42]

In the last section of this chapter we explore how religious communities engage this new challenge of religious diversity in the global village. Three different approaches to religious pluralism stand out: an individualistic, a particularistic, and a pluralistic response. The first is an individualistic response, which Wuthnow also described as spiritual shopping. In his book *Religion and Globalization* the sociologist Peter Beyer describes two main ways in which religion engages the globalized world. He calls them a conservative and a liberal response. I will refer to them as a particularistic and a pluralistic response. The conservative, particularistic response sees globalization as a threat and asserts the cultural and religious distinctiveness of one's own group. The liberal or pluralistic response is proactive in dealing with global problems and becomes involved in social issues of globalization without always having a clear religious profile.[43]

The individualistic response to religious diversity is shaped by a consumer culture that influences how people practice religion. Wuthnow sees spiritual shopping as one way of approaching religious diversity. Disenchanted by organized religion, numerous spiritual seekers emphasize personal spirituality over institutional religion. Like shoppers they experiment with religious beliefs and practices according to their personal preferences and needs and nurture those through readily available books, retreats, travel, and workshops. They explore different paths, such as Eastern meditation or New Age practices, and incorporate ideas from different traditions into their personal spirituality.[44] While "spiritual shoppers" are open to a wide variety of beliefs and embrace the idea

40. Ibid., 73.
41. Ibid., 255.
42. Ibid., 72.
43. Beyer, *Religion and Globalization*, 86f.
44. Wuthnow, *Challenges of Religious Diversity*, 107.

of diversity, they are less likely to get involved in communities or impact how society responds to diversity.[45] The response to religious diversity remains at an individualistic level. A market mentality also influences church members who understand their faith as a means for personal salvation and self-actualization and seek the community of like-minded persons. Those who visit megachurches often experience worship in an entertainment-like setting. The Internet provides many opportunities to learn about religion and to discuss it with others without making a commitment to a particular community. Individuals and communities who focus on an individualistic understanding of their religion may not necessarily respond antagonistically to globalization and pluralism but may simply not engage these issues. They retreat to a private practice of faith.[46] They avoid the confusion and fear caused by exposure to conflicting truth claims by remaining isolated from other communities.

The particularistic response to globalization emphasizes particular interests. It corresponds to cultural differentialism mentioned above by emphasizing boundaries between cultures. This approach finds its most visible form in new fundamentalist movements, which have grown worldwide in the second half of the twentieth century and are reactive against trends of globalization.[47] They emphasize personal salvation and the community of their own group while dividing the world into "us" and "them."[48] Fundamentalism mobilizes against threats to its way of life. Secularization, the separation of religion and state in democracies, and a growing religious diversity render traditional religious institutions less significant, and this has created a vacuum that fundamentalist movements effectively fill.[49] Non-Western fundamentalism reacts against the dominance of Western culture. A fundamentalist response to globalization within the West attempts to hold on to the notion of a Western Christendom.[50] Waves of immigration have created a wide range of faith traditions in the United States, making it the most religiously diverse country in the world. The New Religious Right, an umbrella term for fundamentalist Protestants, Catholics, and Mormons, has fostered the

---

45. Ibid., 129.
46. Ibid., 128.
47. Schreiter, *New Catholicity*, 21.
48. Beyer, *Religion and Globalization*, 92.
49. Grew, "Cultural Context of Fundamentalism," 29.
50. Mike Featherstone, "An Introduction," 11.

idea of a "Christian America" in the public discourse.[51] There are considerable similarities among fundamentalist movements within Protestant Christianity, Catholicism, Islam, Buddhism, Hinduism, and other traditions. They share contempt for modern contemporary society and aim to reinstate patriarchal norms for family and society. They reject secularization, the separation of religion and state, and religious pluralism.[52] While critical of modern society, they are sophisticated in utilizing modern technology to communicate their message.

The alternative approach of religion in a global context proactively engages global problems and pluralism from a religious perspective. The Catholic theologian Robert Schreiter describes this response with the term global theological flows. Flows are cultural movements across geographical lines.[53] Global theological flows are theologically inspired movements across continents that are centered on global and universal concerns. They address issues, such as social injustice, women's rights, human rights, and environmental problems. The movements are rooted in their local context and address these problems locally, while also addressing issues that impact people throughout the world. While antiglobal fundamentalist movements stress their particular group, members of different contexts and cultures throughout the world support theological flows. They may connect with secular social movements but do so by addressing global problems in the realm of religious beliefs and practices.[54] Members of such movements attempt to tend to suffering and social problems in their concrete and immediate context. At the same time they aim to unite different people toward the goals of social justice, equality, human dignity of all, and the protection of the environment. On the one hand they address problems related to globalization, such as the increasing levels of poverty as a result of untamed free market capitalism. On the other hand they are open to the global community and seek justice and healing throughout the globe.

Concerns about justice, equality, and the environment have brought together people of different faiths as well. The Council for a Parliament of the World's Religions, for example, cooperates on the basis of shared ethical principles: It supports the world's religious communities to en-

---

51. Eck, *New Religious America*, 4–5; Beyer, *Religion and Globalization*, 91.

52. Ruether, *Integrating Ecofeminism*, 26.

53. Schreiter, *New Catholicity*, 16.

54. Ibid.

gage the world and its institutions in order to achieve a just, peaceful, and sustainable world. The well-being of the Earth and all life depends on collaboration. The Council has initiated regional chapters in order to create a local grassroots interreligious movement.[55] Religious pluralism provides a challenge for the identity of particular religions. It also provides an opportunity for cooperation in addressing the many global problems together. Under the leadership of the theologian Hans Küng, the gathering of the Parliament of the World's Religions in 1993 developed the concept of a global ethic. Modeled after the 1948 Declaration of Human Rights, the declaration of a global ethic was later followed up by a universal declaration of human responsibilities. These declarations are inclusive of different religions as well as secular approaches and, together, focus on three principles, which are considered common ground for diverse religions: (1) every human being must be treated humanely; (2) the Golden Rule: We must treat others as we wish others to treat us; (3) a responsibility to foster a better social order locally and globally.[56] The two declarations promote a global ethic and seek to counter religious separatism with dialogue of different cultural and religious traditions. The notion of a global ethic emphasizes the interdependence of the human community. It employs religious traditions and those who practice them to contribute to solutions of global problems. It encourages interreligious contact and cooperation.

The notion of a global ethic raises some questions as well. Principles, such as the golden rule or a better social order, are abstract and may reveal more differences than commonalities in concrete ethical situations. An appeal to a global ethic needs to go hand in hand with an acknowledgement of local differences and an appreciation of particularity. Schreiter's concept of global theological flows or Tomlinson's concept of ethical glocalism holds the universal and particular, the global and local in a creative tension. Rather than one strategy or grand narrative, global theological flows find expression in local projects of community organization and address concrete local problems, such as education or health, with global relevance.[57] The projects may look different and are

55. Council for a World Parliament. For more details about the Parliament, see chapter 5.

56. Küng and Kuschel, *Global Ethic*, 21, 23; Küng and Schmidt, *Global Ethic and Global Responsibilities*, 6.

57. Schreiter, *New Catholicity*, 112.

shaped by their concrete geographical and social locations. A second concern about the declarations of a global ethic and global responsibilities is that it was primarily religious and political leaders who articulated it. In order to create a broader effect, citizens and religious communities at the grassroots need to be involved.

GLOCAL RESPONSIBILITY

Tomlinson's concept of ethical glocalism, Schreiter's idea of global theological flows, and the concern with a global ethic share elements I summarize in the term glocal responsibility.[58] Scholar of Islam, pluralism, and globalization, Patrice Brodeur also speaks of a glocal approach to interreligious dialogue.[59] As mentioned previously, Tomlinson's concept of ethical glocalism means a cultural disposition toward the world that includes a willingness to engage the other.[60] It describes an attitude that allows persons to affirm their own cultural belonging while feeling connected with the earth and the global community. This sense of interdependence is expressed concretely in actions of responsibility to the earth and fellow human beings.

Many individuals and religious communities are already engaged in such glocal responsibility. Their efforts can be summarized in the slogan "Think globally, act locally." The Christian ecumenical movement is a concrete expression of the understanding that the church is one body of Christ stretching across the globe. Consider two examples that illustrate how local churches embody glocal responsibility.

As traveling and communicating via Internet have become easier, a local church decides to develop a partnership with a community in El Salvador. The larger denomination makes resources for planning available, and a group of fifteen youth and adult church members take a trip for ten days. In El Salvador they help with painting and roofing a local school and travel to explore the beauty of the land and its people. They walk to villages and learn about the conditions of rural living. They visit urban churches that confront poverty in their ministry by providing job skill workshops for citizens. The U.S. church members participate in worship and learn new songs and prayers they will introduce at home.

58. They also connect with the model of a correlational globally responsible dialogue Paul Knitter proposes. It will be addressed in more detail in chapter 8.

59. Brodeur, "Transnational Interfaith Youth Network," 52.

60. Tomlinson, *Globalization and Culture*, 183.

Upon their return they share experiences in their home church and begin a partnership with the community in El Salvador involving e-mail contact, financial support, and future trips.

Another church expresses glocal responsibility through stewardship for creation. A group of church members raises awareness in the community of how individual and communal lifestyle choices about energy consumption affect the earth and the body of Christ in distant places. They educate the congregation about environmental issues and suggest steps that help members adjust their life style to sustainable living. They conduct an energy audit and introduce small changes in the church building to save energy, and they encourage members to do the same in their households. The connection with the earth has become a part of worship, learning, and action in this community.

These two scenarios illustrate how glocal responsibility can be practiced within the church. It has become increasingly important for Christians to understand glocal responsibility also in terms of their relationships with neighbors of other religious traditions. First, the proposal of a glocal ethic has brought to light the urgency to work together to solve global problems that affect all of us. The problems we face locally have global dimensions. The global issues of ecological destruction, poverty, and armament are so complex and far-reaching that they require the cooperation of people from different cultures and traditions. Second, the growing diversity and close contact of cultures and religious traditions makes conflict more likely. Cooperation of religious communities on a global and local level provides a voice that counters calls for separation and division.

The Muslim community leader Eboo Patel has brought youth from different faith traditions together for service and study. He feels that we have "dangerously thin relationships between religious communities."[61] While we develop a "private language of faith" in our faith communities, Patel sees a need to develop a "public language of faith" where people can discuss issues of religious diversity. Interfaith work has an important role in developing a public language of faith.[62] The acknowledgement of difference and particularity goes hand in hand with an acknowledgement of our common identity as human beings. The affirmation of plural particular identities is one side of the coin of which the other is an affir-

61. Patel, "Affirming Identity," 19.

62. Ibid., 20f.

mation of our equality and connectedness in a global community.[63] The discussion of the particular and the universal has much relevance for interreligious encounters and runs as a common thread throughout this book. The term "glocal" expresses the productive tension of the global and the local and may inform our understanding of the relationships between particular religious traditions—that particularity does not have to be suppressed or given up in search of universals, but both principles can be held and affirmed, and indeed balance each other.

Let us return to the introductory scenarios. During the church board debate about fund-raising for a larger cross, a deeper question surfaced: What does it mean to have an identity as a Christian community in a multicultural and multifaith environment? The church may decide to purchase a cross to give an outward expression to their identity. However, if the discussion stays focused on the symbolic expression, the church misses an important learning opportunity. What if the board were to facilitate visits to the mosque during which church members could get to know their Muslim neighbors? The church could work together with the Muslim community in tackling problems that affect the city. They could clean up playgrounds to create better spaces of recreation for German and Turkish children. Together they could organize drives for used clothing to support the local homeless shelter. In that process of cooperation they could get to know each other as people. They could learn from each other about important religious beliefs and practices, such as prayer and service. The church might come to understand the practice of "athan," the call to prayer, and be less bothered by it. The two communities could engage in learning processes that would help them affirm their own faith while reaching out to the other. Rather than practicing their faith in isolation from each other they could be proactive in engaging the diversity through concrete local action.

The spiritual care advisory board of the urban medical center is challenged with the task of creating a space for spiritual support and practice in a public setting. The new meditation room could be an embodiment of the public language of faith Patel is talking about. In the process of planning and designing the space, the board members could learn how different religious practices provide comfort in crisis. As the new meditation room incorporates particular expressions of faith in a common space, it would communicate the public language of faith for

63. Tomlinson, *Globalization and Culture*, 192.

the institution and those who frequent it. Such a space would serve as a reminder to the public that religions are different but that their adherents can come together to provide a space of emotional and spiritual healing, of respite and support for all.

SUMMARY

Through the revolution of information and communication technology, through easy travel and access, we live more closely together in the global village than ever before. While the global village provides us with many opportunities and its diversity can enrich our lives, it also presents many problems—from ecological destruction, extreme inequality and poverty, ethnic and religious divisions, to armed conflicts. The problems are so far reaching that we need one another. In the global village diverse religious communities exist in close proximity in our local neighborhoods. Some seek to assert their own identity over and against other groups. It is even more common to keep contact with the religiously other at a minimum and exist in isolation from each other. Engaging religious diversity is one important way of embodying a glocal responsibility. It is a task of our time. A global ethic, ethical glocalism, global theological flows, glocal responsibility—these notions appeal to us to proactively engage the diverse global village with its opportunities and problems. They also provide hope and a direction for how to go about it by affirming what we have in common and maintaining commitment to our particularity.

Interreligious cooperation is an expression of glocal responsibility. Diverse religious communities can join together in care for the world, locally and globally. They bring their faith identity to the encounter and learn from each other. Cooperation can heal divisions between the religions and provide an alternative to separatist and prejudiced voices that make themselves heard so clearly.

In the last chapter I provide a theological foundation for interreligious cooperation. In the chapters between the last and this opening one, I describe what interreligious cooperation looks like in work with local communities as well as with individuals in crisis. I also introduce strategies for interreligious cooperation. Fears of losing one's religious identity when engaging another might shut down cooperative projects before they can take effect. Those fears and concerns need to be taken seriously, and we need to meet people where they are. Chapters 3 and

4 describe group dynamics and facilitation tools that aid cooperation. Before addressing those, we need to understand those forces that keep people isolated and focused on their group. In the following chapter I therefore explore the question of what is keeping us apart.

2

What Keeps Us Apart?

Perceptions, Clans, Labels, Fears

IN 2009, SWITZERLAND MADE international headlines with a majority vote by Swiss citizens to ban the future building of minarets. Minarets are to mosques what steeples are to churches. Both are towers attached to houses of worship used to call believers to prayer. Four hundred thousand Muslims, primarily from Turkey and former Yugoslavia, live in Switzerland, whose total population is about 7.55 million people. There are about 130 Muslim places of worship, of which four have a minaret. As a result of an initiative of populist nationalist parties and against the protest of other political parties and religious communities, 57.5 percent of Swiss citizens surprisingly voted to prohibit any additional building of minarets.[1] Leading up to the vote, proponents used a particularly striking demagogic poster: Its colors are red, white, and shades of black and grey. From the bottom of the red and white Swiss flag rise numerous black minarets arranged in a way that they remind the viewer of missiles. In front of the flag is a woman dressed completely in a black burka, her eyes dark and hardly visible. Underneath is the message: "Stop—Yes to the ban of minarets." The poster triggers associations of secrecy and hiddenness, violence and terrorism, and oppression of the rights of women.

Considering that Muslims make up 5 percent of the Swiss population, and there are a total of four minarets in the whole country, how can this rejection of another cultural expression of belief and religious practice be understood?

---

1. Zeit Online, "Volksentscheid. Schweizer."

The campaign has tapped into fears and stereotypes of citizens that are not just unique to Switzerland but are common throughout the Western world. In this chapter we will look at this and other examples of conflicts between religious and cultural groups and analyze their ingredients. We will mine the rich research undertaken in social psychology to understand relationships between different racial, ethnic, and social groups. The core question of this chapter is this: What keeps neighbors of different religious traditions apart? By looking through a social psychological lens we answer the question in a fourfold way: our perceptions, our clan, our labels, and our fears.

DEFINITIONS

Earlier attempts to understand conflicts between groups are part of the psychoanalytic legacy with its focus on instincts and emotional energies within the individual. As Sigmund Freud had done before them, so too John Dollard and his colleagues see the subconscious alive and active not only in individuals but also in groups. They observed that persons as members of particular groups develop strong instinctual ties to other members within their group or to a powerful group leader. The stronger one's ties to one's own group, the stronger is the hostility to persons different from oneself and from members of other groups.[2] In light of the experience of World War II, Theodor Adorno and his colleagues studied the potentially fascistic personality. Their classic study *The Authoritarian Personality* investigates scapegoating of minority groups such as the Jews in Nazi Germany and African Americans in the United States. The authoritarian personality represses certain feelings or aspects in the self, such as fear, weakness, and sex impulses, and projects those onto others so that they are not experienced as a threat to one's self.[3]

The lens of social psychology looks beyond the individual person. Social psychology studies "individual behavior in social contexts."[4] Within social psychology the field of "intergroup relations" understands relationships not just in light of emotional dynamics between individuals but also by looking at relationships of groups. Donald Taylor and Fathali Moghaddam define intergroup relations as "any aspect of human

2. Taylor and Moghaddam, *Theories of Intergroup Relation*, 19f.; John Dollard et al., *Frustration and Aggression*.

3. Adorno et al., *Authoritarian Personality*, 492.

4. Taylor and Moghaddam, *Theories of Intergroup Relations*, 3.

interaction that involves individuals perceiving themselves as members of a social category, or being perceived by others as belonging to a social category."[5] Some theories from the field of intergroup relations help us better understand the conflict or distance between people of different cultures and faiths.

I will introduce social identity theory, which explains intergroup behavior, by studying how we process our perceptions. Social identity theory claims that change of group conflict begins with a change of perception followed by change of our emotions and our behavior toward others. I will then explain stereotype as an ingredient of intergroup relations and articulate a clearer understanding of the anxiety that underlies intergroup conflicts and separation.

By the end of the chapter the reader will have gained familiarity with the concepts of social categorization, social identity, social comparison, stereotype, bias, and one important emotional reaction in intergroup relations, fear. These concepts help us understand what keeps people apart who are different in gender, age, class, ability, ethnicity, culture—and religion.

Before tackling these ideas I define terms from intergroup relations theory that will appear throughout the following chapters. Theories of intergroup relations investigate the relationships of different groups. Social psychologists use the term "in-group" to describe groups of which persons consider themselves to be a part. The term "out-group" is used for groups with which persons do not identify or which they consider those to be part of who are different. "Group" is not used in the narrow sense of a small group in which people actually interact with each other but rather primarily means membership in a category.

For example, opinion pollsters established that the bulk of votes supporting the ban of minarets came from rural areas where the percentage of Muslims is very low.[6] It is therefore most likely that the citizens who banned the building of minarets had no actual direct interactions with Muslims. The vote also triggered international reactions. International Islamic organizations expressed concerns about anti-Muslim sentiments in Europe.[7] The vote may reflect a group attitude among Europeans regarding immigrants from Muslim countries. The vote may also be a cat-

5. Ibid., 6.

6. Zumach, "Analyse des Schweizer Referendums."

7. Stern Online, "Volksabstimmung in der Schweiz."

alyst in a solidification of such group boundaries. Fortunately, the story is more complex. A number of political representatives in Switzerland and other European countries were critical of the vote. Many religious communities expressed concern and understood the vote as an attack on freedom of religious expression. Such voices prevent the hardening of in-group and out-group distinctions to frontlines. How do our notions of in-group and out-group develop? We explore this question by taking a closer look at social identity theory.

OUR PERCEPTIONS: SOCIAL CATEGORIZATION

If you want to go on a hike and study a map before you start, you will focus on the legend that provides you with categories that help you to interpret the map. You distinguish red lines, differently colored dotted lines signifying highways, paved roads, dirt roads, and hiking trails. As you determine your route you will make further distinctions and choose from among the numerous dotted lines (hiking trails) only those trails that will take you from your starting point to your destination. This process of categorization describes a fairly intentional preparation for a daylong hike.

We use categorization throughout the day without being aware of it. When you shop in a regular grocery store, its mind-boggling array of products and aisles might actually make a map helpful, though in this case you tend to orient yourself with the help of signs above the aisles. These signs categorize the products according to type: dairy, produce, snacks, and so on. The more of a rush you are in, the more you will rely on the signs and categories to speed up the shopping trip. If you are looking for oatmeal and see an aisle with breakfast cereals, you approach that aisle.

Categorization is a cognitive process that helps us to organize the vast amount of information that bombards us in any given moment.[8] We order and prioritize information according to things that are similar and dissimilar to each other. This basic cognitive process enables us to conduct simple actions such as shopping or finding our way in an unknown area. Without categorization we would not be able to function in our complex environment.

---

8. Taylor and Moghaddam, *Theories of Intergroup Relations*, 67.

We use this same process of categorization not only with objects in our environment but also when we relate to people.[9] Imagine that a friend invites you to a party. You do not know many of the other guests in attendance. As you enter the house and see people standing together in conversation, most likely you will scan the room and make some mental note of the skin color, gender, and approximate age of people you see. In your mind you identify them as African American, Caucasian, Latina, senior, and so on. Gender, age, and ethnicity are obvious characteristics of people. They are social categories, labels we attach to persons based on their belonging to a social group. There are many other distinctions. As you approach guests and engage in some small talk, you may ask, "So, what do you do?" You may be asked, "Where are you from?" or, "Where do you live?" Aside from starting a conversation and establishing some points of commonality, professions, roles, and neighborhoods are also categories that organize our social environment. We belong to different categories at the same time. Your conversation partner may be an African American engineer who is a mother and attends a local mosque. Her ethnicity, profession, role, and religion are part of her social identity. Perhaps your conversation partner tells you that she is from Beverly Hills and you imagine that she is a very wealthy person. Or another guest tells you that he lives in South Central Los Angeles. The images of gangs, crime, and poverty come to mind as well as the riots in this area in 1992. Reading this paragraph you may think that it is highly unlikely to find guests from Beverly Hills and South Central LA at the same party, which proves the point social psychologists make—that social categories are not just mental organizers, but that they are also laden with evaluations, and they trigger feelings. We will come back to this point later. For now let us note that we use social categorization to order and segment our social environment. Social categorization is one of the foundations of social identity theory that has been developed by European scholars Henri Tajfel, John Turner, and others. In a nutshell, the theory explains the significance of membership in social groups for our sense of identity, how we perceive our own and other groups, and how we relate to each other on the basis of those perceptions.

9. Ibid., 68.

We think others are more alike than they really are.

When we organize our environment according to categories, we group objects and people with similar characteristics together and file those with different features under a different category. In this process of organizing we skip over details and often overgeneralize. Returning to our example of shopping in the grocery store, let us imagine you are looking for oatmeal in the cereal section. Oatmeal has much in common with cereals: it is often eaten for breakfast and is made of grain. It is also different from cereals in that it is not as processed, is not necessarily sweetened, and may be used for baking bread and other purposes besides simply being eaten as a cereal. Yet, most likely your search for oatmeal in the cereal aisle will be successful. Categorization helps us to pursue our goal within reasonable time constraints. By categorizing we simplify and oversimplify our environment in order to act.

When it comes to perceiving our diverse human neighbors, this simplification can be problematic. Especially when we do not know a person, we tend to see him or her more as a representative of a category than as an individual. We overlook the person's particular and unique traits and pay more attention to the group to which he or she belongs. The common statement "they all look alike to me" referring to persons of a different ethnic group illustrates what social psychologists call outgroup homogeneity.[10] We tend to perceive members of a group different from our own and as more homogeneous than they are.

As a pastor-in-training I worked in a German urban parish, in "the north," the "bad" part of town. Crime, drug abuse, and unemployment were high while rents were low. Beautiful nineteenth-century apartment houses with embellished but run down façades lined the streets. Some German citizens living in the north were seniors who had lived here all their lives and had seen the streets and inhabitants change over the decades. Many who could afford it had already moved away, and in their places a lot of migrant families had moved in. I liked the diversity of the neighborhood and enjoyed the people in our parish, many of them down-to-earth, warm, and direct in their communication style.

One day I officiated at the funeral of a parishioner who had died at the age of eighty-one and who, like the majority of the parishioners, had been a nominal member and not someone any of the church staff knew

---

10. Stephan and Stephan, *Intergroup Relations*, 94.

well personally. I was getting ready to conduct a bereavement visit with her adult children and extended family. They lived across the train tracks in the southern part of town. The "south" was known as a well-to-do area. Many academics and members of the upper middle class and upper class lived in the "south." As I got into my car and checked the city map for my route, I wondered what this encounter might be like. Usually, there were many unknowns when I conducted bereavement visits just a day after a parishioner had died and I did not know the family. Yet I also knew that in the past on such occasions I had experienced meaningful visits with families, sharing their stories, memories, and tears. "What would this visit be like?" I wondered. Perhaps it would be more distanced, harder to get to the real feelings that were held in check with layers of politeness and appropriateness. I parked the car and met the family. They were welcoming and open and we had some significant sharing of memories and emotions. Driving home I realized how much on my drive to this family I had been preoccupied with thoughts and defined ideas about what a family in the south would be like. I felt embarrassed about how I had labeled people who lived south of the tracks. I had picked up stereotypes about upper-class people such as "emotionally unavailable" and "concerned about maintaining a façade." On the short drive across town, thanks to such categories and stereotypes, I had created a vivid image of the people I was about to meet. Having a chance to get acquainted with the family and talking with them on a quite personal and meaningful level gave me the opportunity to be proven wrong. Until then, my mind had painted all people south of the train tracks with one brush.

The less familiar we are with persons representing an out-group, the more we rely on categories, maintain simplified notions, and see them as more homogeneous than they in fact are.

OUR CLAN: SOCIAL IDENTITY AND SOCIAL COMPARISON

In the following section, I introduce social identity theory developed by Henri Tajfel and John Turner. In "The Social Identity Theory of Intergroup Behavior" they provide an overview of the theory and its underlying experimental data.[11] My focus here is the potential application of social identity theory to the relationships between diverse religious groups.

11. Tajfel and Turner, "Social Identity Theory," 7–24.

Social identity defines a person's place in society.

If someone were to ask us to list what makes up our personal identity, we would include our unique characteristics such as our physical features and genetic material, our personal relationships and history, our gifts, and our limitations. In addition to these unique aspects of our identity, our social identity is derived from our membership in social groups, our ethnicity and culture, as well as our nationality. Age cohorts such as baby boomers, Gen Xers, or the millennial generation can be important social categories. Finally, our social class, and our religious and political affiliations can imbue us with a sense of identity. They define our place in society and give us a sense of belonging.[12] Personal identity and social identity are not entirely different but are interrelated parts of our personality.

Depending on the context and situation, such belonging to different social groups is more or less relevant. For example, in an immigrant society such as the United States, race and ethnicity are significant social identifications, whereas religious affiliation is of great importance in Ireland. A person looking for a job in information technology may feel that age cohort is a significant factor, since for young people the use of that technology has become second nature. In the process of globalization national borders decrease in importance and our sense of our world is more pluralistic than ever before. Against this backdrop the importance of social identity that is derived from persons' participation or membership in cultural and religious groups becomes even more important. As mentioned in the previous chapter, cultural identity is less connected to a local place than it used to be. Therefore, cultural and religious affiliations are significant in giving persons a sense of place and belonging in a very diverse and complicated world.

Social identity is a vehicle to achieve and maintain self-esteem.

Our belonging to a social group does not only define a place in society. People wish to belong to positively evaluated groups. Many persons have a sense of pride in their nationality, their cultural heritage, or their religion. Belonging to a positively evaluated group can contribute to a positive self-image. I once brought a guest visiting from the United States to a confirmation class I was leading in the same German church

12. Ibid., 16.

I described above. During the class question and answer session, I made a rough sketch of a world map and placed Germany and the United States on the map—only to hear loud protest from some of the boys in the group. "You are lying." It was difficult for the students to accept that Germany was such a small country compared to the geographical vastness of the United States. Their passionate reaction illustrates the need and desire for persons to belong to a positively evaluated group, a need that was perhaps magnified in this particular case since the youth were keenly aware of their membership in an underprivileged social class.[13] Within or across groups, there is usually consensus regarding the status of other groups in society. Groups with higher prestige are usually those with more access to resources, education, and wealth, or simply those representing a majority in a given society.

When we categorize, we compare.

When we categorize people, we do so by making comparisons between them and us. Because our membership in social groups can enhance our self-esteem, our perception of our own and other groups is not just an objective cognitive process, but includes evaluation and comparison.[14] Henri Tajfel and John Turner call this process social comparison.[15] Because our self-esteem is at stake, simply our belonging to social groups creates competitiveness among social groups. We compare ourselves not just with any other group but particularly with those groups that are comparable in our shared context. As mentioned earlier, professional groups can be social categories of significance. For example, many chaplains feel that within their denomination their ministry is often seen as "less important" than that of congregational pastors. It is not uncommon for chaplains to feel that they represent "second-class clergy" although their academic education is equal to that of congregational ministers and they are required to complete additional specialized training. They might have a keen sense of this "lower status" when they attend larger denominational conferences or ministers' meetings. This distinction, however, is irrelevant in institutional settings where other professionals are unaware of the status differences among clergy. Of course, institu-

---

13. Regarding the need to belong to a positively evaluated group, see ibid.

14. Tajfel and Turner, "Social Identity Theory," 16.

15. Ibid., 15.

tional settings such as hospitals are also organized according to a clear hierarchy of professionals with physicians, administrators, nurses, and "ancillary" staff; it is just a different hierarchy and therefore one that is more or less irrelevant in the context of the denomination.

Social groups with higher prestige and status often seek to maintain superiority over other groups. When the United States elected the first African American president it provided inspiration and hope to other African Americans as well as all voters who believe in racial equality. At the same time, we note a significant backlash from this same event. Issues of racism have entered the national debate anew, and just from the beginning to the end of 2009 the number of antigovernment militias increased by 300 percent.[16] Social comparison seems to be part and parcel of social categorization.

We feel loyalty to our group.

John Turner, a colleague of the aforementioned Henri Tajfel, conducted experiments in which participants who had never met each other were divided into two different groups. What distinguished them was that one group liked the artwork of one artist, the other group that of another artist. They had no face-to-face contact and were asked to provide small monetary rewards to other contestants. The only information they had about other participants was their group membership and a code number. Test persons allocated money according to what would advantage themselves as well as based on loyalty to the in-group. Turner concluded that simply belonging to a social category causes persons to favor the in-group.[17] Even in these "minimally defined" groups one could observe competitiveness and a tendency to distinguish participants' own group from the other.

The concepts of social comparison and in-group favoritism highlight how important group membership can be for the self-image of persons and how quick we are to emphasize group differences, to compare and to compete with each other.

16. The Southern Poverty Law Center tracked an increase of militia groups operating in the United States from 42 to 127 in 2009. Avlon, "Anti-government hate militias."

17. Tajfel and Turner, "Social Identity Theory," 13f.

If we are unhappy with our group membership, we seek change.

Members of groups with lower status may try to dissociate from their in-group and join a more positively evaluated group. Alternatively, lower group status may motivate persons to be creative and change or redefine their status.[18] For example, the pink triangle originated as a sign in Nazi concentration camps to designate the reason for imprisonment: "sexual deviance, homosexuality." As such it was a symbol of oppression and atrocities against gays and lesbians. However, the gay rights movement later used the pink triangle as a symbol for empowerment. It has become a symbol of positive self-identification and progress in the struggle for equal rights. The GLBT community has completely turned around the meaning of the symbol as it has struggled for and advanced equal rights for its community over the decades. In the struggle for human rights the GLBT community has increasingly redefined its group identity and has thus achieved change not just for individuals but also on a systemic level.

Social identity theory in context

With its notion of social categorization, social identity theory is a foundation for more detailed research on how our perceptions of others and related stereotypes can possibly be changed. I will take advantage of that research in chapters 3 and 4 when I describe strategies that reduce prejudice and stereotypes between persons of different faiths. The concepts of social identity theory can be helpful as we look at the relationships of persons of different religions. Without addressing theological differences or the historical relationships between religious groups, just by looking at the way we organize and perceive information from our social environment, we can understand why our relationships with those who are different in culture and beliefs can be complicated and conflictual. Our perceptions and our communities are basic to our sense of who we are and how we function in the world. Understanding how we form perceptions and how they shape our relationships to other communities can suggest, in the following chapters, ways in which to improve relations.

Social identity theory is limited and does not provide the only explanation of intergroup behavior. Social identity theory developed as a

18. Ibid., 20.

complement to an earlier theory of intergroup conflict named realistic conflict theory, which claims that *real conflict* of group interests causes intergroup conflict. Many intergroup conflicts have their basis in incompatible group interests and competition for power or resources, political or economic influence, or in differences in values and norms.[19] Also, competition for basic psychological needs, such as security, identity, and recognition, can underlie intergroup conflict.[20] In a nutshell, realistic conflict theory identifies real inequalities as sources of conflict and even war. Real power and resource difference can strengthen individuals' loyalty to their own group and bring about conflict with other groups.[21] Some of the examples I have used in this chapter describe not only perceived group differences but real differences in power and rights, as with African Americans and Caucasians or the GLBT community and heterosexual persons.

Realistic conflict theory can be important in understanding interreligious conflicts. After all, wars have been fought in the name of religion. Tajfel and Turner did not understand social identity theory as a replacement of realistic conflict theory but as supplementing it by giving attention to the subjective experience of group membership.[22] Another cause for intergroup conflict is often found in the history of involved groups. The relationships between Caucasians and African Americans in the United States at large are still marked by real differences in access to power, resources, and education. At the same time, the present situation cannot be fully understood without the history of slavery.

I participated once in a small racial relations discussion group in a southern town in the United States. Henry, an African American participant, shared with the group a painful experience from years ago. It was an early evening, the dark had just set in, and he passed through a parking lot downtown. There were just a few cars parked. He saw through the window of a middle-sized sedan the contours of four women. They seemed engaged in a lively conversation. The woman in the driver's seat turned and saw Henry walking by. Seconds later he heard a muffled sound. The locking mechanism of the doors had been engaged. The driver seemed to see a need for extra protection just at the sight of him.

19. Stephan and Stephan, *Intergroup Relations,* 144.

20. Ibid., 150.

21. Taylor and Moghaddam, *Theories of Intergroup Relations,* 36, 145.

22. Tajfel and Turner, "Social Identity Theory," 8.

He turned his eyes away from the car and kept on walking, feeling sadness welling up in him.

We do not know for certain what prompted the women to lock the car. As Henry walked through the lonely parking lot at dusk, it appeared the women engaged the lock because they were afraid of him. Would they have locked a car if a white man had walked by? Did they associate notions such as "gang member," "criminal," and "rapist" with a young black man? The women's fears and Henry's feelings of sadness are part of deeply rooted, complicated, and conflictual race relations, and this history of relations of slavery and oppression finds its way into ordinary present day interactions.

To sum up, some stereotypes are heightened not only through real and present conflict but also because of historical conflict.[23] Social identity theory does not tell the whole story of intergroup relations. Considering real and historical conflicts is important if we want to understand the relationships between different social groups.

Social identity theory focuses on how we perceive others. It envisions the reduction of group conflict beginning with a change of perception and being followed by change of our emotions and our behavior toward others. In chapter 4 I will introduce the notion that the process of change works the other way around as well. If I try a new behavior, for example, having extended contact with persons I tend to avoid or dislike, I may find myself liking and respecting them more than I thought. These new experiences are in conflict with my old stereotypes. I can resolve the conflict by changing my attitude and beginning to perceive others in a more positive way.[24]

It has also been noted that social identity and much of intergroup relations research has focused too much on cognitive perception and neglects the role of emotions when explaining the relationships between different groups.[25] Perceptions and thoughts, feelings, and behaviors are all facets of relationships between members of different groups and can be captured in the umbrella term "bias." Dovidio et al. distinguish prejudice, stereotype, affective reactions, and discrimination as different types of bias. Prejudice is defined as a negative attitude involving thoughts

23. Stephan and Stephan, *Intergroup Relations*, 9.

24. Pettigrew, "Intergroup Contact Theory," 73.

25. Taylor and Moghaddam, *Theories of Intergroup Relations*, 90, 203; See also Vanman and Miller, "Applications of Emotion Theory," 214.

and beliefs; feelings, such as dislike; and behaviors, such as avoidance. Stereotypes are mental notions and beliefs about members of different social groups. Emotional responses toward others can involve anxiety and hostility. Discrimination stands for unjust treatment based on the membership in a particular group.[26] Perceptions, feelings, and behaviors are dynamic and interconnected. They can be conscious or unconscious and are not as neatly separated as this differentiation might suggest. In the remainder of the chapter, I will investigate two more ingredients of intergroup conflict: stereotypes and a particular emotional response to members of out-groups, fear.

OUR LABELS: STEREOTYPES

Is stereotype just another word for "social categorization," the term we introduced above? We categorize people in order to structure and order our social environment. Categorization in and of itself is not stereotyping, but it is a foundation for the development of stereotypes. Stereotypes are not identical with categorization but are consequences of it. Once we have formed a category for a social group in our mind, stereotypes associate with the category as we further process information. In other words, "a stereotype is a set of characteristics or traits associated with a cognitive category," which we use to process information about members of social groups.[27]

Recall the bereavement visit I addressed above. Not only had I categorized the family in a different part of town even before I ever met them, I also connected certain traits with that category, traits such as "concerned about maintaining a façade," and "emotionally unavailable." Yet what I consider to be emotionally unavailable someone else might describe differently and in more neutral terms as "reserved" or "maintaining emotional composure." Having a chance to meet the family and talking with them on a quite personal and meaningful level helped me become aware of the ways in which I categorized and stereotyped people. I learned from the encounter how quickly we develop mental perceptions of another group, without actually having any personal contact with them.

---

26. Dovidio et al., "From Intervention to Outcome," 246–48.
27. Dovidio et al., "Reducing Contemporary Prejudice," 137f.

Stereotypes do not necessarily have to be negative; there are also positive stereotypes. Through personal experiences we may develop individualized stereotypes of other social groups. Yet, most of the stereotypes are collective and based on a larger consensus of categorizations among members of one group toward other groups.[28] We learn stereotypes as part of our socialization and through interactions with our environment.

Let's remember, stereotypes are mental notions, traits and characteristics we think of when we see or hear of a certain group of people. The term "prejudice" signifies a negative attitude toward members of another group. It has an emotional and affective component. The word "discrimination" is used to describe an unfair behavior toward others based on prejudice.[29]

The Swiss campaign poster with which we began this chapter picks up certain stereotypes about Muslims in post 9/11 Western society. Although wearing a burka is customary only in some cultural groups among Muslims, in the poster it serves as a symbol of oppression of women, a notion that often is generalized to all Muslims and misunderstood as intrinsic to the Muslim faith. The minaret-missile association uses a symbol of prayer and worship to evoke stereotypes of Islam as propagating violence. Here, the experience of terrorist attacks and threats by a radical few has been generalized and projected onto Muslims as a group.

Images such as minaret-missiles also evoke strong feelings, such as fear of being overpowered by a different culture. The emotions that are triggered appeal to an individual's prejudicial attitudes toward Muslims.

The possible restriction of minarets on the basis of the vote raises questions about discrimination, behaviors, and actions resulting from prejudice: Is religious freedom of expression only available to some religious communities and not others? How does this limitation relate to the concept of a democratic society that is based on freedom of expression and a pluralism of opinions and views?

Summarizing, we note: While "stereotypes" are cognitive notions, the term "prejudice" describes feelings and attitudes, and "discrimination" signifies behaviors and actions toward persons of different groups.

28. Taylor and Moghaddam, *Theories of Intergroup Relations,* 161.
29. Dovidio et al., "From Intervention to Outcome," 246–48.

Together with emotional reactions, they are facets of bias. With that in mind, we turn now to review some of the research on stereotypes and stereotyping.

Stereotypes are automatic.

Most of us do not like to admit that we have stereotypes about other groups. Often stereotypes are seen as morally inferior and wrong. However, stereotypes are simply cognitive processes, elements of the ways in which our brains perceive the world. Social identity theory explains stereotypes as based in categorization processes that we undertake to orient ourselves in our complex environment. We categorize not only objects but also social information, and we sometimes do so in simplified and undifferentiated ways, especially when it comes to members of out-groups. Seeing a representative of another group may trigger stereotypes we have developed through socialization and in our environment. Additional stereotypes about the particular social group can quickly be activated. This process is automatic and not necessarily conscious.[30] For example, persons seeing a picture of a family living in Appalachia may project on them stereotypes such as "poor" as well as "inbred" and "illiterate." Censoring their own perceptions as morally wrong, they may not articulate their stereotypes openly. Because they feel they should not "be prejudiced," they may not allow themselves to be aware of their stereotypes. Yet, suppressed or below consciousness, the stereotypes continue to influence their attitude toward persons from Appalachia.

By understanding the development of stereotypes as cognitive and automatic processes rooted in categorization, social psychological research has advanced our insights into stereotypes and has removed the moral judgment. It normalizes the process and thus empowers us to acknowledge our stereotypes, to reflect on them, and to critically investigate them.

Stereotypes are persistent.

In their overview of research on intergroup relations Walter and Cookie Stephan note that stereotypes, once established, are persistent.[31] We have a tendency to register information that confirms preconceived notions.

30. Stephan and Stephan, *Intergroup Relations*, 15.
31. Ibid., 18, 20, 22.

For example, the majority of persons get their news from a news source that represents their point of view. Those who intentionally seek out news reports known for representing opposing viewpoints are rare. It is hard work to keep an open mind and look at an issue from different points of view.

We can observe the same tendency when it comes to processing stereotypes. We are inclined to notice and to remember information that confirms the preconceived notions we already have. Once stereotypes are encoded we like to maintain them.[32] After all, it saves us the hard work of revising our notions and attitudes, which is a much more complex undertaking. Indeed, our minds play some sophisticated tricks in order to hold on to our established notions. Such "tricks" include the "ultimate attribution error," "exception-to-the-rule," and "self-fulfilling prophecy."

In trying to explain the world, we use causal attribution. We are inclined to explain behaviors we notice and attribute causes to them. For example, I might pride myself in never having been in an accident and credit this driving record to my internal abilities as a good driver. I might find it much more difficult to accept responsibility for a mistake or oversight that caused a car accident and attribute the casualty to the other driver or external circumstances. Attribution processes are often emotionally motivated and either self-serving or meet the perceiver's needs.[33]

If I am prejudiced toward African Americans I can easily attribute poor academic performances by African American students with internal factors, the students' lack of abilities and effort. If a Caucasian student completes the tests with the very same grade as the African American student I may consider an external reason, such as stress in the family, rather than posit similar lack of ability and effort. Social psychologists call this process the ultimate attribution error.[34]

Another way to hold on to our notions is the exception-to-the-rule explanation. If we see a member of an out-group behaving contrary to our stereotypes about this group, we tend to identify the behavior as an exception instead of questioning our stereotypes.[35] We discount or

---

32. Ibid., 22.

33. Taylor and Moghaddam, *Theories of Intergroup Relations*, 167.

34. Stephan and Stephan, *Intergroup Relations*, 12.

35. Ibid., 23.

react negatively to information that disconfirms our established point of view. Some studies have even shown that persons dislike individuals who disconfirm their stereotypes. According to one study, male supervisors unfavorably evaluated females who performed extraordinarily well in professions that were traditionally held by males.[36]

A third way to hold on to our stereotypes is the self-fulfilling prophecy.[37] I behave toward a person of another social group in ways that reflect my expectation, which in turn will lead the other to behave in ways that confirm my expectation. One day during my work as a chaplain in a community hospital, my on-call pager went off. I dialed the number on the pager. A nurse in the Emergency Room answered. "We need you right away. If you have another chaplain around, bring them along, too." In the triage area the nurse briefed me: "A person who is a leader in the Gypsy community was brought in. He was a dead on arrival. We expect a lot of people to come." When a member of the Sinti and Roma community is hospitalized, usually many members of the community come to visit. It is common for members of the Roma culture to be expressive and show their grief through loud crying and wailing. The expectation of the staff was that the mourners would be extremely hard to handle. Therefore they wanted not only two chaplains rather than the usual one but had also stationed security guards at all the main entrances. The staff's actions displayed a combination of precaution and proactive preparation on the one hand, and fearful expectation on the other hand. Indeed, about fifteen members of the Roma community did arrive, some crying loudly and expressing their grief outwardly. Yet I wondered: did the obvious stationing of security guards not perhaps in turn cause members of that community to feel threatened and thus amplify their anxiety and heighten their emotions? In other words, that hospital staff acted on their expectation that the community members would be hard to handle might have set up an antagonistic relationship between the hospital and the mourners from the beginning.[38]

With this in mind, and with the help of an example, let us review once more the different ways by which we may maintain stereotypes. Imagine you subscribe to the stereotypical belief that "Germans are serious." Upon meeting a person from Germany you will expect that you are

36. Ibid., 24.

37. Ibid., 25.

38. Grefe, "What Chaplains and Clergy Need."

in for a serious conversation. Based on that expectation you may bring up rather serious topics to which your conversation partner responds accordingly (self-fulfilling prophecy). If your German conversation partner is unexpectedly funny, you have a number of options of how to process the experience. Theoretically, you could say to yourself, "Hey, Germans may be a lot funnier than I thought!" and you would question your stereotype. As pointed out above, persons tend to look first for options that maintain their stereotypes and categories. Notions of "funny" and "serious" are fluid and difficult to confirm or disconfirm. You may not pick up on the subtle jokes your German conversation partner makes because you are not expecting him or her to be funny. You may hold on to your stereotype by attributing the humor not to an internal characteristic of the person but to an external factor (which technically is called an attribution error): "Perhaps this person already had one or two of the beers that Germans like so much." Or you may file away the experience in your mind in the "exceptionally-funny-German-I-met-recently" category, considering the funny German conversation partner as an exception to the rule.

Stereotypes are persistent once encoded. However, in chapters 3 and 4 we will demonstrate that they can be changed when approached intentionally.

Stereotypes can trigger emotions.

Stereotypes are cognitive processes, yet they can trigger strong emotions.[39] Meeting a member of a different social group can bring about feelings of dislike or attraction, fear or suspicion. Our feelings can be strong or less intense. We can have ambivalent sentiments toward certain groups. The Swiss campaign poster is controversial because it so cleverly manipulates the emotions of the target audience. The poster plays on certain fears related to stereotypical associations with Muslims, such as terrorism. At the same time it fans the flames of fears of foreign cultural influence by exaggerating and misrepresenting the small number of religious symbols of the Muslim faith that in fact exist in Switzerland. Xenophobia, the fear of anything foreign, is not a stereotype but a feeling connected with stereotypes associated with persons from foreign countries. Negative feelings can intensify and solidify stereotypes.

39. Stephan and Stephan, *Intergroup Relations*, 17; Dovidio et al., "From Intervention to Outcome," 247.

We often process stereotypes differently depending on the mood we find ourselves in. While emotions are specific, moods describe more global states of feelings. If we experience intense moods, such as fear, anger, or elation, we are too excited to bother with the details of careful processing and rely on simplified perception and stereotyping.[40]

To sum up, stereotyping is a cognitive process. On the one hand it can trigger emotions. On the other hand emotional states influence how much we rely on simplified perceptions and stereotypes. We have given much attention to cognitive processes such as categorization and stereotype that influence our relationships with persons from other social groups. Social identity theory reminds us that our investment in our membership in social groups has a strong meaning for our self-image. Intergroup relationships are also shaped by evaluations and affect. Emotions are an important ingredient in intergroup relations. In the next section we focus on one emotion in particular: fear.

OUR FEARS

At the beginning of the chapter, I mentioned the exploration of fear of the other in individuals through a psychoanalytic lens. In this last part of the chapter we seek to understand how fear plays out in the relationships between social groups. Social psychologists Walter and Cookie Stephan have analyzed the role of fear and threat as causes of prejudice. Fear is a result of a sense of being threatened or assaulted. The Stephans distinguish four different types of threat that contribute to prejudice: realistic threat, symbolic threat, negative stereotype, and intergroup anxiety. As we introduce the four types of threat, the case of the minaret ban shall once more serve as a concrete example helping us to understand the role of fear in intergroup relations. We will focus in particular on symbolic threat because it is especially relevant in interreligious relationships.

The first type of fear is related to a *realistic threat* to the political and economic power or to the material or physical welfare of a group.[41] The threat may be real in a narrow sense as well as include a perceived threat that is real to the perceiver and contributes to a sense of fear. Members of minority groups, such as Muslim immigrants living in Europe, experi-

---

40. Wilder, "Role of Anxiety," 93; Bodenhausen, "Emotions, Arousal," 21. See also "Anxiety" in chapter 4.

41. Stephan and Stephan, "Integrated Threat Theory," 25.

ence real disadvantages due to lack of citizenship, language abilities, and educational resources. They also may fear physical harm, as numerous immigrants have been beaten or had their houses set on fire by gangs and extremist groups.

Members of the majority groups in Europe in turn may feel a sense of threat related to terror attacks in the United States and Europe as well as violent attacks on public individuals who have outwardly criticized behaviors of some extreme Muslim groups. It is the motivation and result of terror attacks to create a constant state of fear that a violent attack could happen at anytime. Terrorist groups harm not only their victims and society at large but also the Muslim community. Fear of terror has spread and been generalized to Muslim immigrants in general. This heightened sense of fear in the population can easily be exploited by right wing nationalist campaigns. Given the low actual number of Muslims living in Switzerland, the prohibition of minarets is disproportionate. Fear must have been the primary factor leading to the vote.

Second, *negative stereotypes* serve as a basis for the expectations of conflictual or problematic interactions with members of the out-group.[42] As outlined above, negative stereotypes color the way we interact with members of out-groups and may unnecessarily stir conflict from the start.

Third, *intergroup anxiety* signifies the anticipation of negative consequences during interactions with members of out-groups.[43] In-group members may feel incompetent and unfamiliar when interacting with out-group members. For example, joining a family celebration or a religious ceremony of a friend from another culture can be enriching and exciting. At the same time we feel somewhat nervous, as we do not know the customs, what to wear, or how to greet fellow guests. We fear making a mistake. Members of minority groups may be nervous when interacting with those from a majority or more powerful group for fear that they will be rejected or ridiculed.[44] Especially when we do not know much about the other group and have not had much prior contact with them or with their ilk, our anxiety may be higher.[45] The more anxious we are, the more cautious we are about what we reveal about ourselves,

42. Ibid., 27.

43. Ibid.

44. Ibid.

45. Stephan and Stephan, *Intergroup Relations*, 128–29.

especially during initial interactions.[46] I remember clearly my first interactions as a chaplain with Jewish patients and as a pastoral educator of chaplains working with rabbinical students who completed their hospital internship in my training courses. As a woman born and raised in Germany I was worried how Jewish patients or students might experience me. Would my accent trigger painful memories for older Jewish patients? Would my Jewish students find it harder to trust me as their mentor? Those were my fears. In reality, I experienced much openness and grace. Since I worked intensively with my students for months at a time, I had a chance to address my fears directly. At the beginning of the training courses I raised issues of the complex relationships between Christians and Jews and talked about my understanding of my history as a German. Once attended to, my fears lost their power.

We may experience our intercultural anxiety indirectly not as fear but as a closed attitude toward other persons. At times, it is easier to express disdain for another group than to acknowledge that we are afraid. Finally, a way to remain in our comfort zone and avoid feelings of anxiety altogether is to avoid contact with those who are different from us or who represent a foreign culture or belief system. We avoid close contact and remain ignorant, which just increases our fear of future interaction. This tendency may be part of the reason why Swiss voters in rural areas with little or no contact with Muslims supported the prohibition of minarets.[47] The less they know about the other, the more they fear the other. In turn, intercultural anxiety and fear of negative stereotype may cause some Muslim immigrants to avoid an active engagement with Western society, the language and culture of their new home. Cultural integration is a mutual process, which can be hindered by intercultural anxiety on both ends. Often Muslim immigrants feel that they have to choose between their old society and the new one. The older generation is attached to the old society, while the children often identify completely with the new, causing extreme stress in the families since there is no hybrid role model as a choice.[48]

Finally, *symbolic threats* are threats experienced on the basis of different worldviews.[49] As people of different cultures and traditions live

46. Ibid., 130.

47. Zumach, "Analyse des Schweizer Referendums."

48. Explanation offered by Sarah Badran.

49. Stephan and Stephan, "Integrated Threat Theory," 25.

closer together they also encounter more intimately their diverse views of how to live a good and moral life and how to organize society. Symbolic beliefs and a sense of threat through the different values of others are especially relevant for the relationships of interreligious groups. Religious paths, while having some common approaches to understanding life, also have differences in morals, values, beliefs, and attitudes. One can experience the worldviews of others as a challenge to one's own beliefs.

Considering social identity theory, not only our religious beliefs but also our membership in religious groups can give us a sense of belonging and identification. We may experience this belonging as threatened by the existence of groups with a very different set of beliefs. These threats arise in part because the in-group believes that its own values are morally right.[50] The differences may be perceived as being in competition with each other. For majority and dominant groups, worldviews and religious beliefs can serve to rationalize and legitimize their sense of superiority. Different symbolic beliefs can contribute significantly to negative attitudes and prejudice toward members of out-groups.[51]

Looking through the lens of social psychology, we see interreligious dialogue in a new light. Much of interreligious dialogue focuses on an exchange of ideas and belief systems. However, religious beliefs and traditions have not only a theological but also a psychological significance. They give persons a sense of belonging and identity. Different beliefs can thus represent a sense of competition or threat and contribute to interreligious conflict. This does not mean that interreligious dialogue is irrelevant or obsolete. It does not mean that it is meaningless to sit down with persons of other faiths and to articulate what we have in common or what distinguishes us. A social psychological lens demonstrates the complexity of interreligious dialogue by considering the social and relational factors that may enter into the encounters. Engaging neighbors of different faiths needs to include awareness and intentional consideration of intergroup relations.

The vote to ban minarets in Switzerland can be understood as a reaction to a symbolic threat. The minarets symbolize a different belief system and way of worship. The burka represents common stereotypical associations with Islam such as sharia law, honor killings, and other issues of authoritarian power, especially over women. While gender in-

50. Ibid., 25–27.
51. Esses et al., "Values, Stereotypes, and Emotions," 139, 159.

equality and oppression are not representative of the Muslim faith and are part of cultural traditions of some immigrant cultures, they clash with Western norms of democracy and equality. Among supporters of the ban were also numerous liberal female voters protesting a culture they experience as authoritarian and oppressive toward women.[52] The case demonstrates the role of symbolic beliefs and values in intergroup relations. It also makes apparent the importance and complexity of sorting through perceptions and emotional reactions.

The four threat components—realistic threat, negative stereotypes, intergroup anxiety, and symbolic threat—influence attitudes toward out-groups and contribute to emotions, such as hatred and disdain, as well as to evaluations, such as dislike or disapproval. The stronger the attachment to the in-group, the greater will likely be the sense of threat from out-groups.[53] In a time of strong social transitions and pluralism of cultures and worldviews, it is understandable when people find in their cultural and religious group a place of belonging, support, and security. The more important our membership in our particular group is for our sense of self and identity, the more we tend to experience other groups as a challenge and even a threat.

SUMMARY

In order to function and process the vast amount of information in our environment, we categorize it. We categorize objects as well as persons we meet. We group together what is similar. Especially when we are unfamiliar with persons, we rely on categories to understand people and neglect their individual and unique traits. We often see groups of persons whom we do not know well and who are different from us as much more similar to each other than they really are.

Our membership in social groups gives us a place in society and enhances our self-esteem. We quickly develop a sense of loyalty to the group to which we belong. We strive to belong to groups with a positive image and higher status. By categorizing, we often compare social groups and do so in a competitive manner. Stereotypes are traits and associations we develop automatically on the basis of our categorizations. Often we are not even aware of them. While stereotypes are cognitive

---

52. Zumach, "Analyse des Schweizer Referendums."
53. Stephan and Stephan, "Integrated Threat Theory," 37.

notions they can trigger more or less intense emotions and are persistent once they are encoded in our minds.

Social comparisons as well as stereotypes can contribute significantly to conflicts between different groups in society. Perceptions, expectations, and emotions are dynamic and interrelated. Fears of one another also play a role in intergroup tensions. Different groups may represent real or perceived threats to one another. Lack of contact and negative stereotypes keep members of different groups apart from each other.

Finally, different cultural and religious groups often experience the existence of other belief systems and values as a symbolic threat to their own way of life. Symbolic threats, therefore, contribute to conflicts and separation in religiously and culturally diverse societies.

The controversy around the ban of minarets also tells a hopeful story we have neglected so far. Many Christian churches openly criticized the campaign for the ban and called for the freedom of religious expression for all citizens.[54] The society of minority groups in Switzerland countered the right-wing initiative with its own poster and a completely different vision. This poster depicts a large sky with a white cloud surrounded by sunshine. Different steeples of houses of worship of diverse religious traditions rise from the bottom into the sky. The poster's slogan is: "The sky above Switzerland is big enough." Non-Muslim groups with their own and different symbolic beliefs developed the poster motivated by values of equality and respect for human rights.[55] They showed solidarity with Muslim immigrants and presented a different vision, in so doing subverting the power of fear and introducing a more expansive view of interreligious and intercultural relations. In the following chapters we will pursue strategies and paths that help reduce and change stereotype and move beyond fear of those who are different.

54. Fistarol, "Der Himmel."
55. Ibid.

3

Religious Communities in Connection

Intergroup Contact

"THAT WAS A PRETTY weird idea you presented today." Mr. Mueller, a parishioner in a German congregation where I visited as a guest preacher, approaches me, passing small groups of people who chat and crowd the foyer during social hour after church. Coffee cup in hand, he sits down next to me. "I've never heard the scripture passage presented in the way you did today," he says, skeptical of the sermon of this young guest preacher right out of school. "An eye for an eye, a tooth for a tooth: you just can't soften that message. It calls for retaliation."

Although he seems critical, I am glad that he wants to talk to me. In my sermon I talked about the passage: "If any harm follows, then you shall give life for life, eye for eye, tooth for tooth, hand for hand."[1] Commonly the passage is understood as a statement of revenge, of re-paying like with like. However, the notion of justice in this passage is not that of retaliation but of restitution: If my behavior causes harm to my neighbor, I am liable and it is my responsibility to fully repair the damage my actions have brought about. That's what I had read in a book about the law in the Hebrew Bible and that's what I had hoped to convey in my sermon at this congregation: the principle guiding the laws is humane, based on a notion of reparation rather than revenge.

Mr. Mueller continues: "An eye for an eye, that's very much the spirit of the Old Testament. Remember all the stories about a punishing God. That's only overcome in the New Testament, when Jesus reveals the God of love." I am familiar with Mr. Mueller's attitude, contrasting

---

1. Exod 21:23.

48

the God of punishment in the "Old Testament" with the God of love in the '"New Testament" and the "old covenant, Israel's religion of the law" with the "new testament, the liberating gospel of freedom."

I had encountered this pattern of thought before in the theological library of the university where I was studying, in numerous commentaries, even those published in the 1950s and 1960s. I was shocked. Even the horrifying experiences of the Holocaust had not reversed many Christians' understanding of their faith as superior and more developed than the Jewish tradition. These anti-Judaistic mind-sets made it from commentaries into sermons and lesson plans for confirmation classes and religious instruction. They still shaped the beliefs of many Christians. So Mr. Mueller was hardly alone in his thinking.

Mr. Mueller and the scholars who wrote their commentaries would probably protest my labeling their interpretation as anti-Judaistic. They might insist that their understanding of the Hebrew Bible is based in theological belief and not in stereotype. However, theology is alive in social contexts, and religious beliefs can serve as rationalizations of stereotype and prejudice.

This chapter has two major parts. First, we will continue to look at the relationship of religion and intergroup relations. The discipline of social psychology will help us to develop a broader understanding of conflicting beliefs and religious teachings. Second, we will introduce a first remedy for interreligious conflict in the form of intergroup contact theory. If interreligious conflicts are not just a matter of incompatible beliefs, but are shaped by relational and social dynamics, we will only resolve them by addressing teachings *and* relational issues. I had hoped to raise questions and introduce a new way of thinking through my sermon. Over coffee I had a theological discussion with Mr. Mueller about how Christians read the Hebrew Bible. I wonder, what would it have been like to visit the local synagogue with him and a group from the church and ask questions in that context and with that congregation about this same passage? Personally meeting members of a Jewish community and learning from them in their terms how they understand their tradition might more powerfully change minds.

In the second part of the chapter we will see how personal contact between different cultural and religious groups can open new horizons of understanding. I will outline how these personal encounters will have to be structured in order to change mental models and lessen stereotypes.

RELIGION AND INTERGROUP RELATIONS

Many religious people are open to persons of different backgrounds because their faith calls them to respect each individual human being. Others who identify as nonreligious are skeptical toward religions because they see people of faith as judgmental and closed-minded toward other systems of belief. When it comes to religion and bias we seem caught in a contradiction. History is full of acts of compassion rooted in religious beliefs. At the same time we find many examples of wars and prejudice that are carried out in the name of religion.

I will introduce Gordon Allport's intergroup contact theory in detail in the second part of this chapter. Allport also studied the relationship of religion and prejudice.[2] He summarized the contradiction of religion as follows: "It makes prejudice and it unmakes prejudice."[3] In the 1950s and 1960s Allport conducted studies exploring attitudes toward other cultural and religious groups. He found that prejudice was lower in individuals who reported no religious affiliation. On the other hand, deeply religious persons reported that their faith taught them to see all other human beings as equal.[4] For Allport, the root cause of prejudice is not religion itself but rather the role it plays in a person's life. People practice their religion in different ways. Allport distinguishes between two types of religious practice, between "institutionalized" or "extrinsic," and "interiorized" or "intrinsic" religion.[5] Extrinsic religion focuses on particular religious institutions and conventions and gives a person a sense of security and social status. Extrinsic religion shows a stronger investment in established forms of religion and can emphasize tribalist instincts. We might picture extrinsic practitioners of religion as persons who attend religious services and practice certain rituals primarily because they have been raised that way. That's what they know, and they feel comfortable with those traditions. Rarely do they personally reflect on the meaning of their practice or question their beliefs. In contrast, intrinsic religion pursues religion as an end in itself and provides a per-

---

2. Batson and Stocks provide an overview of Allport's theory as well as subsequent studies of the relationship of religion and prejudice in "Religion and Prejudice," 413ff.

3. Allport, *Nature of Prejudice*, 444.

4. Ibid., 451.

5. Batson and Stocks, "Religion and Prejudice," 415; Allport, *Nature of Prejudice*, 454.

son with a comprehensive view of life.[6] Persons who practice intrinsic religion have internalized religious teachings and practices. Their beliefs have significance in the way they approach their daily life. Extrinsic religion is associated with increased prejudice and intrinsic religion with reduced prejudice.[7]

Allport's studies were limited by their reliance on self-report questionnaires, for when reporting about personal attitudes participants may not always admit their prejudice, not even to themselves. One of my Christian chaplain students saw his Jewish peers in his learning group as brothers and sisters. He acknowledged that the Christian faith was deeply rooted in the Jewish tradition, yet—like Mr. Mueller—he understood the Christian tradition as a fulfillment of the Jewish faith, the new covenant. He had difficulty understanding that his Jewish peers did not feel that he was treating them as equals. His bias was covert and hidden behind a benevolent attitude. One concern about Allport's initial studies was that the self-reports could not capture covert prejudice.[8]

What complicates matters is that religion seems to reject prejudice toward some groups while at the same time endorsing stereotypes toward other out-groups. For example, many religious believers feel that their faith teaches them to respect people no matter what their racial identity is. There was a time, however, when Christians used certain passages in the Bible to justify slavery. Likewise today, many Christians quote biblical passages to reject homosexuals. Their religion encourages prejudice toward GLBT persons or at least discourages them from learning more from their GLBT neighbors about sexual orientation and identity. In the language of social psychology, their religious beliefs may proscribe or endorse prejudice toward homosexuality.

As I was visiting his congregation only to give a guest sermon, I did not know Mr. Mueller well, but he seemed to be a deeply religious person who cared about his faith like an "intrinsic" practitioner of religion. He would hardly understand his view as biased. However, the religious teachings he had incorporated had contributed to a bias toward another faith. His way of thinking is still common in parts of the Christian community that understand the Jewish tradition as a religion of the law that is overcome in the Christian "new covenant" revealing the

6. Batson and Stocks, "Religion and Prejudice," 415.

7. Ibid., 416.

8. Ibid., 417.

God of love. From a theological perspective this understanding neglects how the Jewish community understands the Hebrew Bible on its own terms. From a social-psychological perspective, this pattern of thinking represents a covert prejudice that is endorsed by some teachings in the Christian tradition.

Religion, even in its intrinsic form, seems to reject prejudice toward some groups while at the same time endorsing stereotypes toward other out-groups. The extrinsic/intrinsic typology we have been using to distinguish between two types of religious practice cannot fully account for the relationship between religion and prejudice.

To address this quandary, the psychologists C. Daniel Batson and E. L. Stocks have classified a third type of religious practice. In addition to extrinsic religion—which they see as "religion as means," religion that is self-serving and enhances a person's sense of security and comfort—and intrinsic religion—which they see as "religion as end"—they identify this third type as "religion as quest," signifying a deep involvement with questions of life, death, and meaning, resisting simple answers and living with ambiguity.[9] In their studies, Batson and Stock found that religion as a quest is connected with the lowest rate of prejudice, overt and covert, and this may have to do with a generally open attitude of this type of believer.[10]

For Allport as well as Batson and Stocks, different types of personal religious practice account for the different degrees of prejudicial attitudes toward other religious groups. Psychologists Jackson and Hunsberger, however, are not convinced that religious prejudice is best explained by personal differences in the practice of religion. They explored the attitudes of religious believers toward persons who believe differently or identify themselves as nonbelievers. They investigated the sentiments of almost three hundred students at a medium-sized Canadian university. Students who followed fundamentalist and Christian orthodox beliefs favored their own groups as well as Christian believers in general and expressed negative attitudes toward those of other beliefs and particularly toward nonbelievers. Students who identified decidedly as nonbelievers in turn expressed negative attitudes toward religious persons. Individuals with less pronounced religious identities were more tolerant toward persons of a variety of beliefs.[11]

9. Ibid., 417.

10. Ibid., 419.

11. Jackson and Hunsberger, "Intergroup Perspective," 512–19.

Jackson and Hunsberger claim that instead of individual differ-ences, intergroup dynamics are best suited to explain stereotypes.[12] In particular, realistic conflict and social identity theories can shed helpful light on interreligious relationships. Let us recall briefly the main tenets of these theories.

Social identity theory suggests that our membership in social groups provides us a sense of identity. Belonging to a certain group can enhance our self-esteem. We tend to favor our own group and compare ourselves with other groups, often with a sense of competitiveness. Accordingly, in Jackson and Hunsberger's study, participants favored their own groups and groups similar to their own beliefs. In the debate about the minaret ban in Switzerland, opponents selectively address negative aspects of some Muslim cultures, such as inequality between males and females. This is done without differentiating between cultural customs and re-ligious teachings and without developing a broader understanding of Islam. This selective perception serves to maintain the notion of superi-ority of one's own tradition over another.

Realistic conflict theory explains intergroup conflict as a competi-tion for resources and influence. Different social groups are in conflict because there are real differences in their access to resources such as land, education, money, political influence, and status. Like other social groups, some religious groups lobby for their values among political rep-resentatives or in elections. Some religious organizations seek for their values to be represented in school curricula.[13] Attempts to introduce prayer in public schools come to mind by way of example.

As I am writing this chapter, a firestorm of protest and controversy about a planned Islamic community center in lower Manhattan has erupted. The project, Park 51, to be located a few blocks from Ground Zero, is envisioned as a Muslim cultural center providing a place for worship, dialogue, the arts, and education. The announcement regard-ing the community center has been countered by loud protests stating that a Muslim center close to Ground Zero is a provocation and stands in the way of healing from the terrorist attacks on September 11—as if there had not been hundreds of Muslims among the victims and those who came to their rescue. The outcries of protest strike Welton Gaddy, a Baptist minister and interfaith leader, as a great irony: There have been

12. Ibid., 519.

13. Jackson and Hunsberger, "Intergroup Perspective," 510.

many calls for Muslims to counter extremism. However, when they come forth in helpful and meaningful ways, they face a severe backlash, "indicating a continued fear and ignorance of the Muslim faith, even as its most peaceful."[14] At first, the controversy smoldered rather quietly in the right-wing blogosphere. Once people discovered the issue's potential to electrify midterm election campaigns, however, political leaders chimed in, made headlines in the media, and kindled the fire of prejudice toward Muslims and their faith.

The building of a Muslim community center and mosque is not only experienced as a provocation in lower Manhattan but across the United States. In Murfreesboro, Tennessee, protestors with "Vote for Jesus" t-shirts demonstrated against the building of a mosque in town. People here as well as in other cities fear that mosques will be breeding grounds for Muslim extremism. The new mosques are built to accommodate a growing number of Muslim immigrants. Diana Eck, a theologian who has devoted her work to understanding religious pluralism, sees the building of mosques in the larger context of the American history of immigration. As groups of immigrants and their religious communities have settled, they have begun to put down roots and build something, indicating: "We're here! We're not just camping."[15]

In terms of realistic conflict theory we can explain the recent protests against the mosques as follows: As different ethnic and religious groups make their home in the United States, established groups feel threatened and seek to assert their influence. Moreover, nonreligious interests for media headlines and political votes exploit the controversies for their gain. On a deeper emotional level, deep-seated fears of the other are stirred up and brought to the surface. Realistic conflict theory provides a significant explanation for strong reactions and prejudice as different and minority religious groups establish their presence in a society.

Jackson and Hunsberger conclude that "religious intergroup relations are no different from any other form of intergroup relations, and . . . for a variety of reasons, group identifications can generate intergroup antagonism."[16]

What can we take away from these social-psychological studies of religion and intergroup relations?

14. Gaddy, "Great Irony."
15. Loller, "Opponents Fight New Mosques."
16. Jackson and Hunsberger, "Intergroup Perspective," 521.

Jackson and Hunsberger claim that intergroup dynamics foster stereotypes, no matter how individuals practice their religions, because group identification is so important to traditional forms of religiosity.[17] It would be a mistake to conclude that individualized faith practiced apart from religious institutions would be a solution to the problem of religion and prejudice. Most religious practices are connected to the life of a community. For example, Christian identity is fundamentally shaped through the sacraments of baptism and communion. Both rituals affirm the understanding of the church as the body of Christ. Christians, as well as believers in other traditions, rely on the support and nurturing of the community. One origin of the word religion is *religare,* "to bind fast," proposing the notion of a bond between humans and God as well as between human beings. Community relates to religion like food to the body. Just as food sustains our bodies, someone following a religious path cannot survive without community. In a more basic sense, human beings—whether they practice religion or not—are communal, deeply social beings. We seek community by associating with friends, family, colleagues, and members of organizations. We enjoy the benefits and suffer the troubles connected with social existence. Jackson and Hunsberger remind us that religion is not above the problems that come with communal living. Religious groups, just like other groups, are vulnerable to the very human dynamics of intergroup competition and conflict. With their study, Jackson and Hunsberger want to challenge religious and nonreligious persons to recognize their susceptibility to prejudice. The researchers hope that an awareness of intergroup dynamics will lead to more harmonious intergroup relations.[18]

From studies conducted by Allport, Batson, and Stocks we learn that religion is not only vulnerable to prejudice but can potentially contribute to the overcoming of prejudice. They take religious institutions seriously as settings where intergroup relations can be practiced and improved. Religious teachings of compassion and interconnections between people can "unmake prejudice." Batson and Stocks therefore encourage the development of prejudice reduction programs in religious settings, programs that not only focus on the teaching of compassion and prejudice reduction but also give religious communities a chance to practice these teachings.[19]

17. Ibid., 511.
18. Ibid., 521.
19. Batson and Stocks, "Religion and Prejudice," 425.

In summary, psychological studies of the relationship of religion and intergroup relations offer important insights to religious communities and leaders. The studies teach us that, as religious communities, we can use our religion as a buffer in relation to other social groups. Or we can use our religious settings to connect to other groups, to "unmake prejudice," and to work toward more peaceful relationships between people of different religious paths. Batson and Stocks point out: "Even if one's religion talks the talk of universal acceptance and compassion, this talk needs to be combined with opportunities to walk the walk."[20]

As a local church in Germany, we once tried to do just that: We wanted to move beyond the preaching and teaching of peace. We created opportunities to get together in the hope of contributing to a better understanding and to stronger relationships with Turkish citizens in our neighborhood. We wanted to expand our knowledge of the customs, traditions, and beliefs of our neighbors and to overcome our ignorance and our stereotypes. Our leadership team felt parishioners would not respond well to educational seminars. The Christian and Muslim houses of worship were just one block apart and we wanted to create connections and get together. A street festival was our first approach. The leaders of the Islamic community joined in our efforts and welcomed us on their grounds. We set up tents in the parking lot. Volunteers from both communities prepared food and organized games for the children. Our good intentions soon met some obstacles. The language barriers made it difficult for participants to communicate, and we had underestimated how hard it was for them to interact with each other. We learned that face-to-face contact has the potential to open minds but that such contact in and of itself will not reduce stereotypes and is not a quick fix. As we cleaned up from the festivities we wondered what we might have done differently to facilitate connection between our church and the Muslim community. We wished we had known of methods and steps that would have helped us direct the event in more effective ways.

We did not know that in the middle of the twentieth century social scientists had indeed brought people of different ethnic and racial backgrounds together. Those social scientists developed insights and strategies regarding how these encounters would best have to be structured in order to help persons engage each other and become less prejudiced. They articulated what they learned in the intergroup contact hypothesis.

20. Ibid.

This theory helps us to create purposeful interactions and experiences in religious communities, interactions in which we learn how to overcome prejudice. In the second part of the chapter we will take a closer look at the intergroup contact hypothesis that would have helped our local church to interact with our Turkish neighbors in more fruitful ways.

MEETING THE OTHER: INTERGROUP CONTACT THEORY

The movie *Remember the Titans* tells the success story of a high school football team in Alexandria, Virginia, during the 1970s. The team won the state championship and in the process also succeeded in developing bonds between its African American and Caucasian members. While the movie is based on a true story, many details are idealized in service of the plot about the overcoming of racial prejudice. The movie serves in this chapter as an illustration of the influential intergroup contact theory, which was formulated by Gordon Allport in the 1950s. This theory is concerned with the development of practical strategies to combat stereotype and prejudice by bringing members of out-groups together in small group encounters. Although numerous scenes in the film are fictional, they demonstrate the main tenets of the intergroup contact hypothesis, a hypothesis that has been widely tested and further developed since its inception. The story in *Remember the Titans* is rich with scenes that can explain elements of intergroup contact in the context of racial relations. We will explore intergroup contact as a tool for improving intergroup relations, which can be applied to the complex relationships of diverse religious groups.

In 1971, in a desegregated school in Virginia, the African American Herman Boone is assigned as head coach to the high school's football team, replacing the popular white coach Bill Yoast. After many players of the all-white team threaten to leave the team and risk their college scholarships, Yoast agrees to stay on as assistant coach. African American and Caucasian team members work through conflict and tension during a rigorous training camp. Through group building strategies they come together as a successful athletic team that eventually wins the state championship. The film describes the growing partnership of the two coaches as well as the close friendship of team members Gerry and Julius, one Caucasian and the other African American. Gerry suffers an accident, becomes paralyzed and is not able to join his team during their final victory. He goes on to win a medal in the Paralympics. The film ends with a reunion of the team at Gerry's funeral after he dies in another car accident. Their sense of a shared community has lived on, although everyone has gone their separate ways.

Gordon Allport's 1954 study *The Nature of Prejudice* is considered a classic in social psychology and provides a succinct summary of the intergroup contact hypothesis. After World War II Allport and other social scientists studied racial relations with the goal of making a difference and eliminating prejudice.[21] The intergroup contact theory has generated further study, influenced U.S. policies on desegregation in schools, and shaped approaches to multicultural education.[22] The scientific research and impetus for social change connected with the contact hypothesis generated the kind of environment and policies that would bring a coach like Herman Boone to Alexandria high school and make it possible for African American and Caucasian students to study, train, and play together on one team.

Summarized, Allport's intergroup contact hypothesis is as follows:

> Prejudice (unless deeply rooted in the character structure of the individual) may be reduced by equal status contact between majority and minority groups in the pursuit of common goals. The effect is greatly enhanced if this contact is sanctioned by institutional supports, (i.e., by law, custom, or local atmosphere), and if it is of a sort that leads to the perception of common interests and common humanity between members of two groups.[23]

Allport specifies four facilitating conditions for prejudice reduction when persons of different ethnic or racial backgrounds come in contact with each other: equal status, common goals, cooperation, and authority support. After more study, a fifth condition was added: the groups have to create friendship potential.[24] We will take a look at each of these facilitating strategies of intergroup contact.

---

21. Other theorists are R. M. Williams, S. W. Cook, and T. Pettigrew. Pettigrew, "Intergroup Contact Theory," provides an overview of major developments of the theory.

22. Pettigrew, "Intergroup Contact Theory," 66.

23. Allport, *Nature of Prejudice*, 281.

24. Pettigrew, "Intergroup Contact Theory," 80.

Small contact groups are based on equal status of the participants.

In the film, rapport between African American and Caucasian team members develops slowly against the backdrop of racial divisions in their town. The high school students have a strong bonding experience during their training camp. While their attitudes toward each other have changed, upon their return home they realize that life at home has not changed and racial segregation still remains. As the bus taking them back from training camp pulls into the parking lot one team member sighs: "Back to the real world."

The team members greet their parents, who still resist the idea of a racially mixed team. Their old friends do not understand their newly developed friendships with members of another race. When some team members want to celebrate a successful game in a local restaurant, the owner refuses to serve the African American member of their small group. Herman Boone, the African American coach, stands out not only because of the color of his skin but also because he personifies the transition to a desegregated football team. One evening, as Boone and his family are gathered, a brick is thrown through the window of their living room. Racial prejudice and tension persist in the town.

The scenes we considered illustrate that small group situations cannot undo or negate the divisions and status differences of their participants in the larger social context. Some group members come from majority or dominant groups while others come from minority and less powerful groups. They bring their group status as well as feelings connected with that status, feelings such as superiority and inferiority, with them into the group experience. Status differences outside of the contact situation cannot be overcome. However, studies have established that even if members have different status from one another in society, equal status within the intergroup contact situation enhances successful intergroup contact. It is important that both groups perceive equal status within their small group setting.[25]

The film illustrates a few strategies that create equal status of group members within their group situation. Whereas team members had been accustomed to traveling separately to school along the dividing lines of race, black and white, Coach Boone creates new categories neutralizing those old divisions. Now the team is differentiated by whether

25. Pettigrew and Tropp, "Allport's Intergroup Contact Hypothesis," 264.

they play offense or defense, with Boone coaching offense and Yoast coaching defense. African American and Caucasian offensive players sit together; African American and Caucasian defensive players share the bench. Regardless of skin color, team members room, eat, and play with either their offensive or defensive teammates. At training camp, black and white players are equal and old patterns of status are irrelevant.

While old social categories have provided *some* team members with a sense of self-esteem, egalitarian norms can create a new positive sense of identity for *all* group members.[26] However, the new sense of equality can also be experienced as a threat to those members who previously held a higher group status. There are some Caucasian team members who remain resistant to the changes most of the team is undergoing. Later, during a competitive game, one of them will try to undermine the success of the team and will ultimately be suspended from the team.

Attempts to neutralize previous status differences can backfire when they are experienced as a threat.[27] When a group leader redresses status differences she or he may be perceived as unfair.[28] In the movie, coach Boone is at times particularly tough with African American team members, perhaps to counter the impression that he favors team members that share his ethnic identity. His behavior is at times so harsh that coach Yoast raises Boone's awareness, telling him that he is walking a fine line between being tough and being crazy.

I learned how challenging it can be to establish equality within a group when I supervised a culturally diverse group of chaplain interns. The students from Africa and South America were unfamiliar with our spiritual care training methods shaped by Western values of individualism and by communication patterns foreign to them. I tried to level the playing field by raising the awareness of culturally diverse communication styles and adjusting our ways of interacting in order to accommodate the students from different cultures. My Western students experienced my behavior as "overcompensating" and taking sides for some students over others. I realized that allowing more room for disadvantaged students ran the risk of isolating them even more if they then were perceived as "teacher's pets." Creating group equality turned out to be a delicate balancing act. The backlash against affirmative action

26. Brewer and Miller, "Beyond the Contact Hypothesis," 295.

27. Hewstone and Brown, "Contact Is Not Enough," 15.

28. Worchel, "Role of Cooperation," 290.

policies in admissions to colleges and universities is perhaps another representation of such resistance against leveling the playing field.

Establishing equality within the group situation also entails the avoidance of power hierarchies. Getting help from other group members can create feelings of indebtedness among those at the receiving end.[29] Perceiving oneself consistently as the helper maintains feelings of superiority, which defeats the purpose of intergroup contact. Of course, this does not mean that group members should not be encouraged to assist each other. Through helping we can learn much about persons of other groups as it brings us closer to them and exposes us to their life stories. Serving regularly in a soup kitchen for the homeless can help a person learn about the situation of homeless people and reduce stereotypes. A pastor who ran a homeless program told me that he once replaced the service model of the traditional Thanksgiving meal with a shared potluck. Participants did not know who was homeless and who was not. It made some "givers" uncomfortable. The shared potluck was a powerful equalizer. Egalitarianism within the group implies opportunities for reciprocal helping and mutual relationships.

By way of summary, small groups cannot change the inequality that exists outside of their group, but egalitarian status within the group situation can replace old categories of inferiority and superiority. Being part of a community of equals can feed a sense of identity so we do not have to rely on being superior in order to feel good about ourselves. As group leaders seek to establish equality in a group situation, they need to be mindful of a possible backlash when group members who are used to their privileged situation outside the group feel threatened. Group leaders also need to be on the lookout for subtle power hierarchies in the group through one-sided helping, which can jeopardize parity.

Group members work toward common goals.

Athletic teams, such as the Titans, represent prime examples for prejudice reduction through active goal-oriented efforts.[30] Every team member is charged to work toward a shared goal in a competition against other groups. The shared efforts in reaching a common goal create a new group identity. Athletic teams can be successful in achieving group

29. Ibid., 292.
30. Pettigrew and Tropp, "Allport's Intergroup Contact Hypothesis," 265.

cohesiveness because their cooperation is not just focused on one single event. They work together over time in order to win games. Not a single superordinate goal but a series of cumulative goals is required in order to reduce intergroup conflict.[31] The idea of superordinate goals has been further developed in the concept of the common in-group identity model, which I will discuss in more detail in the following chapter.

The power of a superordinate goal is illustrated when coach Boone welcomes the players to the training camp with a motivational speech. He holds up their team uniform with the words: "Now you are the Titans. When you put on this jersey you work toward perfection." He asks them to put aside their differences in order to unite around their common task and to give their best to achieve the shared goal. Team uniforms, names, mascots, huddles before and during games—all instill members with a shared identity as they work together toward a common goal.

Group members are asked to cooperate.

Not a football training camp but a boys' summer camp was the setting of a psychological study investigating the impact of cooperation on persons' relationships to each other.[32] Initially, investigators created competitive conditions by dividing the boys into two teams competing in sports, games, and cabin inspections. The competition increased contention between the teams, culminating in quarrels and vandalism. Then investigators created emergency situations, such as a break in the water line, requiring cooperation from both teams to solve the problems. Slowly, the boys from both groups developed friendships and became motivated to work together. The study demonstrated that competition leads to hostility toward out-groups while interdependence increases attraction to members of another group.

Muzafer Sherif, who conducted the classic Robber's Cave study, was interested in the role of competition and cooperation in intergroup relations. His and subsequent studies validate that cooperation in groups improves intergroup relations. Referring to several studies on cooperation, Stephen Worchel states that when persons or groups cooperate, the gain of one party is also to the advantage of the other.[33] Situations call-

31. Hewstone and Brown, "Contact Is Not Enough," 23.

32. Stephan and Stephan, *Intergroup Relations*, 84; Sherif et al, *Intergroup Contact and Cooperation*, 209–12.

33. Worchel, "Role of Cooperation," 292.

ing for cooperation emphasize the interdependence of group members. Each member has an important role to play and other members need her or his contributions.

Scenes from the movie *Remember the Titans* illustrate the importance of cooperation in improving relationships between racially different group members. Before the Caucasian player Gerry and his African American teammate Julius become friends, they confront and challenge each other to overcome selfish play by acting for the sake of the whole team. They have been used to looking out for themselves when interacting with peers from another ethnic group. Now, they have to work together to move the team forward.

Cooperation is not a simple recipe for reduction of intergroup conflict, but it can be successful in concert with other strategies. The conditions of the collaborative interactions need to be carefully observed.[34] For example, when cooperation between previously competitive groups results in defeat, the result may be scapegoating.[35] Imagine if the Titans had experienced a losing streak: the new coach and the new approach of a racially mixed team could easily have been blamed for the failure. The experiment in interracial relations would have backfired.

Personality factors of those involved may influence the effect of cooperation. Some persons expect cooperation while others thrive on rivalry. Competitive behavior of individual group members may disrupt the cooperative group dynamic.[36] Even if the goal is cooperation, the group process may be hampered if there are individuals present who function primarily on a competitive level.

In summary, three strategies underscore positive effects of intergroup cooperation: a consistent number of cooperative contacts, increased communication, and successful outcomes of mutual cooperation.[37]

Intergroup contact enjoys institutional support.

The film depicts institutional policies in an ambivalent fashion. The viewer can feel the pain when the new coach, Herman Boone, is assigned to the football team and replaces popular coach Yoast. Boone himself feels uncomfortable taking Yoast's old job, having experienced

---

34. Worchel, "Role of Cooperation," 297.
35. Hewstone and Brown, "Contact Is Not Enough," 25.
36. Worchel, "Role of Cooperation," 295.
37. Ibid., 295, 304, 298.

that kind of "theft" when he was turned down for previous jobs not on the basis of his qualifications but on the basis of his skin color. He offers Yoast a position as assistant coach. To move the project of a desegregated football team along, Boone must assert his leadership and does so from the beginning. The policy of desegregation creates a situation that is uncomfortable and stimulates conflict in the short run, but has the potential to create change in the long run. Once Yoast accepts Boone's offer, once he participates as assistant coach and contributes his own style of managing the team, the players experience strong leadership support and school board endorsement of their new racially mixed football team. At one point in the story Yoast is presented with a proposal to be reinstated as head coach if he undermines the winning streak of the team. He resists the temptation, as he feels loyalty to the desegregated team and internally supports the principles of cooperation. The growing partnership and understanding between Yoast and Boone is crucial for the team's success.

The intergroup contact theory postulates that explicit social sanction makes intergroup contact more readily acceptable. The passage of civil-rights legislation has been instrumental in establishing antiprejudicial norms in American society.[38] Studies have supported that intergroup contact of group leaders alone is not an effective method to improve intergroup relations. Members at the grassroots level need to be engaged. However, when the group leaders and institutions support intergroup contact on the basic level, it increases the effectiveness.[39]

The group settings provide opportunities
for participants to develop friendships.

During the initial phase of the training camp teammates are still suspicious of each other and quarrel. In one of his motivational speeches Boone makes the point: "I don't care if you like each other but you will respect each other." The boys' relationships are based on cooperation. However, the coach pursues an additional strategy. Ethnically different team mates not only play, they also eat and room together. As their close contact begins to intensify fights and arguments, Boone assigns them homework. The boys are to interview their roommates and to find out about each other's families, likes, dislikes, and interests. They have to

38. Pettigrew and Tropp, "Allport's Intergroup Contact Hypothesis," 266.
39. Worchel, "Role of Cooperation," 290f.

report their findings to the coach. This strategy illustrates the finding of intergroup research that constructive contact relates more closely to long-term close relationships than to initial acquaintanceship. As the teammates get to know each other, their friendly interactions develop more spontaneously, and initial suspicion gives way to laughter and friendly teasing. The potential of a friendship in overcoming prejudice is illustrated in the close relationship of Gerry and Julius.

Evolving intergroup research has suggested, "The contact situation must provide the participants with the opportunity to become friends."[40] Therefore, a fifth facilitating factor was added to Allport's initial four: friendship potential. In the previous section we pointed to the significance of institutional support in intergroup relations. This fifth condition emphasizes the interpersonal orientation. Intergroup relations are improved as group members get to know each other as individuals and develop personal bonds. In order to maximize friendship, potential group settings need to be extended over time and include different contexts where members can get to know each other.[41] They should not be too structured and should allow for informal and open communication. As the friendship of the coaches and their families develops, they respect each other as persons. When Yoast's daughter visits the Boones during the evening when Boone's house is vandalized, Yoast is introduced to institutional racism. At one point during the film Boone says to Yoast: "Welcome to my life." Over time the communication between Yoast and Boone as well as Julius and Gerry becomes more honest and self-disclosure becomes more significant. At that point Julius can tell his Caucasian friend Gerry: "I was afraid of you."

Intergroup contact that allows for the development of friendships extends over time and different situations, is informal, allows for open communication, and is not centered on just one goal or on a formal group structure.[42]

Working through conflict: Harnessing aggression.

At the beginning of the training camp, conflict seems ever present. Teammates resist eating meals together, quarrel over their taste in music

---

40. Pettigrew, "Intergroup Contact Theory," 76.

41. Ibid.

42. Brewer and Miller, "Beyond the Contact Hypothesis," 294.

as they share rooms, and get into fistfights. Early on coach Boone addresses the tangible team conflict directly: "You will harness your aggression to work toward perfection." He challenges the teammates to use their aggression not against each other but constructively in their efforts of training. Instead of pitting themselves against each other they are to pour all their energy into becoming the best football team. Boone acknowledges the conflict but does not seek easy resolution of it, instead helping teammates to understand its roots and confront their prejudices. He redirects the aggressive energy and refocuses members on one common goal. He manages the conflict at hand so it does not get out of control.

Intergroup contact theory proposes a group design with conditions that facilitate prejudice reduction. The theory does not raise the issue of how to manage conflict if and when it occurs in a group situation. The literature surrounding intergroup theory speaks to the possibilities of conflict and offers direction on how to tackle it.

In preceding text I mentioned the possibility that the new contact situation can backfire. Previously privileged group members can experience the new group equality as a threat and resist it. Also, personality factors influence group dynamics. Not everyone thrives on cooperation, and competitive personalities may dampen efforts to motivate a group to work together and develop cohesiveness toward a shared goal. Intergroup contact situations bear the possibilities of conflict that may have to be addressed or redirected.

On the other hand, Donald Taylor and Fathali Moghaddam point to the illusion-of-contact phenomenon, when persons tend to keep contact with members of out-groups harmonious by keeping the contact superficial.[43] Or they may keep their discomfort at bay by denying that tensions between members of out-groups exitst.

Almost always, conflict is a part of group development toward authentic relations. Moderate amounts of conflict are healthy and motivate participants to engage in problem solving.[44] Gerry and Julius, Boone and Yoast engage in honest arguments and exchange harsh words as their relationships grow. Mutual trusts deepens as they confront discord and disagreements openly. Like other group processes, intergroup contact groups move through a phase of conflict that pushes members to work

43. Taylor and Moghaddam, *Theories of Intergroup Relations*, 182ff.
44. Worchel, "Role of Cooperation," 304.

toward resolution, and this typically results in a deepened sense of shared identity.

As we consider conflict in contact groups, we see a range of possibilities. At one end of the spectrum is a conflict that gets out of control and threatens to destroy a common group identity. Conflict that is not contained may fail to improve intergroup relations. At the other end of the spectrum, group members or leaders suppress and deny conflict out of fear and discomfort. They indulge the illusion that they get along while bias and aggression smolder under the surface.

Psychologist Stephen Worchel points out that a group situation without frustration, competition, and conflict would be a rather antiseptic environment that is not only unrealistic but also unstimulating.[45] As persons from different social groups come together in a small setting, conflict is to be expected. It should not be avoided and it may not be eliminated. But it can be managed constructively and reduced. Moderate conflict can teach conflict resolution and move participants beyond a superficial level of relationship as long as the overall aim of reducing prejudice and intergroup tension is kept in mind.

SUMMARY

In this chapter we have learned that religious groups, like other social groups, are susceptible to intergroup dynamics. As is the case in other groups, prejudice and bias contribute to tensions between different religious communities. Our separation and isolation from each other distorts our view of each other and reinforces tensions. The good news: religious communities can also help to "unmake" prejudice. Religious communities can provide their members with opportunities to learn about others and to build healing and constructive relationships with their fellow citizens in different religious traditions.

One might think of education as a starting point for building inter-religious connections: by changing our thinking we will change our behavior. By learning about other belief systems— say, the way Buddhists, Hindus, Jews, or Muslims look at life, its meaning, and order—we can better understand our neighbors of different religious paths.

45. Ibid., 288.

However, intergroup contact approaches interreligious relationships from a decidedly different angle: by changing our behavior we create a change in our thinking.

Religious leaders combat prejudice by bringing people together. As we experience each other in small group settings as people, we can dispel the myths we hold about each other. As people of different religious paths encounter each other regularly in small groups, they have opportunities to disconfirm their stereotypes. Intergroup contact initiates new experiences to create new thinking, new feelings, and new behavior. At least the potential for transformation is present in every human group if we study and apply insights from group dynamics.

Bringing people of different faiths together in and of itself does not reduce tensions. Intergroup contact theory provides parameters and prepares the ground for fruitful, constructive interreligious relationships. We spelled out the intergroup contact hypothesis in the context of its birthplace—race relations. Research shows that constructive intergroup relations consist of the following ingredients: group members have equal status within the group setting, work toward common goals, cooperate, enjoy authority support, and can develop friendships.

The process of unmaking prejudice happens as a byproduct of shared activities. The point is that people of different groups come together, work together, and get to know each other as people in the process. The strategies can be useful when addressing the relationships of different religious groups.

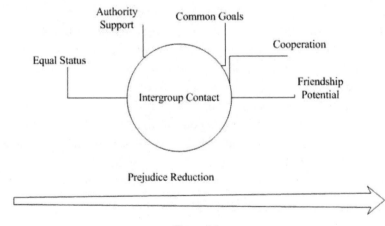

Figure 3.1.

Facilitating Conditions for Prejudice Reduction

Near the beginning of this chapter I told the story of our local German parish's well-meaning but ineffectual attempt to reach out to members of our neighboring Muslim mosque. Knowing the powerful ideas of intergroup contact theory might have helped us tremendously. We had a hunch that our church members might be resistant to educational discussion groups about Christian-Muslim relations. Instead we wanted to bring them together. Had we considered the facilitating conditions of intergroup contact theory, we would not have planned just one event in the form a street festival but a series of events with smaller groups. We already had authority support. The wider church conference encouraged local churches to engage their Muslim neighbors. Leadership teams of our church and the mosque spearheaded our endeavor.

A partnership project with the local Catholic parish was already in place that could have been utilized to enhance relationships with the Muslim community. We cooperated with our Catholic partners in a visiting ministry. Joint teams from both parishes visited families in a large housing complex with many economic and social needs. Our teams made the initial contact to introduce our religious communities and to inform them about local social resources agencies and provide simple assistance as needed. We could have shared these efforts with our Muslim neighbors and broadened our visiting teams to include Christian and Muslim, German and Turkish members. In the context of such cooperation, team members could have had a chance to get to know each other personally. Our work toward a shared goal would have modeled to our wider communities how different religious groups can work together and benefit the local community. In local communities throughout the world diverse religious communities already engage in such shared projects. We will learn more about them in chapter 5.

For now, it shall be sufficient to note that intergroup contact theory is applicable to the work of religious communities. Intergroup contact is by no means the only way to improve intergroup relations. Some issues cannot be addressed by bringing people together in small groups. Intergroup conflict occurs in a broader social context, and prejudice is not just an attitude in individuals but is perpetuated and maintained by social forces, such as mass media.[46] For example, communication in mass media can make and unmake prejudice. It was the media that fired up the controversy about the Park 51 Muslim community center in

46. Pettigrew, "Intergroup Hypothesis Reconsidered," 190.

lower Manhattan. So intergroup contact is only one among many means for improving intergroup relations, yet because religious communities function in small groups, it is a particularly fitting means of addressing interreligious relations.

CONCLUDING QUESTIONS

Intergroup contact theory has been tested and applied to many ethnic and racial intergroup conflicts. Some limitations have been discovered and further questions have been raised.[47] It serves more as a loose conceptual framework in intergroup relations than as a precise theory. Intergroup contact theory states when attitudes are changed for the better but not why and how stereotypes are reduced.[48] For now, we note that the theory provides a list of conditions that facilitate changes in attitudes toward members of other groups. These conditions develop parameters and prepare the ground for successful intergroup encounters.

In the following chapters we will take a closer look at the processes of change: How exactly is prejudice reduced when people of different groups come together in small settings? What exactly changes: our thinking, our behavior, our feelings, or all three? When we get to know a person of a different ethnic or religious group, does our understanding expand beyond this person, and do we change our mind about the social group he or she represents? In other words: does prejudice reduction expand beyond the contact situation? Does education about other groups play a role? Intergroup contact theory emphasizes our commonality. How do we address and pay due respect to our existing differences?

These and other questions have contributed to the further refinement of intergroup contact theory. They will take us into our next chapter.

47. Pettigrew, "Intergroup Contact Theory"; Pettigrew, "Intergroup Hypothesis Reconsidered."

48. Pettigrew, "Intergroup Hypothesis Reconsidered," 179; Pettigrew, "Intergroup Contact Theory," 70.

4

Transforming Relations
in Interreligious Encounters

WHO HAS NOT EXPERIENCED a change of heart about another person? Initial dislike mutated to appreciation, and antipathy developed into friendship. New neighbors move in next door, a new colleague enters our team at work, a new visitor joins our congregation. Our first impressions are formed based on the person's appearance, physical features, skin color, age, dress, and so on. Our impressions become fixed ideas of what the person might be like. Sometimes he or she turns out to be quite different from what we had initially expected. How does this change in perception and attitude come about? Does it occur only with individuals or can it extend to groups of people, such as culturally and religiously different groups? In this chapter we will explore how attitudes and bias toward out-groupers transform. For if as religious leaders, counselors, and theological educators we are to promote interreligious relationships, we need to better understand processes of attitude change and prejudice reduction.

Intergroup contact is a vehicle for the transformation of intergroup relations. The intergroup contact hypothesis explains when our perceptions are altered but not how and why.[1] To address this problem social psychologists have integrated intergroup contact theory and social identity theory in order to formulate a more complete theory of prejudice reduction. In the previous chapter we described basic conditions that promote connections between different social groups in intergroup settings. In this chapter, we discuss innovative strategies that help reduce bias between the involved groups. The first part depicts how our notions

---

1. Kenworthy et al., "Intergroup Contact," 279f.

and categorizations of others can be modulated. Revisiting concepts of social identity introduced in chapter 2 will help us in this endeavor.

Face-to-face contact with members of different social groups creates new experiences for participants, experiences that include the way they think, feel, and act toward members of other social groups. In the second part of the chapter we examine how intergroup contact can change not only our mental images of others but also how we feel about them and how we behave toward them. We envision possibilities of change of our minds, hearts, and practice in relation to people of other religious traditions.

FACILITATING ATTITUDE CHANGE
IN INTERGROUP ENCOUNTERS

Four different strategies help reduce bias toward persons from different cultural and religious groups, doing so by targeting our perceptions of them. Social psychologists have tested and fine-tuned these strategies in numerous studies.[2] The focus here is not so much on the studies themselves but their practical application to interreligious relationships. I paint a picture of these tools by portraying the experiences of two families from different faith traditions. They are involved in a joint project organized through a local interfaith council. I explore how the four strategies might shape ways in which the interfaith council might approach the joint project.

Abdul and Sadika were born in India and immigrated as children with their families to the United States, where they later met and married. They have two children: Yasmeen, who is seventeen, and Kareem, who is nine. The family regularly attends a local mosque. Robert and Michele attend the Methodist church two blocks away from the mosque in the same town. They were born and raised in town and have a son, Andrew, who is seventeen.

The leaders of their religious communities meet regularly at a local interfaith council, which sponsors a local soup kitchen and encourages its member communities to volunteer their time. Aside from serving the poor, the soup kitchen gives volunteers an opportunity get to know each other and their different faith communities. The two families meet each other in this context.

2. Overviews of Allport's contact hypothesis and studies further developing and refining intergroup contact theory are presented in Pettigrew, "Intergroup Contact Theory," and Kenworthy et al., "Intergroup Contact."

In the second chapter we described the process of social categorization we use to process the complex information we perceive in our environment. Let's recall some of the main tenets of social identity theory. We use categories such as African American, Caucasian, Christian, Jewish, male, female, senior, adolescent and so on, in order to organize data that stream into our consciousness. The less familiar we are with persons, the more we rely on categories when we initially meet them. These categorization processes simplify our complex environment. Our membership in groups, such as ethnic and religious groups or professional guilds and political associations give us a sense of belonging and self-esteem. We have a tendency to compare our groups with others and do so competitively. We favor the groups we belong to and see others in a less favorable light. Figure 4.1: Groups without Contact depicts how, in different groups living side by side without extended contact with each other, group categories and boundaries are emphasized. White squares represent one category and grey squares represent another. Groups without contact relate to each other primarily based on their categories, which define clear boundaries between the groups.

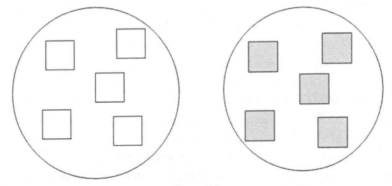

Figure 4.1.
Groups without Contact: Group categories and boundaries are emphasized.

Stereotypes are attributions, which are connected with certain categories. Once established, they are difficult to change. The mind resists new information that would challenge us to revise our way of thinking. However, change is possible. Categories are not static. They can move and adjust. In this chapter we introduce strategies that interrupt and shift the process of categorization when people of different groups encounter each other. Using these techniques we can cross-categorize, decategorize, differentiate, and recategorize. Intergroup contact is a flexible means by which we can shift and adjust our mental categories.

Cross-categorization: "You're a mom, dad, student, citizen like me."

Abdul and Sadika are Indian-Americans. Abdul is an engineer and Sadika works part-time as a dietitian. Their children, Yasmeen and Kareem, were born in the United States and attend a public high school. The family is Muslim and regularly attends the local mosque. Robert is a contractor and his wife Michele works as a substitute teacher. They are Caucasian and were born and raised in the United States. Along with their son, Andrew, they are active in the Methodist church. Each member of the two families belongs to several social groups at the same time. They are students, parents, professionals, and members of faith communities and of distinct cultural groups. They belong to different groups while simultaneously having some group affiliations in common.

The importance of each category depends on the social context persons find themselves in. At work or school their religious affiliation is relatively unimportant, whereas in their religious communities their professional roles are relatively insignificant. Each group membership meets a need for belonging and contributes to a sense of self-esteem. Identifying with multiple groups can create a sense of personal balance, since a person's identity is not wrapped up in one single group membership.

The psychologist Marilynn Brewer, who articulated the concepts of cross-categorization and decategorization, points out that individuals' affiliations across different groups contribute also to balance and stability in the larger social context.[3] In complex pluralistic societies the need for belonging is met in several overlapping categories of ethnicity, gender, religion, age, and occupation. Persons do not depend on one single group to gain self-esteem and in turn are less motivated to put down other groups.[4] As persons navigate multiple group memberships and group conflicts, they are not overly invested in a single conflict. Group tensions are diffused.

The mere fact of having a variety of group affiliations can enable persons to become more tolerant and open to complex identities. On the other hand, overlapping group memberships can be overwhelming for some persons who desire a sense of certainty through clear group boundaries.[5]

Yet having certain group memberships in common does not necessarily bring people closer together. At work it is known that Abdul is Muslim. He uses his Friday lunch hour to attend prayer services at

3. Brewer, "Reducing Prejudice," 169.

4. Ibid., 170.

5. Ibid., 177.

the mosque. His colleagues do not ask him about his faith and rarely inquire about his cultural background. Just sharing a work environment and a certain social category with a member of a different social group does not automatically increase understanding or reduce bias toward the other person's other group memberships.

In summary, the term "cross-categorization" depicts overlapping group affiliations, which occur naturally in a person's and in society's life. Cross-cutting group memberships can be a basis for personal and social balance. They do not automatically reduce bias toward members of other groups.[6] However, they can be a foundation for connections.

Figure 4.2: Cross-categorization illustrates how overlapping categories deemphasize group boundaries. Most of the white and grey squares include geographical shapes, such as circle, octagon, star, and triangle. The squares are connected with each other based on the geometrical shape they have in common.

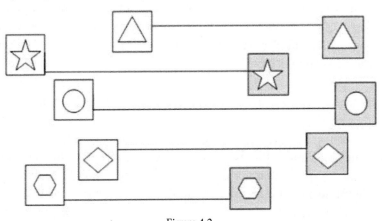

Figure 4.2.
Cross-Categorization: Overlapping categories deemphasize group boundaries.

How does cross-categorization contribute to a reduction in bias? I may have reservations toward a person of a different faith or cultural group. At the same time I recognize that we have things in common. I begin to like the aspects of the person that I share with him or her. This inconsistency between my feelings of reservation on the one hand and my connection on the other hand causes me to adjust my attitude to the other and become more open to other aspects of his or her personality.[7]

6. Miller et al., "Crossed Social Categorizations Effects," 413.

7. Brewer, "Reducing Prejudice," 170.

Cross-categories can also be used intentionally to improve inter-group relations. As described in the previous chapter, coach Boone introduces new categories that neutralize the old dividing categories of "black" and "white." He divides the football team members according to their roles as offensive or defensive. African-American and Caucasian team members share rooms, eat, play, and work together within their newly created teams. He used the strategy of cross-categorization by introducing new subgroups to replace old conflictual subgroupings.

The interfaith council likewise can introduce cross-categorization in the way it conducts the soup kitchen service. So far, the practice has been that the Methodist church takes responsibilities for serving food on Mondays, the Presbyterians cover Tuesdays, the mosque takes care of Wednesdays, and the local synagogue Thursdays. The council can change this pattern and introduce new categories by establishing interfaith teams for the different weekdays. Abdul and Robert now have a chance to serve together as members of one of the Tuesday teams. They meet regularly as they pick up supplies from a food bank and build pantry boxes while Michele and Sadika prepare food in the kitchen. Yasmeen and Andrew can serve food one Saturday a month along with other teenagers from the different faith communities. The teams de-emphasize faith group categories and create new cross-categories by organizing teams according to weekday and not faith community.

During their work in the soup kitchen, the helpers can find out that they have many things in common aside from their different faith affiliations: "Our faith traditions and cultural backgrounds are different. At the same time we are moms and dads with similar joys and worries about our children." "We are Muslims, Christians, and Jews. At the same time we are teenagers and students with similar struggles in school and similar interests." By mixing volunteers from faith communities the council can cross-cut the familiar group affiliations and emphasize shared teamwork.

Decategorization: "I knew you as a Muslim man. Now you are Abdul."

Cross-categorization capitalizes on existing overlapping group affiliations or is achieved when new categories replace old dividing categories. Psychologists Marilynn Brewer and Norman Miller give us a second way in which intergroup contact can disrupt categorical responses. Through decategorization group members come to rely less

on categories. They begin to see members of out-groups in differentiated and personalized ways.[8]

When we have only superficial or no contact to members of other
groups, we relate to them as members of their category rather than as
individual persons. We see them in oversimplified ways and as more
homogeneous than they really are, as is expressed in the common statement: "They all look alike to me." When we develop extended and closer
contact with members of another group, we realize that our simplified
categories do not do them justice. We begin to draw distinctions between different members of the out-group. Personalized contact allows
a person to see a member of a different group not primarily in terms of
their category identity but in the context of a relationship to them as
individual human beings.[9]

Figure 4.3: Decategorization shows how personalized contact allows for differentiation and de-emphasizes group boundaries. As connections between individual white and grey squares are made, group
categories and boundaries become less important.

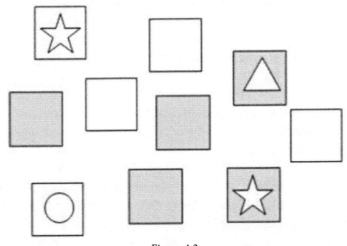

Figure 4.3.
Decategorization: Personalized contact allows for differentiation
and deemphasizes group boundaries.

In chapter 3, I delineated five conditions that facilitate successful intergroup contact. The contact situation should be structured in

8. Miller and Brewer, "Categorization Effects," 213ff; Brewer and Miller, "Beyond
the Contact Hypothesis," 287–89.

9. Brewer and Miller, "Beyond the Contact Hypothesis," 287–88.

such a way that participants have equal status and are able to develop friendships. These two facilitating conditions form a basis on which de-categorization can take place. For prejudice reduction to occur, group participants need to be on equal footing within the group. Group members should share tasks equally and independent from their category.[10] Egalitarian group norms allow for open communication between participants. In the soup kitchen duties are divided among all volunteers, independent from their faith affiliation. Task oriented roles need to be limited so members have enough opportunity for informal contact. Also, group encounters should be set up frequently enough and over different contexts so that extended contact among members is possible. The more frequently group members meet and the wider the diversity of members of each category, the more likely group participants will be open to other members of the same out-group in different settings.[11]

In addition to establishing mixed weekday service teams, the interfaith council can employ an additional tool to mediate decategorization. The council can periodically invite teams to informal dinner gatherings at which the soup kitchen project is coordinated and the volunteer service is celebrated. The gatherings acknowledge the accomplishments of each of the weekday teams. During conversations over dinner participants from the different teams can get to know each other better. They can learn about each other's lives, what moves them, what gives them joy, and what concerns them; young children have a chance to play with each other. Participants can meet a diversity of representatives of the faith communities, allowing all to develop a differentiated view of the partner community.

Robert and Michele meet Abdul and Sadika, as well as other families of the mosque from Iran, Indonesia, and Pakistan. Monolithic perceptions about Islam begin to break down. Michelle finds one of her assumptions and stereotypes about Muslim women challenged.

"Sadika, you are not wearing a head-scarf. I thought Muslim women are supposed to wear one."

"I used to wear a hijab since I was a teenager. My mother had one, my sister did. I wanted one, too. In my twenties I decided not to wear it anymore. I have a friend who started wearing one when she was eighteen years old, much to the bewilderment of her family. It's part of her religious identity. She likes it. I no longer do. It's a personal choice."

10. Ibid., 291.
11. Ibid., 292.

Differentiation does not dissolve group boundaries and categories but allows for greater complexity in the perception of the other. Over time the soup kitchen volunteers get to know each other as individuals. After some time working in the same team, Robert and Michele see in their teammate not primarily a Muslim man but Abdul. As Yasmeen gets to know Andrew, she relates to him less as a Christian fellow teen but as Andrew.

Getting to know other group members personally and developing more differentiated views of them allows participants to see commonalities and develop a liking. Newly gained personal appreciation for members of other groups can bring about a change in attitude and behavior toward the out-group.[12]

Intergroup contact theory in general as well as the strategies of cross-categorization and decategorization focus on what people of different cultural and religious groups have in common. By concentrating on the similarities between various groups, however, we can easily overlook and minimize real differences that contribute to the diversity and richness of our religious and cultural landscape. Also, emphasizing interpersonal relationships between individual group members leaves the question: Will group participants transfer their changed attitudes from their group partners to other members of the same religious or cultural groups? In other words, will prejudice reduction generalize and improve not only individual but intergroup relations? The concepts of cross-categorization and decategorization are limited in addressing the issues of generalization and difference. Therefore, the concept of mutual differentiation has been developed.

Mutual Differentiation: "In some ways we are alike, in some ways we are different."

Positive intergroup relations include both the discovery of similarities and the appreciation of diversity. Blurring the differences between outgroups does not assist in creating more open attitudes toward members of different social groups. Psychologists Miles Hewstone and Rupert Brown have proposed the strategy of mutual differentiation, holding that categorization occurs naturally. They remind us that the identification with a particular group has a psychological function by contributing to a positive social identity. Therefore, rather than aiming to do away with stereotypes, the goal of the intergroup encounter is to challenge the

---

12. Brewer, "Beyond the Contact Hypothesis," 288.

simplicity of out-group stereotypes.[13] The model of mutual differentiation maintains the original group boundaries but in the context of intergroup cooperation where similarities and differences are acknowledged and valued. Mutual differentiation aims to create more differentiated perceptions of the out-group. Each group should value itself positively while also cultivating positive attitudes toward the out-group.[14]

Figure 4.4: Mutual Differentiation illustrates the process of intergroup contact that maintains group distinctiveness: white and grey squares are connected while group categories and differences remain prominent.

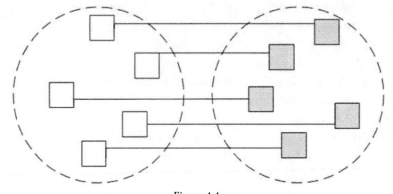

Figure 4.4.
Mutual Differentiation: Intergroup contact
maintains group distinctiveness and differences.

We've learned that the mind is resistant to integrating information that disconfirms stereotypes. We tend to ignore as long as possible information that will disrupt our established mental field. First, we tend to see what we expect (self-fulfilling prophecy). Second, when we have a pleasant interaction with a member of an out-group, rather than opening our mind we tend to explain that interaction as an exception to the rule and our mental field is once again "refenced."[15] A pleasant and positive interaction with a representative of another social group does not change our stereotypes but persuades us that the person is an exception to the rule.[16] Numerous studies have shown that stereotype-disconfirming information is generalized more effectively to the whole group when we see the other group member as a typical representative

13. Hewstone and Brown, "Contact Is Not Enough," 30.

14. Ibid., 35.

15. Ibid., 19f.

16. Ibid., 19.

of the out-group.[17] If positive encounters with others only change our personal relationships but not perceptions of the out-group, intergroup conflict remains unchanged.

The overall goal of intergroup encounters includes the improvement of the relationships between group members, but it goes further: it aims to generalize positive experiences with individual out-groupers beyond the interpersonal relationship to other members of the out-group.

The interfaith council soup kitchen project can maintain mutual differentiation and involve elements that maintain the differences and uniqueness of each faith in respectful ways. The dinner meetings can include programs where volunteers learn about each other's faiths. Educational sessions about Christian, Jewish, and Muslim teachings about serving the poor and about the social implications of each faith help participants to develop a more differentiated understanding and appreciation of each other. The different communities can take turns hosting evenings with different foods that celebrate and honor each other's cultures and customs. It is ideal if several members from each faith group participate in the soup kitchen service project so the whole group can experience a variety of representatives of the other group.

This set-up creates opportunities for Abdul, Robert, Michele, Sadika, Andrew, and Yasmeen to develop a better understanding of the Muslim and Christian communities. When Robert and Michele get to know Abdul and Sadika they are surprised to discover that both work and are involved in the raising of their children. They had assumed that Islam confines women to the home and devalues the rights of women. As long as their exposure to Islam is limited to one particular couple, they may see Abdul and Sadika as exceptionally progressive Muslims. As Robert and Michele realize that Abdul and Sadika are not unique and that other Muslims also understand their faith to teach gender equality, they develop a more differentiated view of Islam. In turn, Abdul and Sadika develop a personal liking of Robert and Michele and experience them as exceptionally open-minded. Based on portrayals of the media they had assumed that most Christians in the United States seem to see Islam as a threat to Western culture. Through their exposure to other Christians in the soup kitchen project they learn that there are many Christians who are not afraid of Islam and welcome the religious diversity in this country.

17. Hewstone and Lord, "Changing Intergroup Cognitions," 370, 388.

Intergroup encounters need to create opportunities that allow participants to see the other as representative of the other group. They should not blur the distinctiveness of the groups, but rather help participants to understand and appreciate not only their commonalities but also their differences.

Recategorization: "We work together now."

Decategorization reduces our reliance on categories when interacting with another person. Recategorization introduces a new group category encompassing all group participants. Social identity theory holds that we tend to favor our in-group. In other words, we tend to have a pro–in-group bias.[18] Psychologists Samuel Gaertner and John Dovidio articulated the concept of recategorization, which is achieved by creating a common group identity. Members of two different groups are induced to see themselves as members of a single, more inclusive group. The process of recategorizing transforms "us" and "them" to "we," and we transfer our pro–in-group bias to the new superordinate group. As a consequence, attitudes toward former out-group members become more positive.[19] Coach Boone used recategorization. African American and Caucasian football players now wear the same team uniform and call themselves the "Titans." Many people from different cultural and ethnic backgrounds understand themselves as Americans. The national identity encompasses many cultural and ethnic identities of those who have immigrated to the United States, whether a long time ago or more recently.

Recategorization is closely connected to the idea of introducing common goals and cooperation into the contact situation. Introducing a superordinate identity brings about personalized interactions with out-group members with the potential of enduring positive relations between groups.[20] Recategorization is therefore compatible with decategorization. The development of a common group identity does not require that members give up their former less inclusive membership. Persons can hold dual identities simultaneously, and social cohesion does not require that individuals deny their particular cultural identity.[21] So, recategorization is also compatible with mutual differentiation.[22]

18. Gaertner et al., "Across Cultural Divides," 182.

19. Ibid., 179f., 185; Dovidio et al., "Reducing Contemporary Prejudice," 153.

20. Gaertner et al., "Across Cultural Divides," 200.

21. Ibid., 195.

22. Dovidio et al., "Reducing Contemporary Prejudice," 152.

Figure 4.5: Recategorization shows how common group identity overcomes old group boundaries while maintaining differences. White squares and grey squares are connected. Group distinctions and boundaries are maintained, while a new superordinate group encompasses all members.

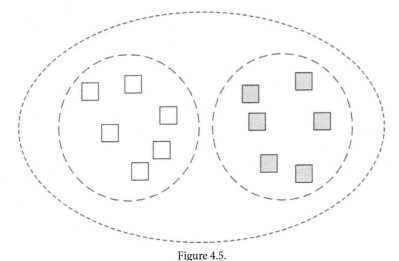

Figure 4.5.
Recategorization: Common group identity encompasses all members while maintaining differences.

Simple strategies for introducing a common in-group include seating arrangements that interrupt group boundaries and encourage intimate contact between members of different groups.[23] Also consistently expressing the common group identity by referring to the whole group as "we" can influence a more positive perception of former out-group members.[24] However, consider the following caveat. Members of majority groups have an interest in assimilation of the out-group members into one single culture that is dominated by the majority. Minority groups are concerned that the new inclusive group can threaten their positive distinctive group. They have an interest in retaining their cultural identity. Thus, in some cases the introduction of a superordinate group could threaten a person's or group's distinctive social identity, which in turn intensifies intergroup conflict.[25] Therefore, when recategorization is considered as an intervention one needs to bear in mind power dynamics and different interests of the groups involved.

23. Gaertner and Dovidio, *Reducing Intergroup Bias*, 56.

24. Ibid., 105.

25. Dovidio et al., "Reducing Contemporary Prejudice," 157.

The soup kitchen project brings together different religious communities for the purpose of shared service and teamwork. During shared gatherings and meals their identities as Muslims, Christians, and Jews are celebrated. Their distinct perspectives are valued. At the same time the interfaith council can employ strategies that emphasize the common group identity. They can introduce a common name, "The Interfaith Soup Kitchen Project," and make t-shirts for volunteers with the group name.[26] Representatives of the teams can present and celebrate the project in gatherings of their respective faith communities and in the wider local community.

A Combined Approach

The strategies for the reduction of bias presented so far move between two poles. One pole emphasizes what people have in common (cross- and decategorization); the other is concerned with maintaining distinctiveness (mutual differentiation). The tension between the particular and the universal, which is an issue in globalization theory, also emerges as a theme in intergroup contact theory. The notion of the creative tension of the global and local, the concrete and universal, forms a red thread throughout this book. As pointed out in chapter 1, the emphasis on either similarity or difference is guided by the underlying vision of a pluralistic society with models such as cultural differentialism, cultural convergence, and hybridization. Similarities as well as differences are important in intergroup encounters and need balanced attention.[27] On the one hand personalization and empathy (disrupting the categorization process and emphasizing common humanity), and on the other hand mutual differentiation (maintaining difference and group boundaries) are approaches that are both needed and that balance each other.

Recent studies support combining these different approaches, emphasizing the importance of personalization while maintaining an awareness of category to a certain degree.[28] Decategorization should occur first, and the next stage would reintroduce the group category (mutual differentiation). A third stage is represented by recategorization, the introduction of a common superordinate group identity.[29]

26. Regarding the effect of cognitive priming, see Gaertner and Dovidio, *Reducing Intergroup Bias*, 113.

27. McCauley et al., "Contact and Identity," 325. See also Taylor and Moghaddam, *Theories of Intergroup Relations*, 189.

28. Kenworthy et al., "Intergroup Contact," 282; Brewer, "Reducing Prejudice," 166.

29. Kenworthy et al., "Intergroup Contact," 284.

Table 4.1 summarizes the use of strategies facilitating intergroup contact in a community project.

Table 4.1: Facilitating Intergroup Contact in a Community Project

Project Phases	Intergroup Contact Facilitating Conditions	Facilitating Methods	Interfaith Project
Structuring of Group/Project	Group structure allows for the development of friendly bonds.		Needs assessment in local community for service project Group experience structured over an extended period of time Teams not exceeding ten members
	Institutional Support	Project enjoys support of local religious communities.	
Beginning Phase	Common goals/ equal status	Cross-categorization Normalizing and monitoring of anxiety	Project teams formed of members of different faith communities
		Decategorization	Space for informal contact and conversation
Working Phase	Cooperation	Mutual differentiation Perspective-taking Working through conflict	Uniqueness of faith traditions maintained Opportunities to learn about and celebrate each other's traditions Open communication
Closing Phase	Common goals	Recategorization	Shared name of project Shared presentation of project in faith communities and local community (media)

Studies have shown that mood can have positive and negative effects on the success of intergroup encounters. Positive affect and affirming experiences in the contact situation have been found to increase a favorable orientation toward others and enhance openness to others when group relations are cooperative or neutral.[30]

However, when groups have competitive or antagonistic relations, positive affect may increase perceptions of distrust, intensifying bias.[31] When a group experiences heated conflict, the group needs to work through it and will perceive positive affect as manipulation or cover-up. When groups have no history of previous conflict and the groups cooperate with each other, a positive mood produces more inclusive representation and people have more favorable out-group attitudes and lower levels of bias than those in neutral moods.[32] Heightened anger and anxiety, but even very elevated happiness influences how we process information. Under stress, positive and negative, we tend to be simplistic in our perception. We tend to think in superficial terms and process information with stereotypes.[33] Facilitators need to be aware of the mood that accompanies the group experience. Ideally, participants experience an overall positive mood, yet a sense of safety that allows for the expression of authentic emotions. Negative feelings and conflicts should be allowed to surface and worked through constructively.

In summary, decategorization, mutual differentiation, cross-categorization, and recategorization together represent strategies that group facilitators can underscore and introduce to reduce prejudice and improve intergroup relations.

These change processes concentrate on the cognitive process of categorization. At the same time participants' feelings, motivations, and behaviors are involved. Intergroup contact impacts feelings of belonging, group loyalty, fear, dislike, hatred, liking, attractiveness, and competitiveness. It also influences behaviors, such as avoidance, belittling of other team members, teamwork, or cooperation. Intergroup contact creates experiences that move the whole person. It can serve as a catalyst transforming our thinking, our emotions, and our behavior. We will

30. Miller et al., "Crossed Social Categorization Effects," 413; Dovidio et al., "Positive Affect," 340ff.

31. Dovidio et al., "Positive Affect," 348, 360.

32. Gaertner and Dovidio, *Reducing Intergroup Bias*, 127.

33. Bodenhausen, "Emotions, Arousal," 24.

take a closer look at theses change processes in the second part of the chapter.

CHANGE OF MIND, CHANGE OF HEART, AND CHANGE OF PRACTICE

I participated once in a workshop on cultural competency for health-care professionals. Culture shapes how patients and treatment teams understand the body, health, life and death, and how we communicate with each other. The keynote speaker co-edited a reference guide for diverse cultural beliefs and practices related to health care. The book can come in handy on the nursing unit when a quick answer on cultural issues is needed in the midst of multiple other demands. Our speaker opened her lecture with a disclaimer about her own book. She emphasized that reference guides and informational clips cannot fully address the complexity of cultural customs and beliefs and the variety of individual practices within a culture. Educational material can give partial orientation but is not sufficient to develop cultural sensitivity. Therefore, her lecture was short and she spent the balance of the time engaging us in experiential exercises that demonstrated how differently people across cultures experience and organize space, time, eye contact, body language, and communication. Complex issues require complex approaches: Intercultural and interreligious learning involves an expansion of knowledge as well as experiences that reach our emotions, attitudes, and practices.

When facilitating interreligious relationships, our goal is to change the bias that keeps us at distance and alienates us from each other. The word "bias" has been used by a number of psychologists as an encompassing term for a phenomenon with different facets.[34] Bias encompasses how we think about others, how we feel about others, and how we act toward others.

Psychologists distinguish four types of bias. First, stereotypes represent a constellation of cognitive beliefs about members of different social groups. Second, bias includes emotional reactions toward members of different social groups. They can range from attraction and respect to discomfort, fear, and hostility. Third, discrimination denotes how we act toward each other and implies inappropriate actions toward persons based on their membership in a particular group. Fourth, the term prej-

34. Dovidio et al., "From Intervention to Outcome," 243.

udice describes an attitude with cognitive and emotional components and a behavioral predisposition.[35]

These different forms of bias are not neatly separated but influence each other. Let's say I am a member of the board of my local Presbyterian church, which is involved in the social issues of the community. A new colleague, Jeff, joins my team at my job. Chatting during a break, Jeff tells me that he belongs to an evangelical church. Right away certain stereotypes about evangelicals are triggered in me. Some are neutral images. For example, in my mind I see Jeff in a worship setting that is very informal. Other thoughts may be laden with judgment: "I wonder if he's one of those Bible-thumping Christians who don't tolerate other views." These thoughts spark feelings. I experience discomfort. I find myself more guarded in Jeff's presence whenever water cooler conversations in the office involve talking about our opinions about social issues. My stereotypes influence my feelings and behavior toward Jeff. On the other hand, stereotypes can serve as rationalizations of my discomfort and avoidant behavior. "I would be more open with Jeff if evangelicals weren't so judgmental." Over time, as I get to know and to like Jeff, I feel more comfortable talking with him. I find out that his views about faith and social issues are more complex than I had assumed.

Cognitive, emotional, and behavioral aspects of bias are closely connected. At the same time they represent particular aspects of bias that can be targeted with particular interventions.[36] In the following paragraphs we will explore strategies that address primarily one dimension of bias over the other.

Change of minds

A basic vehicle for changing the way we think about others is a knowledge-based approach, such as multicultural education. Education about different cultures and religions and about beliefs, values, and practices in different cultures and religions include readings, listening to personal stories, watching videos, and visiting worship sites of other traditions. They create an expanded and more differentiated knowledge and contribute to a reduction in stereotypes and mental perceptions of other systems of belief.

35. Definitions of the four types of bias in ibid., 246–48.
36. Dovidio et al., "From Intervention to Outcome," 249.

I have experienced a change in a chaplain student who had reservations about engaging Muslim patients based on his belief that they believed in a different God. While Muslims understand the word "Allah" to be a name, it is also the Arabic word for God used by Arabic-speaking Christians and Jews as well as Muslims. Just learning about the use of the word "Allah" opened this student's mind to learn more about Islam and its differences and commonalities with Christian beliefs. Our thinking about persons of different cultures and religion can be changed through exposure to information.[37]

Being exposed to different cultures not only provides information but also implicitly introduces the notion of pluralism. Multicultural and multifaith education models an appreciation of diversity, which can effect values of learners and reinforce values of equality. Those who engage in intergroup contact not only learn about the out-group but also about their own group, as they realize that their own norms and customs are not the only ways to manage living and understanding the world. Intergroup contact leads individuals to reevaluate the norms and customs of their in-group. They begin to understand that their way of viewing the world is one among many, a process that can be described as "deprovincialization."[38]

While face-to-face contact with members of different religious groups has the potential to touch all three dimensions—cognitive, emotional, and behavioral—it clearly aims to have an effect on cognitive processes. As outlined above, our perception of others, our categorizations, change as we develop differentiated and personalized knowledge of members of other groups (decategorization), appreciate our similarities (cross-categorization) and differences (mutual differentiation), and see ourselves as members of the same larger group (recategorization). As intergroup contact affects our perceptions of members of other groups and changes our categorizations, it has the potential to change our minds.

Change of hearts

The imprecise term "change of heart" stands as a metaphor for the effect intergroup contact can have on emotional aspects of bias. Intergroup contact theory as well as social identity theory places a heavy empha-

37. Stephan and Stephan, "Intergroup Relations Program Evaluation," 433f; Pettigrew, "Intergroup Contact Theory," 71.

38. Pettigrew, "Intergroup Contact Theory," 71f.

sis on the cognitive elements of bias. They zoom in on our perceptions of others and how to change those. A number of psychologists have pointed out the need for more research regarding the role of emotions in prejudice and the integration of affective and cognitive processes in intergroup relations.[39] Discoveries in neuroscience about emotions, the brain, and the biological basis for empathy, for example, can contribute new insights to the field of intergroup relations. As I focus on the application of intergroup contact theory and social identity, the evolving research on emotions is beyond the scope of this book.[40]

All this is not to say that the primary theories we rely on pay no attention to emotional components of bias. As we categorize others and ourselves, we often do so competitively, favoring our own group and putting down others. Our sense of self is tied to the groups we belong to and we feel a sense of loyalty to them. When persons cooperate with each other and even develop friendships, liking, trust, and empathy often increase. As mentioned previously, our categories of other persons are cognitive notions, but even these are often deeply connected with motivational and emotional elements.

Next, we will take a closer look at two emotions in particular. In chapter 2 we explored fear as a feeling that keeps us apart from those who are different from us. In this chapter we revisit this emotion and investigate the role of anxiety in stereotyping. The second sentiment we examine is empathy and how it can mediate the reduction of bias in intergroup relations.

Anxiety

Imagine you are just about to make an important proposal in front of a group of persons you experience as critical. You are waiting before the closed door in the hallway until it is your turn. In your mind you go over the important points you want to make. Most likely, you feel restless. Your pulse is elevated and your hands are sweaty. These are automatic physical responses over which you don't have much control. If your anxiety is moderate, it can assist in concentration and motivate you to give the best presentation possible. Perhaps you employ some techniques to

39. Pettigrew and Tropp, "Allport's Intergroup Contact Hypothesis," 272; Pettigrew, "Intergroup Hypothesis Reconsidered," 181; Bodenhausen, "Emotions, Arousal," 33.

40. See, for example, the essay collection by Mackie and Hamilton, *Affect, Cognition, and Stereotyping*.

center yourself and breathe in order to keep your anxiety in check. Too much anxiety gets in the way of your presentation.

What we know intuitively about anxiety has been confirmed in psychological tests. As Galen Bodenhausen points out, the physical reactions of high anxiety are similar to those of anger: both involve the amygdala and both heighten pulse and blood pressure, as well as stimulate the secretion of epinephrine.[41] Moderate anxiety can be functional, motivating persons to solve problems constructively. High anxiety, however, reduces our capacity to cognitively perform and to process complex issues.[42] Too much anxiety and a lack of safety can trigger our reliance on stereotypes.[43] A person who feels anxious is distracted and therefore relies more on existing schemas and stereotypes rather than carefully analyzing the actions of another person. Too much anxiety can create a negative mood that colors our judgment and thus contributes to conflict.[44]

Bodenhausen, a psychologist, distinguishes between integral and incidental affect. Anxiety that is integral to the contact situation is directly related to the presence of someone from a different group. This intergroup anxiety has been described in chapter 2; let's review the main ideas again here.

Members of other cultural or religious groups can present a real or perceived threat. At times the different beliefs and religious practices represent a symbolic threat to our worldview. Meeting people from different cultural and religious groups may increase feelings of insecurity because we don't know how to approach them and how to interact with them. Finally, because of distant relationships with members of other groups we may expect that the encounter will be tense or turn out badly, or we fear that the other may harbor negative feelings toward us. These types of fear are integral to intergroup conflict. As pastoral theologian David Hogue explains, brain science teaches us that our evolutionary history has tuned our brains to the frequency of fear.[45] We are wired to scan our environment with vigilance in order to make sure we are safe.

41. Bodenhausen, "Emotions, Arousal, " 18.

42. Ibid., 19.

43. Ibid., 32.

44. Wilder, "Role of Anxiety," 93f, 104.

45. Hogue, *Remembering the Future*, 49.

Incidental emotions are not related to the contact situation but may originate in other situations.[46] Even if anxiety is unrelated to the outgroup, it can color judgment and influence how we rely on stereotypes. Imagine that the Interfaith Soup Kitchen Project suddenly has problems. The building is in need of repair, funds are limited, and food donations have declined. Dealing with such stressors creates incidental affect and has the potential to dampen the teamwork and spirit of interfaith cooperation.

Intergroup contact initially produces a certain level of anxiety. Especially at the beginning participants experience intergroup anxiety because they feel unfamiliar with the customs and beliefs present in members of another religious group. They may be influenced by negative stereotypes even if they do not acknowledge those to themselves and others. As they learn about different beliefs of the other group throughout the course of the project they may experience symbolic threat. Thus, the participants in programs such as the interfaith soup kitchen project may enter the endeavor with a great deal of insecurity about what experiences lie ahead of them. Establishing group norms together, such as respect for different views and reflective listening, can create a critical sense of safety from the program's outset. Group leaders also can deflate intergroup anxiety by acknowledging and normalizing the presence of anxious feelings and insecurities at the beginning of the project.

Moderate anxiety can be motivating and can be acknowledged and normalized as being part of the encounter. Elevated anxiety requires intervention to be used constructively. Overall, a basic sense of safety is necessary so participants become less vigilant of each other and can begin to engage each other.

In summary, too much anxiety in intergroup contact amplifies alienation and distance of different social groups and needs to be monitored and addressed. Now we turn our attention to an emotion that can mediate connections and build bridges to the other.

EMPATHY

The psychologists Stephan and Finlay distinguish three forms of empathy: cognitive empathy and two types of emotional empathy, parallel and reactive. First, cognitive empathy describes the ability to entertain

---

46. Bodenhausen, "Emotions, Arousal," 14.

the perspective of another and is also called "perspective-taking."[47] Dialogue between conflicting parties often relies on perspective-taking, attempting for a moment to see the world from the partner's perspective and understanding where he or she is coming from. Perspective-taking engages our understanding of another person's view, cultural customs, beliefs, and practices. As the other's viewpoint is actively considered, the perspective-taker sees the other as more like him- or herself. In the process intergroup contact and trust increase and stereotypic responding decreases.[48]

We distinguish two types of emotional empathy: a parallel emotional response and a reactive emotional response.[49] When I experience parallel empathy I have feelings that are similar to those the other person experiences. Veronica, one of my chaplain interns, relied primarily on a wheelchair to get around. During the time she worked at our hospital I began to see our work setting with different eyes. Passing through crowded small work areas to access charts and computer stations, I became aware of the lack of space. Everything took longer and simple routine tasks were cumbersome. One time we attended a meeting in a building in close proximity to our hospital. Making my way together with Veronica I suddenly noticed the lack of ramps on the sidewalks. As we tried to cross a street with pedestrian crossings far apart, I found myself feeling vulnerable in traffic. I had a glimpse into Veronica's feelings as she experiences the world in a wheelchair. I also experienced reactive empathy: I had emotional reactions to Veronica's experiences. I was saddened about the challenges she had to face. I changed the furniture arrangement in our office to make it easier for her and others who rely on a wheelchair to get in and out of our small office space. I also admired her for her resiliency to manage the bumps of everyday life and function like able-bodied colleagues.

Learning about Veronica's daily life exposed me to the experiences of persons with disabilities who rely on a wheelchair to get around. Psychological experiments have established that empathy can not only

---

47. Stephan and Finlay, "Role of Empathy," 730; Galinsky and Moskowitz, "Perspective-Taking," 708.

48. Galinsky and Moskowitz, "Perspective-Taking," 709, 720.

49. Stephan and Finlay, "Role of Empathy," 730.

change our attitude about one individual, but also that feeling easily transfers to the social group he or she represents.[50]

Implicitly, empathy develops in intergroup contact groups as members of different out-groups work together. In the process of increased contact they not only know more about each other but also develop emotional bonds and emotional insight into the other's situation. Neuroscience has discovered that we are wired to "catch" the emotional experience of another. Often beneath our consciousness we not only react to an emotion in another person, but what they feel may trigger the same emotion in us.[51]

Empathy can also be taught and encouraged.[52] An explicit method of encouraging cognitive empathy involves dialogue groups. For example, dialogue groups have developed on college campuses to facilitate relationships between different ethnic and cultural groups.[53] They include face-to-face dialogue, reflections, and experiential activities. Dialogues enable participants to listen and to value different perspectives even when they are radically different from their own. Often empathy can be directly encouraged by asking participants to describe their feelings as they hear another's story or by inviting them to express how they might feel as they imagine themselves in the other person's situation.

Emotional empathy can be boosted through role-playing exercises. Students in a medical school affiliated with our hospital complete a course on professionalism in the practice of medicine. Alex gave a presentation to his fellow students on providing care for patients with disabilities. As part of his preparation of the topic he was asked to spend half a day navigating the campus in a wheelchair. When Alex first learned about the assignment he was skeptical that prescribing himself a disability and spending just a few hours in a wheelchair could help him to comprehend the full extent of being disabled. Yet he kept an open mind and navigated the campus in a wheelchair, using elevators, bathrooms, and the library, at times needing the assistance of others. He states: "Though it didn't replicate the experience of being disabled, it nevertheless served its purpose of giving me a clearer picture of what challenges wheelchair users face both physically and socially."

50. Batson et al., "Empathy and Attitudes," 117.

51. Hogue, *Remembering the Future*, 42; Goleman, *Social Intelligence*, 16.

52. Stephan and Finley, "Role of Empathy," 732–34.

53. Nagda and Derr, "Intergroup Dialogue," 134, 138.

Facilitators need to consider some caveats. Empathy without respect can lead to condescending attitudes.[54] Alex was skeptical of the wheelchair exercise out of respect for the experience of persons with a disability. He thought the exercise was problematic if it suggested that someone could spend a few hours in a wheelchair and comprehend what it is like to be disabled. In the end he concluded that the exercise served its purpose. His awareness of the limitations of the exercise comes from a place of respect for experience of persons with a disability.

Empathic connection can stimulate complex feelings that are not always experienced as positive.[55] Becoming aware of the difficult plight of others may bring about feelings of vulnerability. As Christians, for example, develop a deeper understanding of anti-Judaism and the persecution of the Jewish people throughout history, they may experience feelings of guilt. Some persons may react to these complex and uncomfortable feelings with avoidance.[56] They may choose to not enter deeper into feelings of empathy and the complex emotions connected with the experience.

We usually develop empathy for another individual whose story and experience begins to touch us. In order to improve intergroup relations, insights into systemic issues need to complement such feelings of empathy. I may gain emotional insights into the experiences of a person living with a disability. Yet my understanding of the other person's situation remains incomplete without an understanding of larger systemic issues of discrimination. As intergroup contact facilitators are aware of these pitfalls, they need to model constructive ways of dealing with vulnerability, guilt, anger, discomfort, and other issues that complicate empathy.

Summarizing, empathy can build bridges to members of other social groups. Emotional empathy seems to change attitudes more directly than a cognitive change of perceptions. Studies have shown that empathy generalizes easily beyond the individual to the whole group and can create long-lasting attitude change.[57] Empathy increases the perception of a common humanity and aids the development of connections to the

54. Stephan and Finlay, "Role of Empathy," 737.

55. Ibid.

56. Ibid., 738.

57. Batson et al., "Empathy and Attitudes," 106; Pettigrew, "Intergroup Contact Theory," 72.

other.[58] The encouragement and teaching of empathy clearly is part of the strategies of reduction of prejudice.

Changed practice

Changed perceptions and expanded emotional responses toward others, such as empathy, can lead to self-evaluation and can encourage us to change our actions toward others. We may move from avoiding to actively engaging persons from another group. We may shift from dismissing or belittling others to respectful speech.

A change in our practice can also work in a reverse order, from the bottom up. When I find myself working together with persons I used to avoid, I begin to think and feel differently. Intergroup contact creates new experiences and practices that allow persons to experiment with new ways of relating. I begin acting differently, and my thoughts and feelings have to catch up to this new reality.

This new behavior of cooperation can lead to a change in attitude; the dissonance between old prejudices and the new behavior can be resolved by a revision of attitudes. Repeated contact makes intergroup encounters more comfortable.[59] As individuals feel more at ease with members of different groups they begin to accept them because they seek to reduce the dissonance they experience between their newly attained attraction and their former stereotypical attitudes.[60]

SUMMARY

We have analyzed how our thinking, our feelings, and our behavior toward people from different social groups can change. We explored tools that can promote this change in attitude. Knowledge-based approaches, such as multicultural education, target the way we think. Processes of cross-categorization, decategorization, mutual differentiation, and re-categorization aim to shift our perceptions and notions about others. They also involve emotional aspects. Managing anxiety and encouraging empathy promote a change in the way we feel about others. Bringing people together in face-to-face contact creates new experiences and ways of relating to each other. These experiences are often accompanied by a

58. Kenworthy et al., "Intergroup Contact," 287.
59. Pettigrew, "Intergroup Contact Theory," 71.
60. Worchel, "Role of Cooperation," 298.

change in thinking and feeling. These tools are best used in combination. At times we emphasize one over the other, but together they represent a repertoire of strategies that equip religious leaders, counselors, and educators to tackle the humbling task of bringing together people of different religions and of helping their connection along. In the following chapter we take a look at some examples of interreligious connection and cooperation and examine the lessons learned.

5

"Not Only in Disaster!"

Religious Communities Working Together

CERTAINLY CRISES CAN BRING people together. After the terrorist attacks on September 11, 2001, across the nation Christians, Muslims,
Jews, Buddhists, Hindus, and people of other faiths came together in
interfaith services. But prejudice and hate crimes against Muslims have
increased since then as well. An ecumenical church council in Seattle
was concerned about a backlash against Muslim citizens when a fire was
set in the parking lot of a local mosque shortly after the 9/11 attacks. The
council organized volunteers to patrol the school campus and surround-
ings of the mosque to offer protection.[1] In 2010, Muslims joined in support of their Christian fellow citizens following a New Year's Eve bomb
attack on a Coptic church in Alexandria, Egypt, that killed 23 people.
Thousands of Muslim Egyptians supported the minority Christian community as it celebrated Christmas on January 6 and 7, 2011, holding
candlelight vigils and even functioning as human shields as they surrounded the Christian churches.[2]

In these spontaneous actions people of different faiths expressed
a level of solidarity and engagement that reaches beyond tolerance and
peaceful co-existence. The actions of people of faith against prejudice
and hatred contrast with the intolerance and division, which also are a
reality in interreligious relations. As opposed to the voices of religious
extremism, these actions do not make the headlines in the media and
are beneath the radar of wider public awareness. Are these actions of

1. Niebuhr, *Beyond Tolerance*, 6.
2. Butt, "Muslims' Support."

98

support isolated and rare events limited to crisis situations, or are they fruits of a broader current of increased acceptance of religious diversity in our communities more generally?

In the last three chapters I have employed selected theories of intergroup relations to understand the relationships of different religious groups and to develop strategies to bring these groups together and reduce prejudice. In this chapter I explore what religious communities are already doing to nurture interreligious relationships and what we can learn from these activities. To find out about such activities, I sat down with religious leaders who shared their experiences with me. A growing body of literature documents multifaith activities of religious communities who seek to live together, and who serve with and learn from each other. These projects of interfaith dialogue and cooperation often grow out of concrete local situations and are not centrally organized. Therefore, it is not possible to provide a systematic or panoramic overview of the landscape of interreligious activities in the United States. Instead, I take snapshots, tell stories, and lift up themes. Some of the emerging themes resonate with concepts from the field of intergroup relations, validating that this field of study provides rich resources, ready to be mined and put to use in the interest of bridge building between different religious groups.

INTERFAITH WORK IS ABOUT RELATIONSHIPS

It's a sunny afternoon as I am visiting with Rev. Alexei Smith on the Plaza of the Cathedral of Our Lady of the Angels close to downtown Los Angeles. Los Angeles is the most religiously diverse metropolitan area in the world with more than six hundred separate faith communities and a large number of ethnic neighborhoods.[3]

Father Alexei is the director of the Office of Ecumenical and Interreligious Affairs for the Archdiocese of Los Angeles. He represents the Archdiocese on interfaith and ecumenical councils as well as in many dialogue initiatives. The Archdiocese nurtures bilateral dialogues with Buddhist, Hindu, Sikh, Jewish, Muslim, and Christian evangelical communities. It would take many hours of his busy schedule to give me a thorough overview of all of them. So we concentrate instead on one project, the long-established dialogue with the Buddhist commu-

3. Orr, "Religion and Multiethnicity."

nity that is sponsored by the Buddhist Sangha Council and the Catholic Office of Ecumenical and Interreligious Affairs.

All major Buddhist schools and ethnic traditions are found in Los Angeles. In 1980 the Buddhist Sangha Council of Southern California was formed as an intrareligious umbrella for these different forms of Buddhism. At the same time, the council began to explore interfaith dialogue.[4] On the Roman Catholic side, "the document Nostra Aetate of Vatican II prepared the groundwork for the Catholic church by encouraging the church to reach out to other traditions in respect for their particular paths," Fr. Alexei says. "Here in LA the Buddhist-Catholic dialogue has been in existence for over thirty years. The priest who had this job before me was standing in a line at a bank. Behind him was a Buddhist monk. They struck up a conversation, which led to this dialogue."

An ongoing, core group consisting of approximately eight Buddhist and eight Roman Catholic representatives meets every six to eight weeks, rotating between Buddhist and Catholic locations. Topics of discussion come up by suggestion. Last year, the group focused on education and reviewed textbooks for courses on the world religions in Catholic high schools. "The texts were written by Catholic authors," notes Fr. Alexei. "Sometimes they highlighted aspects that a Buddhist wouldn't even think of. As a result of our joint study, the dialogue group submitted re--visions and corrections to the publishers of the textbooks. Also, our high schools often bring in guests from other traditions. When our Buddhist friends visited one of the schools, the students had just finished studying Buddhism and had a chance to talk to our Buddhist guests. It was a great experience for them."

The dialogue group sponsored the seventh conference on Christian-Buddhist studies and celebrated a joint service here at the cathedral. Fr. Alexei explains, "Our cornerstone at the cathedral says: My house shall be a house of prayer for all people. It's my job here to enflesh that." The visits of each other's houses of worship are reciprocal. Fr. Alexei and other Catholic representatives join the Sangha Council for Vesak, the commemoration of the Buddha's birthday. "Historically, there has been some tension between Catholics and Buddhists in Vietnam. Those old conflicts tend to live on, even in a new cultural context. Sometimes,

4. Buddhist Sangha Council and Archdiocese of Los Angeles, Buddhist-Catholic Dialogue.

people are divided not so much by religion but by cultural or historical issues. It's important that Buddhists and Catholics are seen together," he concludes.

Currently, the dialogue group is discussing end-of-life issues. "There are real differences in our beliefs about what happens after this life, eternal life or reincarnation," says Fr. Alexei. "Nobody is going to deny that. We are asking each other: Where are you coming from? What does this really mean for you? Sometimes you hear interfaith dialogue being critiqued for participants overlooking their differences in order to get along. I haven't seen that in our dialogues. You have to be solid in your faith in order to credibly dialogue with someone else. But because of the relationships we have with each other, there is a respect for the other tradition. Interreligious dialogue does not take place between religions but between believers of those religions. Nobody wants to convert the other, nobody expects you to deny your faith. It's about coming to a deeper understanding of the other. It's about letting the differences enrich us rather than divide us."

The dialogue group plans to facilitate a joint memorial service for those whose lives have ended tragically, due to armed conflict, in military service, or because of gang-related issues. The conversations about end-of-life issues lead to a concrete pastoral service for the wider community.

I ask Fr. Alexei if the dialogue group ever encountered difficult issues in their conversations. "We learned we had to be more sensitive and tread lightly when it comes to political issues," he notes. "Our Buddhist friends seemed to be more reluctant to take a stance on political issues. Political issues can be controversial and we learned to be sensitive to that."

I ask what roadblocks they have encountered in their interfaith work.

"Well, there are still some people who think we should not do this kind of work. I facilitated interfaith services at a Catholic high school and elementary school. I invited a rabbi, an imam, a Buddhist monk, and a Hindu swami to celebrate the service along with me. One of the parents took me aside afterwards and said: 'Father, what was that? You can't do that. You're going to hell.' I hear those comments every once in a while in response to our interfaith activities. I try to explain that the church has moved on and that our critics are coming from a pre–Vatican II mindset.

On the other hand, visual images of representatives of different faiths joining together to celebrate worship or to distribute hygiene kits to the homeless, although provocative to some, are so significant. When we co-celebrated in the elementary school, the kids were fascinated. They had never seen the saffron robes of the Buddhist representatives and thoroughly enjoyed it when the monks along with the Muslim, Hindu, and Jewish clergy spent time with them. It's helpful for them to visually experience the embrace of diversity. Because stereotypes are something we learn early, exposing children to diversity is so important."

Fr. Alexei continues to share about another program that helps Catholic lay persons to welcome the religious diversity in the community. Periodically he leads bus tours to houses of worship in LA. After a Lutheran morning prayer the tour group gets in a school bus and visits a Hindu and a Buddhist temple. After a stop at the Greek Orthodox cathedral they have lunch across the street and finish the day with a visit at a neighborhood mosque. "You allow someone to enter into someone else's house of worship and encounter them there in their worship space. It's a changing experience when you can put a face on a person of a different cultural and religious tradition. I had one lady stop me when we were coming from the mosque. She said: 'Father, I am so happy you brought us here.' 'Why is that?' ''Cause I live down the street and I've never been in here.' 'Why didn't you go in?' ''Cause I was afraid. I wouldn't have known how to act.' Once she got in she said: 'They're just like us.' When I spoke at a Thanksgiving service not long ago, I was beseiged by people interested in another tour. We have to help create more of these experiences that enable people to say, 'They are just like us.' We are all human beings; we follow different paths. We need to do more to bring this work to the men and women in the pews. The majority of interfaith dialogue happens on the level of academics and religious leaders. There is a hunger at the parish level to understand and learn."

I ask, "Father Alexei, has there been something that has moved you and given you encouragement in your interfaith work?" He replies, "This is personal. A few years ago, when my mother died, many of my interfaith friends and dialogue partners came to the service. They did not know my mother. But they came to be with me. It was a feeling of acceptance and shared grief. We can be people with different paths but we can share each other's sorrows and joys. This work is about relationships."

"THERE IS A SPECIAL PLACE FOR PEOPLE OF FAITH IN PEACE-MAKING."

About ten miles west of the cathedral is the building of the Jewish Federation of Greater Los Angeles. As I am making my way through security and my bag is scanned, I remember the 1999 shooting at a Jewish Community Center close to LA by a white supremacist. Many synagogues and Jewish organizations are equipped with security systems, a tangible reminder that anti-Semitism is still alive. I am on my way to visit Rabbi Mark Diamond, the executive vice president of the Board of Rabbis of Southern California, which brings together more than three hundred rabbis representing the Conservative, Orthodox, Reconstructionist, Reform, and transdenominational streams of Jewish life. One of the programs of the board is the Interreligious Action Center, which nurtures interfaith engagement and action within the diverse religious community of Los Angeles. The Board of Rabbis has an impressive list of interreligious activities. I primarily ask Rabbi Diamond about a unique project he initiated in 2005. He shares how the idea for the project evolved: "I go to Israel often, about twice a year. Christians and Jews travel to Israel because it's a holy land for both of our traditions. Jewish and Christian tour groups may very well be in Israel at the same time and never run into each other. When I take a Jewish group we stay in West Jerusalem, Tel Aviv, and Haifa; visit the Jewish holy sites; and talk with Israeli government officials. We have an Israeli tour guide. If you took a Christian group you would stay in East Jerusalem; visit Bethlehem, Nazareth, Ramallah. You would visit Christian holy sites, have a Palestinian tour guide, and meet with Palestinian journalists."

Since 2005 Rabbi Diamond has organized three trips, taking judicatory officials, clergy, community leaders, and academics from faith-based universities on trips to Israel and Palestine. Jews and Christians from different denominations as well as Muslim representatives joined the trips. Rabbi Diamond says: "I am not so naïve as to think that anybody here in LA can ever solve the conflict in the Middle East. But there is a need for a balanced and nuanced perception of any complex problem, especially the conflict in the Middle East. If we're ever going to achieve any progress towards peace and if we are ever to come to a better understanding of the complexity and multiple narratives of the conflict, we need to make these trips together. On my trips I have been trying to strike this balance, meeting with Israelis *and* Palestinians. That's not always easy. What I consider a balanced program may not look balanced to you." With a smile he says: "I try to lop off the extremes and pray for the best." The participants need to bring openness to the experience as well. "It's important that people can talk from their hearts and speak the truth as they see it. You may feel passionately about Israel or feel passionately about Palestine. Are you open to hear another perspective?

In our communities we have a tendency to cherry-pick. We hear what we want to hear and don't expose ourselves enough to other views. My hope is that by meeting with diverse groups of officials, journalists, and academics we can gain a richer understanding of the complexities of the conflict in the Middle East. We can agree to disagree about the solution to problems facing Israel and Palestine, and ultimately it's not up to us in Los Angeles. At the same time there's a lot to do for us right here in LA. There are many problems in our own community that require our help.

It often takes getting away from our own communities and traveling with a group of people to develop close and special bonds. When you come back you have a working partnership. We have relationships with almost all religious denominations, but those bonds are strengthened when ten or twenty of us travel together. I find that there is a greater depth and breadth to our interreligious work. What happens after the trips is as important as the trips themselves. When we return we conduct interreligious programs with fellow trip participants. At the synagogue where I am a member, three travelers—a Muslim, a Christian, and I—delivered a sermon together and invited the community to a luncheon afterwards. In short, when we come back from our trips we model that kind of civil discourse to the wider community. There is a second aspect of our travels: we bring a flavor of LA with us when we go on these trips. For example, during our most recent trip two female professors, a Jew and a Muslim, roomed together. The Muslim member was wearing a headscarf. A staff member of the hotel approached her Jewish roommate in disbelief: 'Are you Jewish? What are you doing rooming with a Muslim?' I believe that the warm and close relationships we share among faith communities in LA are special and precious. If we can make it work here, we can make it work almost anywhere. There's been a lot of progress in interfaith relations but there's still a lot of anti-Semitism, Islamo-phobia, prejudice, and misunderstanding."

Rabbi Diamond tells me about an encounter during a visit of religious leaders from Arab countries under the auspices of the International

Visitors Council of Los Angeles. The visitors were on a multicity tour of the United States with a focus on religious diversity in this country and on interfaith work. "We were happy to host them. After a visit to a synagogue and time for Muslim prayers, we gathered for a kosher/halal dinner. An imam from Iraq asked through a translator: 'Rabbi, I appreciate what you have been sharing. But what you share with me about Judaism as a peaceful religion doesn't square with what I know about Judaism. I have read a book on the Internet called *The Protocols.*' I was shocked, but as I looked at him I found no malice in his eyes. I proceeded with the assumption that he really did not know any better. I explained: '*The Protocols of the Elders of Zion* is a notorious anti-Semitic treatise fabricated in the Russian empire about a hundred years ago. It creates the lie of a group of Jews planning global domination, has been translated into many languages, and is circulating on the Internet. It is a fraud and has caused a lot of suffering to my people.' I promised him that I would find a refutation in Arabic, which I was able to send to him after the trip. He asked me: 'What can we do?' I responded: 'You and I have met, that's a beginning; let's start with the two of us.' He promised that he would disseminate the book I had shared with him. Interreligious work is about changing relationships, one person at a time.

One of the tragic mistakes is that religious voices are excluded from the peace-making table—in the Middle East as well as in other conflicts. Religion has a bad name. The only voices we tend to hear when it comes to conflicts are the extremes, voices of intolerance and division. But there are plenty of voices of moderation, tolerance, reconciliation—those voices need to be at the table. There is a special place for people of faith in peace-making. And there is a special mandate for the children of Abraham—Jews, Christians, and Muslims—to try to work together to bridge differences and understand each other."

GLOBAL AND LOCAL CONNECTIONS

Rev. Dr. Jeffrey Utter is a minister of the United Church of Christ. He is pastor of a local congregation and frees up time to serve as the secretary of the Southern California Committee for a Parliament of the World's Religions. He has been involved in this movement for many years. Every five years people from diverse faiths and from all over the world meet to talk with each other, learn about each other, celebrate together, and reflect on issues that concern all. In connection with the World's Fair in 1893 in

Chicago, the first Parliament of the World's Religions convened. It was planned mostly by American Protestant Christians and drew representation from the Jewish, Buddhist, and Hindu traditions. It introduced the religious traditions of Asia to the United States.[5] Muslims, Native Americans, African-Americans, and women were underrepresented at this first meeting. Still, the gathering can be seen as the first act in the modern interreligious movement.[6] The Council for a Parliament of the World's Religions was formed in 1988 in preparation of a centenary celebration for 1993 in Chicago. Since then, the parliament has met every five years: 1999 in Capetown, 2004 in Barcelona, and in 2009 in Melbourne.

Dr. Utter has attended the last three global meetings. While global ethical issues related to justice, violence, and the environment are discussed, the parliament is not an institution with decision-making power. Dr. Utter says: "You get together with people from around the world for a week of intensive exchange and celebration. These are peak experiences. You can tangibly feel the reality of the interfaith movement. Speaking biblically for a moment, this is something completely new that God is doing. Not that people of different faiths have not interacted before; but the extent to which this is moving to the grassroots—from a Christian perspective I see it as a movement of the Holy Spirit." While Dr. Utter speaks with respect and admiration about the spiritual traditions in India and a female Hindu leader he will be hosting this year, he comes to his interfaith work from a commitment to his Christian faith: "I don't believe that Christianity is superior, but I assert that the sense in which we believe that Christ is the savior of the world cannot be said about anybody else. In that sense I may be called conservative. But it hasn't kept me from engaging in this interfaith work. It's more about how you believe and how you relate to others on the basis of your belief."

In the process of interreligious dialogue and relationships the communities participating in the World Parliament have discovered shared ethical principles. The impetus for this global commitment is the realization of our interdependence: The well-being of the earth and all life depends on collaboration. The Council for a Parliament of the World's Religions seeks to cultivate harmony among the world's religious and spiritual communities and to foster their engagement with the world and its guiding institutions in order to achieve a just, peaceful, and sustain-

5. Roberts, *Religion, Theology, and the Human Sciences*, 248.

6. Eck, *Encountering God*, 24.

able world. It has initiated a Partner Cities Network as well as regional chapters in order to create a local grassroots interreligious movement.[7]

The Southern California chapter meets once a month. Most participants are not ordained religious leaders. Members from the different traditions take turns in leading the group in one hour of spiritual practice according to their tradition. On occasion, the group has held interfaith healing services in support of members who are ill. In addition to this spiritual exchange, the group organizes local events. For example, they have sponsored a lecture on the influence of Indian spirituality in the United States at the Vedanta Society as well as a banquet with a lecture on ecological challenges all communities are facing together. Currently, they are planning a concert, "Sounds of Peace." The group consists of Hindus, Buddhists, Sikhs, Jews, Christians, and Muslims. "We are especially active in preparing for the international gatherings," says Dr. Utter. "For example, for the meeting in preparation of the Barcelona parliament at a Buddhist university we had more than hundred participants. It's a bit harder to maintain the momentum during the periods between meetings."

The Parliament of the World's Religions is one of a number of global interfaith organizations. Other international organizations are Religions for Peace, an international coalition of representatives of major religions dedicated to practical help in conflict situations.[8] The United Religions Initiative (URI) also seeks to bring together at a local level people in different nations to work for the common good by addressing social and environmental issues.[9] Like the Council for a Parliament for the World's Religions, these international organizations function through decentralized local grassroots projects where people of different faiths get to know each other and their traditions through shared action and service projects.

The experience of religious pluralism, especially in churches in Asia and Africa, has challenged Christians to take a fresh look at their relationships with other religious traditions. Father Alexei mentioned the significance of the document Nostra Aetate of the Second Vatican Council in opening the Roman Catholic Church to dialogue with other traditions. For Western Protestantism, religious pluralism came to the surface along with the beginning of the modern ecumenical movement

7. Council for a Parliament of the World's Religions.

8. Religions for Peace.

9. United Religions Initiative.

at the beginning of the twentieth century when churches from all over the world sought to reflect the unity of the church.[10] Dialogue with other religious traditions was introduced and practiced in concrete historical situations in Asia, for example, where younger churches worked together with peoples of different traditions in the development of nations. In 1971 the World Council of Churches (WCC) created an interfaith program now called Interreligious Dialogue and Cooperation.[11] It makes educational materials available that assist churches in initiating and conducting dialogue with people of other faiths on a local level.[12]

On national and regional levels, a number of churches and religious bodies employ staff dedicated to intra- and interfaith relations. In the United States, the Interfaith Alliance was developed in 1994, based on an understanding of the importance of religion in public life while being committed to maintain clear boundaries between state and church. It promotes policies that protect both religion and democracy and—challenging extremism—seeks to build common ground among diverse perspectives.[13] The Pluralism Project at Harvard University brings together a network of researchers and affiliates under the leadership of comparative religion professor Diana Eck; it is in itself representative of the diverse religious landscape in the United States. The project seeks to help Americans engage the reality of religious diversity in the United States through research and the dissemination of resources.[14]

Locally, the interfaith movement finds expression in interfaith councils, which at times developed out of ecumenical councils or which exist alongside of them and have adopted their structure.[15] Like their ecumenical counterparts many interfaith councils focus on dialogue and service to the community. They organize interfaith services for civic holidays, such as Thanksgiving or the Martin Luther King Jr. holiday. They respond to community crises, organize workshops, address social justice issues, or organize service projects, such as soup kitchens. In

10. Ariarajah, "Interfaith Dialogue," 281.

11. Ibid., 285; see also the World Council of Churches website.

12. World Council of Churches, *Guidelines on Dialogue*; World Council of Churches, *My Neighbour's Faith*.

13 Interfaith Alliance.

14. Harris, "Pluralism Project," 92.

15. McCarthy, *Interfaith Encounters in America*, 87.

2006 about five hundred of such councils existed.[16] Fr. Alexei Smith and Rabbi Mark Diamond are both members of the Interreligious Council of Southern California. The majority of councils consist of religious leaders and represent Protestants, Catholics, Jews, Muslims, Buddhists, Unitarians, Orthodox Christians, Hindus, Sikhs, and Baha'is. They may also include Latter Day Saints, Wiccans, Adventists, and others. Ethnic minority churches and evangelical churches are underrepresented. At times, theological reasons, such as concerns about syncretism, may prevent active participation in interfaith activities. Many ethnic churches represent poor communities and are pressed to deal with the immediate needs of their communities.[17] The imbalance in ethnic representation may also point to cultural and racial divisions that are still prevalent and exist side by side with religious differences. In *Interfaith Encounters in America,* Kate McCarthy investigates interfaith connections in America in different contexts, such as academia, national community organizations, family, and cyberspace. She surveyed interfaith councils in the United States and interviewed members of such councils. McCarthy points out that the opportunity to develop personal and informal relationships is very significant for participants. They value councils as forums where people can come together and experience a connection in an otherwise divided society. She concludes that the greatest value of interfaith councils may not lie in dialogue or community programs, but "simply in people of different religious identities being present to one another."[18]

Journalist Gustav Niebuhr has traveled the United States and visited with different interfaith activists. In his book *Beyond Tolerance,* he tells the story of the "quiet countertrend" to extremist, exclusive, fundamentalist movements within the religions.[19] Niebuhr has seen a new degree of religious diversity as well as an increasing number of persons who want to work constructively with that diversity.[20] While the numbers of interreligious activities have increased nationally and internationally, they lack any central organization.[21] Approaches to interfaith work are diverse and depend heavily on religious leaders and those who already

16. Ibid., 85.

17. Ibid., 95.

18. Ibid., 124.

19. Niebuhr, *Beyond Tolerance,* xix.

20. Ibid., xxi.

21. Ibid., 189f.

bring an openness and interest to this kind of work. In the following section we look at different types of interreligious partnerships between local communities and social groups.

INTERRELIGIOUS PARTNERSHIPS

Gustav Niebuhr tells the story of a partnership of a synagogue and a mosque on Long Island, a local expression of Jewish-Muslim relations. In an effort to get to know each other better, members of the two communities met in their homes and began to talk about things they had in common, such as family rituals, life cycle events, and their sacred scriptures. Initially, they stayed clear of sensitive topics, such as the Middle East conflict, but as relationships grew stronger their discussions included such controversial issues. When the mosque was criticized by a polarizing politician, the rabbi spoke out in support of the mosque.[22]

Professor of religious studies Michael Kogan helped his synagogue develop a better understanding of Jewish-Christian relations.[23] He has taught adult education classes in his synagogue that take a fresh look at Jesus as a Jew and that study early Christian scriptures from a Jewish perspective. He also taught Christian communities delivering guest sermons in churches, which explored themes common to Jews and Christians.[24] Rabbi Diamond wishes more congregations would develop partnerships with religious communities, which often are just blocks away. Pulpit exchanges, guest sermons, and joint educational classes are easy ways into such partnerships. Fr. Alexei tells me about a six-week curriculum for local parishes and mosques about Islam and Christianity. The Catholic Church in cooperation with other Christian churches and with Muslims develops this curriculum in the hope that it will increase mutual understanding as well as encourage partnerships between mosques and churches in local neighborhoods.

Examples of partnerships among religious communities are still the exception. For many clergy, interreligious work is on the bottom of the to-do list. In addition, it is much easier to raise donations and funds for services that are focused on the particular faith community than for programs that engage in bridge building across religious boundaries. Social scientist Robert Wuthnow conducted a three-year research study,

22. Ibid., 93–96.
23. Kogan, "Bringing the Dialogue Home," 61.
24. Ibid., 71.

the Religion and Diversity Survey. He reviews its results in *America and the Challenges of Religious Diversity*. Wuthnow reports that only one church member in six has participated in a worship service in their congregation in which a non-Christian leader spoke. Only one in nine has participated in a study program focusing on beliefs and practices other than Christianity and Judaism.[25] Wuthnow points out, "Although it is common to give lip service to the value of diversity, many Americans regard religions other than their own as fanatical, conducive to violence, closed-minded, backward, and strange."[26] The religious leaders with whom I spoke expressed candidly that more needs to be done to move interreligious partnerships from the level of religious leadership and academia to local congregations and rank-and-file members. It will be important that interreligious work takes root on a broader platform and does not remain largely an expertise of the elite. At the end of the chapter, we return to the issue of interreligious partnerships of local communities. Now, we take a look at some programs that have created partnerships across particular projects and social groups: partnerships among women and young people and the exchange of spiritual practices.

In the 1980s a number of conferences brought women of different religious traditions into dialogue.[27] Participants in these conferences discovered that dialogue among women of different religions was uniquely possible because they shared common concerns, such as experiences of violence and reproductive issues.

The experience of being excluded from leadership roles and rendered insignificant in their own religious institutions has made women sensitive to the need of listening in openness to the dialogue partner from a different religious tradition.[28] Religion does not exist apart from practical social aspects of life. For women, as for minorities and the poor, concerns for justice form a common starting point for action and dialogue. Conference participants discovered commonalities and cultural differences between dialogue participants. For example, what appears to Western eyes to be oppressive practices toward women may not be perceived as such by women from within another culture. Wearing

25. Wuthnow, *Challenge of Religious Diversity*, 229.

26. Ibid., 228.

27. Two essay collections give insights into interreligious conferences of women: Mollenkott, *Women of Faith in Dialogue*, and Eck and Jain, *Speaking of Faith*.

28. Powers, "Women of Faith," 3.

the headscarf, or *hijab*, is very controversial in Europe and the practice has been banned in French schools, along with other religious symbols. Many Westerners perceive the *hijab* as a symbol of repression. However, many Muslim women choose headscarfs from a variety of different and fashionable designs and wear them as a positive expression of their religious and cultural identity. Numerous Muslim women choose to adhere to a modest dress standard because they see it as taking a stand against the exploitation of the female body by a male dominated culture.[29] Through interpersonal and direct conversation during the conferences, participants could come to a deeper understanding of their differences and commonalities.

In their contribution to the essay collection *Interfaith Dialogue at the Grassroots,* Edith Howe and Mark Heim write about an interreligious partnership that began as a book club named "Daughters of Abraham." Women of the three Abrahamic traditions came together to share meals and read books, primarily novels, which were in some way related to Judaism, Christianity, and Islam. As the group evolved the members traveled together to Spain and Jerusalem. One Jewish participant of the book club commented: "We are learning that there are different kinds of Christians. We thought you were just all the other (the group we have had so much anti-Semitism from, a monolithic group that all basically think alike), but now we see that you have all these different groups."[30] For another member this group was the only place where she was comfortable talking about issues of faith. The members became a close support to each other during times of illness and trauma in their personal lives. The group did not need experts or special preparation; instead, members talked about the stories they read and how they connected to their lives.

Muslim community leaders Eboo Patel and Patrice Brodeur collected descriptions and reflections of interreligious activities for youth and young adults in *Building the Interfaith Youth Movement.* Eboo Patel has founded the Interfaith Youth Core, an organization that involves young people ages fourteen to twenty-five in relationship building, dialogue, and service. The young people tutor refugee children, build houses, and clean up neighborhoods. The service is accompanied by small group discussions in which they share how their service is inspired by

29. O'Neill, *Women Speaking, Women Listening,* 57f.

30. Howe and Heim, "Next Thing to Dialogue," 53f.

their faith tradition. Conversations are free of proselytizing and respect the private space of the other tradition.[31] Aside from their activities in Chicago, Interfaith Youth Core helps to resource and network similar projects nationally and reaches out internationally through publications and conference presentations.

College campuses represent a rich cultural and religious diversity. Patrice Brodeur, Chair on Islam, Pluralism, and Globalization at the University of Montreal, describes a campus program he organized under the auspices of Religions for Peace on the campus of Harvard University.[32] Students had the opportunity to attend lectures and workshops on nonviolence. Through Amnesty International they wrote letters on behalf of prisoners, as well as sent them greeting cards and prayed for them. They engaged in fund-raising for local service projects and international humanitarian crises. The activities included the preparation and facilitation of interfaith prayer services. When members could not agree on the specific words for collective prayer at those services, the group decided to pray in silence, which was experienced as a powerful way of enhancing group cohesion. The programs intentionally involved education, spirituality, and action, and they aimed to help young people become global citizens navigating their engagements on local and global levels. Numerous theological schools expose their students and future religious leaders to other religious beliefs and practices through shared study programs, such as conferences and mutual visits of their schools.[33] Patel reaches out to young people for primarily two reasons. First, young people are targeted and recruited by extremist religious organizations. Second, they bring special gifts of vision and enthusiasm to interfaith work.[34]

Interfaith dialogue often involves the exchange of ideas and cooperative community service. It can also include spiritual exchange in shared worship, prayer, and meditation. In 1987, the World Council of Churches facilitated a consultation in Kyoto, Japan, bringing together Christian laypersons and monastics from different denominations who lived in a multifaith environment in Asia and had deeply engaged the spiritual practices of their host cultures. Participants reported how they were enriched by the spiritual life of other traditions. Like many

31. Patel and Neuroth, "Interfaith Youth Core," 176f., 170.
32. Brodeur, "Transnational Interfaith Youth Network," 54f.
33. Wood, "Seminarians Interacting," 102.
34. Patel and Neuroth, "Interfaith Youth Core," 169.

Westerners who cross over to Eastern meditation and yoga practices in the search for a meaningful spirituality, these Christians explored Eastern spiritual practices because many of them felt that something was missing in their tradition.[35] Participants in the Kyoto consultation stated that the practice of other traditions deepened their own Christian faith: "We have seen the unexpected Christ and have been renewed."[36] Father Alexei Smith shares with me that spiritual exchange has also been an aspect of the Buddhist-Christian dialogue in Los Angeles. "Joint monastic retreats have taken place between Buddhist and Catholic nuns and monks," he says. "Catholic nuns stayed at the Buddhist temple and participated in meditation and chanting there. In turn they hosted Buddhist nuns. Everyone lived for a while with the spiritual practices of the other to the level of one's comfort. The boundaries can be fluid."

Father Alexei talks about an experience during one of his bus tours for Catholic parishioners. At their stop at a Buddhist temple they participated in a meditation facilitated by a Buddhist monk. "The monk asked us to focus on the light within us. He said, 'For you Christians, that light is Christ dwelling within you.' That's total understanding, what more can you ask? The exposure to the spiritual practices of other traditions can be enriching. It has caused me to deepen my own theological studies. I wasn't much of a meditator. Well, I started hanging with the Buddhists and now in my own little parish we have a contemplative prayer group."

BRINGING DEPTH TO INTERRELIGIOUS DIALOGUE

Two kinds of fears can be roadblocks to interfaith dialogue: the fear of blending religious traditions and the fear of conflict. Both concerns point to the need to address differences constructively. As Rabbi Diamond puts it, we need to dig deeper in our interreligious work.

The fear of syncretism speaks to the concern that shared prayer or even the dialogue with others blurs the boundaries and creates a mishmash faith. Some people stay away from interreligious partnerships and especially interreligious worship for fear that such exchange would water down the identity of their particular faiths. In my conversations and in reviewing literature on interfaith dialogue, the opposite seems to be

35. Arai and Ariarajah, *Spirituality in Interfaith Dialogue*, 1; Eck, *Encountering God*, 153.

36. Arai and Ariarajah, *Spirituality in Interfaith Dialogue*, vii, 2.

generally true. For example, the projects of the Interfaith Youth Core are guided by ground rules that state respect for the other traditions. Patel, who has developed the program, is very clear about boundaries between areas of connection, such as shared service, and the private space of traditions in differing concepts of the divine, salvation, and prayer practices.[37] Participants in interfaith encounters have shared that, while they learned about other traditions, their own faith deepened because they had to rethink and reflect deeply about their own tradition in exchanges with others.[38] A number of projects facilitate simultaneous inter- and intrafaith dialogue groups, deepening one's own spiritual identity while developing solidarity among different faiths.[39] Father Alexei describes the fruits of the Buddhist-Christian dialogue in Los Angeles as allowing the differences to enrich rather than divide participants. Because interreligious dialogue is not a dialogue between abstract belief systems but a dialogue between believers, interfaith work is not about finding a compromise but about respect for the religiously other and his or her path, and being enriched in one's own religious practice.

The second roadblock is the fear of conflict and disagreements, which can keep interfaith conversations at a superficial level. Rabbi Diamond states: "I am not a strong proponent of the neutral interfaith services where we water down our own traditions. In the end that does not feel authentic to you or me or anyone who's involved. Sometimes interfaith activities feel superficial, when, for instance, we all sit in a big circle and say that we are brothers and sisters. Some people jump into interfaith work with a certain naïveté that's dangerous. They fail to recognize the nuances and complexities. Their motto is: can't we just all get together and get along? But it's more complicated than that; there's a lot of history we bring to interfaith encounters."

The Board of Rabbis cosponsored an interfaith conference with the title "Troubling Traditions: Wrestling with Problem Passages." Presenters and participants examined passages from the traditions of Judaism, Christianity, and Islam that suggest superiority over the other faiths. Rabbi Diamond says, "Each of our faith traditions has passages that speak of peace and love and so on, but we also have passages that are blemished and set us apart; we need to wrestle with these problematic

---

37. Patel and Neuroth, "Interfaith Youth Core," 171.

38. Goggin, "High School Youth Program," 191.

39. Keen, "Young Adult Development," 40.

texts. We have to deal with what's troubling in our own tradition and gives offense to other traditions."

Father Alexei tells me about a program for Catholic high school teachers, developed by the Anti Defamation League, "Bearing Witness." "It immerses secondary school teachers in Holocaust studies and assists them to present the Holocaust accurately: the development leading up to it and role of the Catholic church in it. The teachers have a chance to meet with a Holocaust survivor. It's an excellent program to combat anti-Semitism in schools."

After the Holocaust many Christians began to wrestle with their tradition. Although anti-Semitism and Nazi ideology are not to be confused with Christian beliefs, anti-Jewish prejudice within the Christian tradition has contributed to anti-Semitism and the oppression of Jews throughout the centuries and by the Nazis.[40] In 1987 the Institute for Christian and Jewish Studies was founded in Baltimore. It is one of a number of similar projects that challenge theological distortions that contributed to the conflict between Christians and Jews. The Institute studies sacred traditions and develops resources that honor the legitimacy and distinctiveness of the other. It seeks to disarm religious hatred and misunderstanding and to promote a better understanding of the tradition.[41]

Rabbi Diamond calls the work of engaging differences "bringing depth to interfaith dialogue": communities confront their complicated histories, carefully face prejudice and shadows in their own traditions, and talk honestly with each other. He says, "We need to move beyond politeness. As important as it is to appreciate our commonalities, it is also important to appreciate our differences."

AN INTERGROUP RELATIONS PERSPECTIVE

While I have not encountered direct reference to theories of intergroup relations in the surveyed literature or in my interviews with religious leaders, their stories resonate with its concepts and strategies. Reviewing this chapter so far, we can identify some elements of this theory that have been used successfully to promote better contact and communication among people of different social groups.

40. Niebuhr, *Beyond Tolerance*, 125.
41. Ibid., 126; Institute for Jewish and Christian Studies.

Chapter 4 concluded that bias involves cognitive, emotional, and behavioral components. It is most effectively addressed with multifaceted approaches that involve all three dimensions—cognitive beliefs, emotional reactions, and our actions toward others. Many interreligious activities employ not just one but various approaches, such as study, prayer, and action. As Patrice Brodeur puts it, they engage the head, the heart, and the hands.[42] The cognitive dimension is addressed in study of sacred scriptures and learning about beliefs and values of other religious traditions. Scholars and religious leaders often concentrate on this intellectual exchange. Some interreligious programs promote education about other religious traditions in schools and congregations. Other programs engage the behavioral dimension and tackle concrete problems of the local and global community. They engage in service and advocacy. Participants come together for action projects, cleaning up a neighborhood, building a house for a homeless family, or helping in a food bank. The emotional dimension is addressed when participants visit each other's houses of worship, share food, listen to each other's stories, and pray or meditate with each other. In these activities, empathy for another's religious identity and perspective develops.

While programs may emphasize study, action, or prayer, many try to include all three elements. The *Guidelines on Dialogue with People of Living Faiths and Ideologies* by the World Council of Churches recognizes the dialogue of life, of study, and of spirituality.[43] The Interfaith Youth Core gives young people an opportunity to serve, but their day of service is framed with a reflection on the spiritual values that move them to serve as well as some time of prayer. Rabbi Diamond feels that all three elements should be employed. "We could easily jump into action, which seems to be the most obvious starting point. But it is also important for participants to realize how their actions flow from their respective faith traditions. When Rabbi Abraham Joshua Heschel supported the civil rights movement and marched along with Martin Luther King, he said that he was praying with his feet. Study, prayer, and action cannot be separated from each other. All three components are part of a healthy interfaith engagement."

The previous chapters highlighted the effectiveness of *cooperation toward shared goals* in reducing prejudice (recategorization). Rabbi Diamond summarizes his interfaith trips to Israel and Palestine: "It of-

---

42. Brodeur, "Transnational Interfaith Youth Network," 54.

43. World Council of Churches, *Guidelines on Dialogue*, vii.

ten takes getting away from our own communities and traveling with a group of people to develop close and special bonds. When you come back you have a working partnership." The Council for a Parliament of the World's Religions finds commonalities among the religious traditions in core ethical principles and engages in action projects promoting justice, peace, and the well-being of the earth. On a local level, interreligious councils work together in community projects.

Friendship potential is another facilitating condition in intergroup contact. The accounts in this chapter overwhelmingly emphasize how important and enriching personal relationships among dialogue partners are. Through direct contact and cooperation in interreligious programs participants develop personal relationships with each other. Rabbi Diamond describes the interfaith relations in Los Angeles as special and precious. Fr. Alexei recounts how partners from other traditions came to support him when his mother died. Dr. Utter experiences the global gatherings at the World Parliament as peak experiences. Friendships and relationships are highly valued and important vehicles in interfaith work.

In dialogue and cooperation among particular social groups, such as women and young people, there are points of connection that cut through religious differences and categories. Women across religious traditions find commonalities in their roles and concrete challenges, such as their exclusion from leadership roles in their traditions and societies. Participants typically experience *cross-categorization* and develop bonds across faith lines as other concerns are shared.

In this chapter we have encountered classic statements of *decategorization*. A Jewish participant in the book club "Daughters of Abraham" describes how her view broadened from seeing Christians as a monolithic group to realizing their diversity. Intergroup relations theory calls this process differentiation. The visit to a mosque opened the eyes of a Catholic woman, who now sees the Muslim fellow citizens in her neighborhood as persons rather than in terms of a category; as she tells Father Alexei, "They are just like us."

Finally, the importance of *mutual differentiation* has been pointed out as well. Rabbi Diamond talks about the need to appreciate our differences as well as our commonalities. For Father Alexei an important aspect of the dialogue with the Buddhist community is the deeper understanding of our different paths, letting the differences enrich rather than divide us. It is a condition of credible interfaith dialogue to affirm the other's path and to respect boundaries. Both aspects of intergroup relations, the appreciation of commonalities and and of differences, of universals and of particulars, have to be maintained for there to be effective interreligious contact.

These concepts from the field of intergroup relations resonate with many experiences shared above and can be capitalized upon as religious local communities develop methodological steps for interreligious work.

There is a consensus that interfaith work needs to broaden and reach the rank-and-file members of the religious communities. Much of the dialogue takes place on an academic level by theological specialists and religious leaders. Wuthnow has found that local church leaders deal with the religious diversity in their communities largely by strategies of avoidance or minimizing. One half of local churches have no interreligious activities whatsoever, while activities of the other half do not move beyond a symbolic level to a substantial one.[44] There are theological reasons for this disengagement, which we will address in chapter 8. I suspect that many leaders and members of congregations feel ill-equipped and do not quite know how to engage the religious diversity in their communities. In the first chapters I have described opportunities and challenges of religious pluralism. I have tried to understand and take seriously the ways in which many respond, consciously and unconsciously, when they encounter the religiously other in increasingly diverse neighborhoods. Stereotype, fear, prejudice, and isolation are common responses. Chapters 3 and 4 develop tools that equip religious communities for the kind of interpersonal and intergroup dynamics they may encounter as they engage in interreligious programs. These tools based in research of intergroup relations can deepen our understanding and broaden our methodological repertoire in interreligious work. They help us to respond pastorally to religious pluralism and embrace it in ways that can enrich us. I believe that they can expand interreligious activities to the grassroots and community level.

Intergroup contact can be achieved through explicit and implicit approaches. Explicit approaches are found in dialogue groups and educational programs that face differences, prejudice, and troubling histories between religious groups head-on. These programs are very important but may be a steep entrance path for those who have their first contact with persons of other faiths. Their intergroup anxiety may be high. Joining a faith discussion group and taking on different beliefs

44. Wuthnow, *Challenges of Religious Diversity*, 255.

that represent symbolic threats to their own religious identity may be too daunting for some people. In contrast, implicit approaches pursue more modest goals and lower the threshold. Implicit approaches focus on small steps of cooperation toward a shared goal (recategorization), such as joining in a neighborhood cleanup, running a food bank, or raising funds for a homeless program, accompanied by learning and prayer. Participants get to know each other by way of working together (decategorization). Informal relationships develop much in the way described in the previous chapters. As they participate in joint activities, people share personal stories about their identities as people of faith, and they share spiritual practices to the level that is comfortable, even if that only means being present during the worship service of another tradition. When they develop friendly relationships, empathy shifts perceptions and softens categorizations. In the process, participants get to know each other as people, discover commonalities and differences (mutual differentiation). As trust develops, differences are discussed; hurt that has been caused through prejudice can be expressed. As different religious communities work together to repair and strengthen their local and global neighborhoods, so too do they begin to heal their relationships. By cooperating in service and by healing suffering in their communities, people of faith can overcome their divisions. While both explicit and implicit approaches to interreligious work are important, implicit approaches are more accessible and seem to be better entrance points for communities and congregations. Implicit cooperation projects allow time and space to develop safety before more difficult and potentially conflictual issues are addressed.

Listening to the stories told in this chapter, I have felt inspired by different and creative approaches to interreligious cooperation. They do not get much press and are beneath the radar of the wider public. They send a message that, though complex, cooperation between religious communities is possible and enriching.

From diverse religious communities who work together to heal their communities and their relationships, we move in the next chapter to interreligious work that addresses the suffering of individuals and families. Spiritual leaders, such as chaplains and counselors, support people of increasingly religiously and culturally diverse backgrounds who are confronting crisis, illness, and death. What are the unique dynamics and challenges for this ministry and how can they be addressed?

6

Tending to Our Souls

Interreligious Spiritual Care

STEVE IS A HOSPITAL chaplain in oncology. As he makes his afternoon rounds, the charge nurse waves at him and tells him about a patient in room 407 who is on the verge of dying. He is a Chinese man in his seventies. His wife and adult children are in the room. The family is Buddhist.

Steve knocks at the door and peeks into the room. The curtains are drawn and dim light comes from the lamp above the bed. The patient labors to breathe; his wife sits by his side and holds his hand. Steve approaches a man who might be in his late forties and could be the son.

"My name is Steve. I am a chaplain—like a priest or pastor. I work for the hospital and support people of all traditions."

The man nods. Steve continues: "The nurse told me that Mr. Yu is dying." Nodding. "Are you his son?"

"Yes, this is my wife, my younger brother and his wife, my sister, and my mother," he says, motioning in turn to each person in the room.

Most likely the family is not familiar with the role of an interfaith chaplain, so Steve tries to be unobtrusive. He wants to offer help but also to allow the family to feel comfortable to decline his services. Steve shakes everyone's hand:

"I am sorry—this is a very difficult and also very important time. Is there something I can do for you? I can check in with you every once in a while or leave you in privacy—whatever you prefer. I also can try to contact someone from your tradition. Our census tells me that your father is Buddhist?"

The son nods, his face lights up a little, he motions toward the door. In the hallway he says that the family sometimes has visited a Buddhist temple in the neighboring city. His father would appreciate hearing familiar chanting. Steve writes the name of the temple in his note pad and offers to return with some more information.

He contacts the temple, and finds out that a priest will not be available right away. He will do his best but cannot promise. Steve begins to get nervous at the prospect of having to move into unfamiliar territory on his own. What if the priest won't be there in time? Can he even try to fill in the gap? He heard from a colleague that it is important to many Buddhists that the dying process be as peaceful as possible. The state of the mind at death is considered to have an important influence on the rebirth process. Chanting certain sutras is believed to have a calming effect on the mind of the dying person.[1] Therefore, burning incense and chanting accompany the dying process and continue for hours after the death. Steve looks in the office for incense—with success. Now the next hurdle: according to safety regulations, there is no way Steve can burn incense in the patient's room. He approaches the charge nurse again.

"I would like to open the patio door in the patient room and burn the incense outside on the patio. It might be helpful to the family."

The nurse thinks for a moment:

"Ok, but all our nurses are very busy. You have to make sure to check in with the family regularly."

Steve walks back to the older son in 407.

"The priest from the temple will try his best, but he could not make a promise. I was wondering whether burning incense is something that might be of comfort to you? If you would like that, we could open the patio door and burn the incense right there on the patio. Unfortunately we can't do it inside because of safety regulations."

"Thank you, it is very kind to bring the incense, we would like that."

"I will stay with you for a while. Will that be all right?"

"Yes, we appreciate all your help."

Steve then walks over to the wife and the patient, holding their hands in each of his and asks the son to translate:

"Mr. Yu, my name is Steve, I work for the hospital as a chaplain and will be here with you and your family for a while. Mrs. Yu, I'm here to support you and to help you if you need anything."

1. Truitner, "Death and Dying in Buddhism," 130.

The wife nods approvingly. Steve lights the incense where Mrs. Yu can see it from where she sits. After a while, its aroma wafts into the room. Steve gets a chair and quietly sits down. The young Mr. Yu shares a little about his father and mother, about how they have come to the United States, and about what their life has been like.

After about two hours a nurse enters and waves to Steve, saying, "The monk has arrived." Steve thanks him for coming and leads him into the room.

The Buddhist priest greets the family members, talks to them for a little and begins chanting.

Steve is present as Mr. Yu breathes his last breath. The family members are visibly sad, expressing their emotions quietly. Culturally, a display of strong feelings is considered to get in the way of a peaceful transition. The chanting continues and fills the room. The wake and meditation continue for some hours. Steve walks back and forth between the nursing station and the patient room, ensuring that the family has the time it needs to be with the body and yet also that the older son knows they will have to leave in a while. After the family says their final goodbyes, Steve leads the priest out, helps the family fill out some forms, and accompanies them out of the hospital.

Steve walks to his office with a mix of emotions. He feels honored that the family allowed him to be part of this sacred moment. He is exhausted from sitting in the midst of grief without being able to do anything to take the pain away. He feels uncertain about having had to improvise for most of the encounter with the Yu family. He had some rudimentary knowledge of how to respond to the needs of a Buddhist family but he had to learn as he went along to support them in this sad and sacred moment in their lives. The Buddhist priest could respond directly to the family thanks to his role and their shared cultural and religious language. Nonetheless, through his presence and quiet advocacy behind the scenes, Steve had facilitated a holding space for emotions and for the ritual. He created a space to honor the dying person and the dying process. He helped create memories that would support the family's grieving process. Steve also feels grateful and enriched for having been a part of this transitional moment. As a protestant chaplain he could experience the power of a ritual in a different tradition, was part of the ritual, and still feels wrapped in the unfamiliar smells and sounds.

This encounter with chaplain Steve and the Yu family demonstrates the close connection of intercultural and interreligious care, and it offers insights into the challenges and opportunities of interfaith spiritual care. Steve meets a family of a culture and religious tradition different from his own. Within a short time of his arrival, questions begin rushing through his mind: How can he connect in brief moments? The family's Eastern culture is not only foreign to Steve but also to the hospital culture of Western medicine. How can he advocate for the support of the family's practices? How does the experience and care relationship affect Steve?

This chapter seeks to answer these questions. We will define interreligious spiritual care and explore aspects of interdenominational and intercultural spiritual care. Prayer between a caregiver and careseeker of different faiths exposes the tensions and possibilities of interreligious spiritual care as if with a magnifying glass. Therefore, we will develop a model of interreligious spiritual care and counseling via an analysis of interreligious prayer. But first we will clarify what we mean by interreligious spiritual care as we explore the use of the term, distinguishing it from interdenominational and intercultural spiritual care.

A WORD ABOUT TERMINOLOGY

In many public health care settings the word "pastoral" is replaced with "spiritual." What used to be "Pastoral Care Departments" or "Pastoral Care Consults" are now "Spiritual Care Departments" and "Spiritual Care Consults." The term "pastoral" has roots in the biblical image of the shepherd and describes the concern of the religious community for the person in crisis.[2] Just as "pastoral care" has connotations with the Christian tradition, "spiritual care" describes more appropriately the helping relationship between persons of different faiths.[3] This change of terminology reflects a growing demand for spiritual care from an interfaith stance because of an increasingly culturally diverse population of patients, families, and staff.

When a chaplain enters a patient's room to introduce herself for the first time, many patients and families most likely will assume that she is a Christian clergy. However, the percentage of chaplains from non-Christian traditions is growing. For example, the website of the Islamic Society of North America hosts a section on Muslim chaplaincy,

2. Mills, "Pastoral Care," 836.

3. Friedman, Jewish Pastoral Care, xvi.

the professional guild for Jewish chaplains is the National Association of Jewish Chaplains, and the number of Buddhist chaplains is increasing as well.[4] The understanding of the profession "chaplain" is undergoing a change and is inclusive of religious workers from diverse traditions.

The word "spiritual" also pops up more often in case discussions, research, and teaching in the world of medicine. Health-care workers, from mental health professionals to physicians and nurses, give more attention to the spirituality of patients and families. In this context the word "spiritual" is not so much juxtaposed to "pastoral" but is used to complement the dimensions of body and mind as a way of considering the human person more holistically. Medical research has established that spiritual beliefs and practices help people cope with illness and suffering as well as affect positive health outcomes.[5] The Joint Commission for the accreditation of health-care organizations requires that hospitals address and provide for the spiritual needs of patients.[6] While chaplains have long been recognized as primary spiritual care providers, today more and more medical students are being taught to take a brief "spiritual history" in order to assess the importance of spirituality in patients' ways of coping with an illness.[7]

Spirituality is difficult to define and is associated with the dimension of the soul, of values, meaning-making, beliefs, community, and religious connections. Pastoral theologian Emmanuel Lartey points to the root of the term "spirituality" in spirit or breath as the "enlivening force of a person." Thus, rather than delineating only the nonphysical, inner dimension, spirituality involves a person's relationship to self, others, the world, and transcendence. It is the integrating center for a person and for a community.[8]

To sum up, the use of the term "spirituality" in health-care setting reflects two trends: (1) Spirituality is taken increasingly seriously in the world of health care. (2) The assessment of spiritual needs and the provision of spiritual care includes persons from diverse cultural backgrounds. Those who seek spiritual support and those who provide spiritual care

4. Islamic Society of North America; National Association of Jewish Chaplains.

5. Mueller et al., "Religious Involvement," 1232.

6. Joint Commission, Standard RI.2.10 EP4.

7. Maugans, "The Spiritual History," 11–16; Puchalski and Romer, "Taking a Spiritual History," 129–37; Puchalski and Ferrell, *Making Healthcare Whole*, 74ff.

8. Lartey, *In Living Color*, 141.

increasingly come from diverse religious traditions. Spiritual care happens in a web of interreligious relationships.

In response to the growing diversity in our society, professionals in health care and counseling are attending far more to cultural competency. Many hospitals have departments of culture and diversity that provide translation and interpretation of different languages as well as assistance in understanding the needs of patients and clients from different cultural and ethnic backgrounds. Literature addressing counseling in multicultural contexts has grown for health-care professionals, psychologists, social workers, and pastoral counselors. For chaplains, interdenominational spiritual care has been a long-standing practice. While the reflection on interreligious spiritual care is in a beginning stage, chaplains and counselors can already find numerous helpful concepts for intercultural spiritual care. *Interdenominational, intercultural,* and *interreligious spiritual care* are closely connected, yet each has a distinct focus. We examine them more carefully in the following paragraphs.

INTERDENOMINATIONAL SPIRITUAL CARE

Even within one's own faith tradition chaplains of Christian denominations have to negotiate theological beliefs and the needs of the spiritual care situation. The diverse spiritual practices they encounter in patients and families may stretch their comfort zones. For example, the Baptist tradition values the conscious decision of a person for baptism, called believer's baptism. In their careers, Baptist chaplains quite often encounter situations where they are called to officiate an emergency baptism for an infant who is about to undergo a serious surgery. Or a chaplain may be faced with the request of Roman Catholic parents to baptize their baby who died in the womb. A conversation and spiritual assessment quickly establish that a blessing would just not have the same meaning for the family that the baptism has. For the chaplain, such a baptism may make no sense theologically. Yet, many chaplains facilitate the ritual because it has the power to comfort and support the parents' grieving process. A core objective in crisis intervention is stabilization by assisting persons in crisis to tap into their resources and to empower them to use practices that make sense within their belief systems. When choosing the appropriate spiritual care intervention, theological considerations are important but must be balanced by the needs of the patient or family whom it seeks to support.

Crisis situations call for decisions and interventions on the spur of the moment. They do not leave time for much theological reflection. Therefore chaplains are well advised to engage in ongoing theological reflection about their beliefs and what guides them as they work with persons with different value systems. In chapter 8 I delineate theological values rooted in my faith tradition that impel me to reach out to persons in crisis, regardless of their faith tradition, and that guide me in providing unconditional spiritual support. Most chaplains expect that the context of spiritual care in public institutions requires them to be flexible. Compared to congregational clergy, chaplains work with persons of very diverse backgrounds in manifold life situations and support the practices of those they serve who are in vulnerable positions. It is part of the chaplain's role to embrace a diversity of theological convictions and to respect and empower the spiritual beliefs that—in careful assessment—seem beneficial to the patient and family.

The professional code of ethics for professional chaplains expresses respect for religious diversity by asking chaplains to "affirm the religious and spiritual freedom of all persons and to refrain from imposing doctrinal positions or spiritual practices on persons whom they encounter in their professional roles as chaplain."[9] Going a step further, in order to effectively support patients, chaplains need not only to abstain from imposing their values and practices but should strive to actively engage those of the patients. When I encounter spiritual practices that are foreign to me, I try to enter what is meaningful to the patient so I can be fully present and assist the patient to draw support from what helps him or her to cope. I may be stretched beyond my comfort zone because I not only tolerate but advocate for a practice that is foreign to me but meaningful for the patient and family.[10] Setting aside personal theological views and responding in advocacy for the spiritual values of the careseeker is integral to the role of the chaplain.

INTERCULTURAL SPIRITUAL CARE

Openness and advocacy for the values of the careseeker are integral not only to *interdenominational* but also to *intercultural* spiritual care. The term "intercultural" spiritual care and counseling increasingly replaces "cross-cultural" or "multicultural" pastoral counseling since these terms

9. Association of Professional Chaplains, "Code of Ethics"; see also Standard 101.4 in Association of Clinical Pastoral Education, "Standard 100 Code."

10. See also Bueckert, "Stepping into the Borderlands," 48.

seem to suggest a rather static understanding of culture.[11] *Inter*cultural spiritual care is congruent with the understanding of culture that has been put forth in the first chapter.[12] In chapter 1 the notion of culture as "human software" has been suggested as a helpful metaphor because it expresses that beliefs and behaviors are learned and shared. The idea of "software" implies that culture is not necessarily bound by space or time but is open to change, is dynamic and fluid.[13] The term "intercultural" also expresses that the interaction between the spiritual caregiver and ca-reseeker is a mutual exchange. Three attitudes help chaplains and counselors develop cultural competency and engage in the caring relationship with those who come from different social, cultural, and religious contexts: self-awareness, respect for difference, and empowerment.

Self-Awareness

When I am providing spiritual care to a person of a different culture, my effectiveness is directly related to my awareness of my personal feelings and assumptions.

Chaplain Steve knows viscerally that he encounters difference in the Yu family by his rising anxiety level when he phones the Chinese temple and finds out there is a chance that the Buddhist priest might not be able to come. He collects the rudimentary knowledge about possible needs of Buddhist patients that he has attained in informal conversation with his colleague. He feels fearful that he might make mistakes when interacting with the Yu family. It is easy to feel overwhelmed in the face of otherness in a patient or family who need our assistance: After all, cultural differences include not only language but how we think, feel, behave, organize our family and social relationships, and approach transitions in life, as well as what gives meaning to us and how we see the Transcendent. In chapter 2 we learned that social psychologists use the term *intercultural anxiety* to capture these fearful feelings related to unfamiliarity with another culture.

Such intercultural anxiety can be managed in different ways. One way is to avoid it. As it is complicated to work with an interpreter or to understand different traditions, health-care workers may—consciously

11. For example, see Augsburger, Pastoral Counseling across Cultures and Conflict Mediation across Cultures; van Beek, Cross-Cultural Counseling; Law, The Wolf Shall Dwell.

12. Lartey, *In Living Color*, 31ff.

13. Nederveen Pieterse, *Globalization and Culture*, 78, 46.

and unconsciously—avoid contact, pass by a particular patient's room, or interact as little as possible. A Christian chaplain may look through the census in the morning and—somehow—the Muslim or Jewish Orthodox family ends up at the bottom of his priority list. One can avoid contact with those who are different or one can avoid feelings of fear and incompetence by pretending there is no difference. Steve could have chosen to behave as if he were talking to a Caucasian family, offer his help in a general way, and move on. He would have missed the needs of the Yu family.

In contrast, Steve uses his anxiety in constructive ways. He asks the family what might be helpful to them. He has some ideas of what might be supportive and explores his ideas with the oldest son of the Yu family. Approaching a person with respectful curiosity entails acknowledging our differences as well as our fears of difference. It requires from spiritual counselors the openness to explore their fears and use them constructively by inviting input from the careseeker.

Awareness of one's feeling toward a culturally different counselee is the foundation for an open and respectful encounter, as is attentiveness to one's own assumptions and bias.

Respect for Difference

Self-awareness about personal values is an important component of cultural competency because chaplains may encounter spiritual beliefs and practices that are not only different but in conflict with their own. For example, immigrants may draw upon the support of indigenous healers, such as curanderos among Mexican Americans, and shamans among some Asian cultures, along with or instead of Western medicine and clergy. The belief in good and bad spirits that intervene in persons' lives, and notions of demon possession may be meaningful for persons from different cultures, but may rub against the values of health-care professionals and spiritual caregivers from Western cultures. In order not to impose one's own values on patients from a different culture, chaplains need to be aware of their reactions to other cultural beliefs and practices and remain open to educating themselves about different cultures. In intercultural spiritual care chaplains not only move into the terrain of diverse beliefs, they also may be challenged to learn new spiritual practices in order to support patients. In a hospital with a large Latino/a Catholic population, for example, Caucasian Protestant chaplains cannot rely on interventions that are meaningful within their own framework. They have to familiarize themselves with devotion to the Lady of Guadalupe, an indigenous symbol of Mary, and integrate images, such as holy cards and statues of saints, into their spiritual care. Chaplains from Western mainline Protestant traditions are most familiar with counseling interventions that are verbal and focus on the mind. In order to work effectively with a Latino/a Catholic patient population they need to integrate nonverbal actions and gestures, such as ritualized forms of prayer and blessing with holy water, touching the patient on head, hands, and feet. Respect for different cultural and spiritual practices involves an awareness of the caregiver's willingness to move into new territory.

German CPE supervisor Helmut Weiß summarizes this attitude of respectful curiosity as follows: "This person is different from me and I don't know anything about her or him."[14] A number of pastoral theologians go back to a simple and memorable formula that can help healthcare workers and counselors to approach difference with curiosity and respect.[15] Every person in certain respects is (1) like all others, (2) like some others, (3) like no other. There are some experiences that we share with other human beings no matter what our background is. We may approach birth, suffering, and death differently, but to a certain degree these experiences are universal. There are some experiences that we have in common with those who also share our cultural, social, political context. Finally, each person is a unique individual and we cannot assume that just because someone comes from a particular culture they hold beliefs or practice customs that are typical for that culture. Especially for persons whose culture represents a minority, it is important that differences are not minimized but acknowledged. We learned in chapter 4 that social psychologists use the term mutual differentiation to point out that respectful encounters between people of different social groups include an awareness of what they have in common *and* where they are different. Persons live on a continuum of universality and particularity. Besides the stances of respect and self-awareness, spiritual caregivers honor their patients from minority cultures with interventions that seek to empower them.

14. Weiß, "Die Entdeckung interkultureller Seelsorge," 17–31; Weiß, "Seelsorgeausbildung," 266.

15. It has been developed by Kluckhohn and Murray, *Personality in Nature,* and is referred to by Augsburger, *Pastoral Counseling across Cultures,* 49–67, and Lartey, *In Living Color,* 171–75.

Empowerment

Power dynamics are present in every helping relationship. They are more pronounced—if not always obvious—in intercultural relationships. As pastoral theologian James Poling points out, when professional counselors are identified with the dominating power they easily underestimate the level of injustice that influences the life of their clients.[16] Caucasian health-care professionals may not be aware of how persons from racial and ethnic minorities feel when they seek assistance or medical treatment from those who represent the majority culture. Most North American health-care settings function on the basis of Western values. *Cultural normativity* often is unconscious, denies minorities their cultural identity, and silences their spiritual identity.[17]

One strategy of addressing power imbalance is the counselors' awareness of inherent power dynamics in caring relationships. This does not mean that counselors have to deny their own values. Differences are best approached with transparency, exploring together different beliefs so they can be respected without one being taken over by the other. Spiritual counselors can bring to the surface cultural differences at play in the pastoral relationship. They can share their perceptions and interventions and invite counselees to reflect on the pastoral relationship together.[18]

Actions of *empowerment* address cultural normativity and the inherent power imbalance in many intercultural helping relationships. Throughout the history of pastoral care and counseling five classical functions of spiritual care and counseling have developed: healing, sustaining, guiding, reconciling, and nurturing.[19] For intercultural spiritual care the Ghanaian pastoral theologian Emmanuel Lartey adds two additional functions: liberating and empowering.[20] *Liberating* involves consciousness-raising about structures that keep persons from living to their full potential. Liberating in the form of consciousness-raising can help them to uncover the predominant assumptions about health and illness and make a more conscious choice of who they are and what they are able to do.

16. Poling, "Wahrnehmung kultureller Differenz," 74.

17. Ibid.

18. Riedel-Pfäfflin and Strecker. *Flügel Trotz Allem*, 33.

19. William A. Clebsch and Charles R. Jaekle, leaning on S. Hiltner, outlined the first four functions. Howard Clinebell adds the fifth function, nurturing. See Clinebell, *Basic Types of Pastoral Care*, 42f., 432.

20. Lartey, *In Living Color*, 67f.

Empowering involves assisting persons to move beyond enforced and internalized helplessness and help them discover resources in themselves, use community support, and become advocates for themselves and others.[21] Counselors who take the stance of empowerment shift their perspectives in relationship to counselees from persons who have deficits to persons with challenges and the resources to cope with those challenges.[22]

The members of the Yu family faced challenges because they were in a state of crisis and grief. Mrs. Yu spoke little English. The hospital team was unfamiliar with Buddhist end-of-life practices and the family likewise was unfamiliar with hospital protocols and with death itself. The hospital's usual practice is to move a body to the morgue after two or at most three hours after death. Chaplain Steve made the needs of the family known to the health-care team, thereby giving them a voice. Once their needs were known, the nurses were open to attend to them as much as possible.

Cultural competency for spiritual caregivers and counselors involves listening to culturally different voices and advocating for them. At times it entails assisting minorities whose values are silenced to listen to their own voices.

So far we have explored attitudes in spiritual caregivers and counselors that assist interdenominational and intercultural pastoral relationships: flexibility, respectful curiosity, self-awareness, and empowerment of careseekers to validate their cultural values. These stances are fundamental to interreligious spiritual care as well. In addition, spiritual support of persons from other religious traditions has unique characteristics, which we will now explore.

CONNECTING: A FUNCTION OF INTERRELIGIOUS SPIRITUAL CARE

Just as Lartey adds *liberating* and *empowering* to the classical pastoral care functions in the context of intercultural spiritual care, I propose an eighth function for interreligious care: *connecting*.

Spiritual care involves linking persons in crisis to their spiritual resources, helping them to tap into what will help them cope. Chaplain Steve obtained incense for the Yu family to enable a familiar ritual, and

21. Ibid.

22. Empowerment as a resource orientation in work with counselees has been outlined by feminist orientation in spiritual care and counseling. Riedel-Pfäfflin and Strecker. *Flügel Trotz Allem*, 34.

he called a Buddhist priest. An interfaith chaplain's spiritual support can go a long way, but at times her or his role may be that of a *resource agent* who connects patients with faith specific resources. A religious leader or member from a patient's faith community can often more effectively help the patient to tap into spiritual resources for coping with a crisis through specific rituals, or through chanting or reciting sacred scriptures in the original language. Interreligious spiritual care does not mean that an interfaith chaplain has to be "everything to everybody" but that the chaplain should know when to make the appropriate referral.

Interfaith spiritual care includes the function of connecting persons to their spiritual resource and community. In order to adequately fulfill this function, spiritual caregivers and counselors do well to invest time and energy to develop connections with religious resources within the local community. Such relationships need to be nurtured and supported. Many chaplains have active relationships with diverse Christian, Jewish, Muslim, Jehovah's Witness, Buddhist, Hindu, and Native American communities and religious leaders. They meet representatives of these communities personally and call upon them when patients need support. Thus, effective interfaith chaplains and counselors are resource agents and know how to connect persons in crisis to their faith communities.

Still, the reality is that, in many spiritual care emergencies during the night and on weekends, faith specific community resources may not be available. As the example of chaplain Steve demonstrates, there are many things a chaplain can and needs to provide. A Christian chaplain might feel tempted to call the local mosque right away before making a thorough assessment and fully exhausting all the possibilities she may have in working with a Muslim family. Perhaps this is so because calling the local imam is more convenient than getting involved with another tradition. Or perhaps it is because the situation leaves the chaplain feeling ill prepared, overwhelmed, or fearful of the difference the other belief represents. Connecting persons of other religious traditions to their resources has its important place but cannot replace the involvement of the chaplain.

In sum, the following are spiritual care functions in the context of interdenominational, intercultural, and interreligious spiritual care:[23]

---

23. Clinebell, Basic Types of Pastoral Care, 42; Lartey, In Living Color, 67f.

1. Healing—supporting persons to move past the suffering they experience

2. Sustaining—helping persons to endure and cope with illness and suffering

3. Guiding—assisting persons in sorting through difficult decisions they may have to make and opening up alternative choices

4. Reconciling—restoring fragmented and hurt relationships with self, others, and the Transcendent

5. Nurturing—assisting persons to develop their potential and facilitating their growth

6. Liberating—consciousness-raising of dominant values and how they may be internalized and prevent persons from living to their fullest potential

7. Empowering—assisting persons in moving beyond a sense of internalized helplessness.

8. Connecting—linking persons to their particular spiritual resources, to their spiritual practices and communities.

Setting aside personal theological views while advocating for spiritual practices of careseekers is a common denominator in interdenominational, intercultural, and interreligious spiritual care. To many chaplains, offering spiritual support to a person of a different faith tradition seems to be more convoluted than providing care to persons of different denominations within the same faith tradition. A spiritual encounter with someone of a different faith can bring about fears and questions of identity. Speaking in the terminology of social psychology, beliefs and practices of another can represent a *symbolic threat*. This may be the case both in the careseeker and caregiver. Many spiritual practices such as prayer and ritual come from the core of one's belief system. Can a chaplain of a different faith enter such practices with authenticity? Interreligious ritual and prayer present more of a challenge to many chaplains than spiritual support through reflective listening, for example. Thus, like a prism, prayer focuses the issues, concerns, and opportunities that are raised when it comes to interreligious spiritual care. In the following paragraphs we will examine interreligious prayer closely. We will untangle what might be behind the hesitancy to encounter careseekers of other faiths as well as discover the potential in such encounters.

INTERRELIGIOUS PRAYER: A PRIME EXAMPLE OF
INTERRELIGIOUS SPIRITUAL CARE

Spiritual support of persons from diverse religious traditions includes reflective listening, spiritual counseling, as well as facilitating rituals from
the spiritual practice of careseekers. Besides listening and exploration,
blessings and prayer are perhaps the most common spiritual resources
and rituals chaplains use in providing spiritual care. They may be offered
at the bedside as well as in public contexts such as interfaith worship
services. The observance of diverse religious holidays in hospitals and
prisons provides opportunities for communal prayer, for example the
sounding of the shofar on Rosh Hashanah or the celebration of Eid al
Fitr, the end of Ramadan. Interfaith services took place in local communities and numerous hospital chapels and meditation rooms during
national crises, such as the terrorist attacks of September 11, 2001, and
Hurricane Katrina. World Aids Day, memorial services for patients who
have died, and transitions in the institutional life, such as the opening of
a new wing or building—all are opportunities and contexts for interfaith
services. The liturgies and rituals in such services need to be sensitive to
the many religious traditions represented in public institutions.

How can chaplains understand such services and relationships with
persons of other faiths in these settings? Several scenarios of interreligious
prayer can be distinguished:[24] (1) *Multi-faith prayers* are often used during
interreligious gatherings. This respects and maintains the various religious
traditions of participants. (2) *Interreligious prayer services* are designed
with a shared representation of resources from different traditions.[25] For
example, they may consist of an opening prayer from the Christian tradition, a song from the Jewish tradition, a reflection by a Buddhist, and a
reading from the Qur'ān. *Interreligious prayers* between a pastoral caregiver and careseeker from different religious traditions are shared as part
of a counseling session or at the bedside in a health-care setting. Familiar
words from specific prayers can powerfully connect to someone's soul and
offer comfort. For example, a non-Jewish chaplain may pray with a Jewish

---

24. These scenarios are partly inspired by and lean on five types of interreligious
prayer as distinguished by Araiarajah, *Not without My Neighbor*, 32–34. I have comple-
mented and modified the types described by Ariarajah for the context of pastoral care.

25. For resources see Heckman and Picker Neiss, *Interactive Faith*. For reflections
on working with persons of different religious traditions in the hospital context, see
Kirkwood, *A Hospital Handbook*.

patient the Mi'sheberach, a prayer for healing. The prayer can comfort in a more meaningful way when recited in Hebrew.[26]

(3) *Generic prayers* use a language that is not unique to any faith tradition and is intended to be inclusive and available to all. They may be used in public worship as well as in the hospital room. The caring presence of a chaplain before surgery who facilitates an inclusive prayer before the procedure can be a powerful source of support at a time of heightened anxiety. Whether a generic prayer or a faith specific prayer is used depends on the situation and persons involved.[27]

Concerns about Interreligious Prayer

Religious language and symbols are expressions of culture. Religious communities celebrate worship and liturgy in a space set apart from the everyday world where they encounter a plurality of beliefs. Cultural customs as well as particular religious rites can be powerful sources of social identity. Persons from other traditions often have difficulty understanding them and experience them as foreign. Most Christians would not know how to act when entering a Sikh temple or attending the funeral of the mother of our Buddhist co-worker. Sometimes the fear of making a mistake may keep us from reaching out. Religions can separate as well as connect. The isolation of different communities in the religious realm can consolidate ignorance and stereotype. Besides a lack of knowledge, theological concerns about syncretism are sometimes roadblocks to interreligious prayer. For example, some Christian clergy express reservations about praying with Muslims. They feel they cannot pray to Allah, because they understand this as a prayer to a different God rather simply a prayer to "God," which is the English translation of the Arabic word Allah. They are concerned that they might gloss over theological differences and might lose their integrity by praying in a different prayer language. The Christian understanding of God is trinitarian, while Muslims understand Jesus not as divine but as a human prophet equal to Abraham, Moses, and Mohammed.

Chaplains need to respect the integrity of their faith in order to be authentically present in a caring relationship. However, a one-sided emphasis on integrity and boundaries of each faith tradition excludes

26. Weintraub, "Mi Sheberakh."

27. The following resources provide prayers from different religious traditions as well as generic prayers: Christian Education Movement, *Praying Their Faith*; Levy, *Talking to God*; Roberts and Amidon, *Life Prayers*.

the possibility of shared expression of faith and spirituality. Based on the diversity of prayer language and images of God in the Bible, especially in the Book of Psalms, it can be argued that prayer is not a doctrinal description of the belief of a community but an opening to God's mystery from very different perspectives. When Christian and Muslim theologians meet in dialogue and consultation about their traditions, precise theological definitions and doctrinal clarity are important. The concerns in a pastoral care situation, however, when a family is grieving the death of a loved one are comfort, support, and guidance, some of the functions of spiritual care outlined in the preceding text.

In the context of the hospital, the patients' preferences need to be respected. A patient or counselee may be hesitant to engage in a prayer with a chaplain or counselor from a different faith tradition. But if a patient finds support in shared prayer, does the idea of the theological impossibility of interreligious prayer hold up?

Not only Christian chaplains voice concerns about the possibility of interfaith prayer. A CPE supervisor told me about his Buddhist student who felt that she could not authentically pray with patients because her practice was not based on a belief in God. Buddhist chaplain Mike Monnett, however, describes his practice of spiritual support, which may include reading from the Bible and prayer in support of a patient. He understands such an intervention as an expression of Buddhadharma, Buddha's teachings, originating from his identity as a Buddhist interfaith chaplain.[28]

Opportunities of Interreligious Prayer

Many chaplains can share stories of amazing openness and connection with patients and families of other faiths. Once I visited with a retired Jewish rabbi who was hospitalized. As our conversation came to an end, I offered a generic blessing for his recovery. In response the rabbi offered to bless me. He placed a paper napkin from his nightstand on my head – perhaps to function as a kippah, an expression of humility before the Divine. If he was Orthodox, perhaps the napkin made it possible for him to touch me. After he placed the napkin on my head he laid his hand on me and blessed me. I was deeply touched and honored to receive his blessing. That the rabbi did not share my belief in a triune God never crossed my mind. The connection to this rabbi as well as his gift was an authentic religious experience and a sacred moment for me. His laying on of hands as well as the use of the paper napkin left a deep

28. Monnett, "Developing a Buddhist Approach," 57–62.

impression with me. The rabbi created a sacred space in the hospital room and ritualized the blessing with his gestures, which enriched and deepened my understanding of blessing and has encouraged me to use more expressive gestures in my spiritual care.

Pastoral care offers care for the soul. A young patient's mother stops by our spiritual care office to express appreciation for the chaplain who supported her. She mentions that she is not religious. As she found herself trying to understand the complicated medical condition and treatments of her boy and spent much time calling her insurance company, the chaplain stopped by and asked her how she was doing. She says: "The fact that someone showed up and cared about my soul and spoke to me as a person was so helpful to me. The simple prayer was calming in this extremely stressful time." To her, the chaplain represented a humanizing aspect in a high-tech, bureaucratic health-care machine. Although prayer is not part of her personal practice, she appreciated it.

For others, chaplains represent the religious community or the Divine in a critical time in their life. Some prefer a representative from their religion; for many others, interfaith chaplains fulfill that function just fine and are appreciated.

Prayer focuses the potential of interreligious interaction as well as the question of how spiritual counselors can theologically understand their spiritual care relationship with persons of other faiths. To this end, I now introduce a model that conceptualizes interreligious spiritual care along a continuum of three concentric circles. This model considers the particular and the universal, boundaries as well as possibilities of interreligious care.

CONCENTRIC CIRCLES
OF INTERRELIGIOUS SPIRITUAL CARE[29]

The outer of the three circles is the realm of *common human experience*. The interfaith movement is based on the fact that we are brought together by global problems that concern of all us: environmental problems, poverty, and human rights. In spiritual care with individuals and families these human conditions are birth, death, suffering, illness, and injury. While different cultures and religions have different rituals and

---

29. Araiarajah, *Not without My Neighbor*, 49–53. The Sri Lankan ecumenical theologian Wesley Ariarajah has conceptualized interfaith worship, which represents a public form of interreligious prayer. When reflecting on the possibility of interfaith worship, he envisions three concentric circles, which inspires the notion of the three concentric circles in the context of interreligious spiritual care.

conceptualizations to approach these issues, we connect to others in these universal experiences. We use our shared common humanity as a connecting point.

The second circle is characterized by *interconnected spiritual practice*. Throughout history religions have been interconnected and influenced each other.[30] For example, beads as means of meditation, concentration, and prayer are common in Buddhism, Hinduism, Islam, and Roman Catholic Christianity. They are being rediscovered by contemporary Protestant Christians as well. Although they are used differently in the different traditions, the similarity of the symbols indicates some interconnections.

The most inner circle of *particular spiritual practice* represents the core identity of a religious community. Interfaith spiritual care finds its boundaries and limits in this circle. Spiritual care in this circle most often includes the employment of particular spiritual resources, such as working with specific rituals and representatives of the religious communities involved. The inner circle speaks to our experience of particularity.

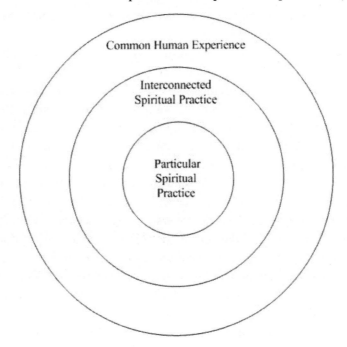

Figure 6.1.

Three Concentric Circles of Spiritual Care

30. Smith, *Toward a World Theology*, 38, 48. See also the concept of hybridization as described in chapter 1.

The three circles are distinct and represent different ways of engaging spiritual practice. Even so, they do not represent separate worlds but are distinguished through boundaries that are somewhat permeable, sharing one center. Interconnections between members of different religious traditions are possible in all three areas. The two outer circles represent areas where interconnections with other religious traditions are most easily possible. The inner circle of particular practice is important as well, as it maintains the need for nurture and preservation of our unique faith identity.

The Circle of Common Human Experience

The outer circle represents spiritual practice in the context of our shared humanity. When I am offering spiritual support to a person from another religious tradition on their terms, I am not moving away from my own spiritual center and tradition. For example, tending to those who are hungry, in prison, and sick is a core practice of the Christian faith. Shared human experiences represent areas where the spiritual center of the careseeker and my own can meet. The outer circle speaks to our experience of universality.

But a word of caution is in order. Within the context of interreligious spiritual care, not only cultural normativity but also *Christian normativity* is often unconscious, as we see in the following example.

Mark, a Christian chaplain, plans a service for the hospital patients, families, and staff in his community hospital during the winter holidays. The hospital population has a considerable percentage of Jewish patients. Because the Christmas season and Chanukah holidays overlap in the calendar, Mark calls a local rabbi to invite him to facilitate together an interfaith holiday service with a generic theme of light. The rabbi explains to Mark that he prefers to offer a separate celebration, because this Jewish holiday and its particular significance get diluted in a context where the majority culture is Christian. Mark realizes that his well-meaning attempt to be inclusive is misdirected. Considering that Christianity is predominant and normative in the larger society and the hospital community, inclusiveness in the form of a generic service would diminish the distinctiveness of this Jewish holiday. This vignette illustrates that the emphasis of supposed "universals" from the perspective of the majority faith tradition can actually deny the spirituality of those in a minority. On the surface it may appear inclusive, but as power structures remain unconscious, it upholds the very structures that minimize traditions that are different from the mainstream.

Nonetheless, our shared humanity can be a common ground for interreligious spiritual support: Barbara, a Jewish CPE student, supports a Roman Catholic family in the Intensive Care Unit whose child is being disconnected from life support after a long illness. Before she offers a prayer, Barbara invites the family members to say words of prayer, thus making room for the religious identity of the family. Barbara moves into unfamiliar ground, as spontaneous prayer is not as common within the Jewish tradition as within the Christian tradition. The prayer she offers is informed by images and metaphors of her own tradition. In her reflection with her peers she expresses how connected she felt to the persons in the room because "there was just something so human about the experience. The pain, the grief, the comfort, the mystery of death. The prayers flowed out of me when I could connect to the most humanizing aspects of the experience." In this chapter's opening vignette, chaplain Steve provides spiritual care through his presence by making sure that the patient could die in a dignified way that is meaningful to him and his family. The chaplain's cooperation and communication with the nursing team about expanding the time the family can spend with the body, his presence, and advocacy—all are spiritual care interventions on this outer circle. Other interventions include empathic listening, exploration, empowering, affirming, consciousness raising, reframing. Some rituals, such as blessing and generic prayer focused on the shared and common experience of humanity and suffering, are possible as well. The primary role of the spiritual counselor in the circle of our common humanity is that of the *companion*.

The Circle of Interconnected Spiritual Practice

Shared spiritual practice is possible because religious history is a web of relationships. We meet in areas where our spiritual traditions interconnect. We will experience difference, but in our experiences and the ways we interpret them we can connect. Both Jews and Christians read and pray the psalms. They understand many psalms through a different lens. When those differences are not overlooked, psalms can form a common ground for interreligious spiritual care. My hospital has a large percentage of Latino Catholic patients. Our CPE program trains numerous rabbinical interns. Frequently they use the psalms to connect to the spiritual practice of our families. They begin the prayer by reading a psalm, pray, and invite the families to close with their own prayer—if they wish. When discussing these experiences in case conferences the peer groups discover that the limitations presented with different faiths are also opportunities. The Jewish chaplain invites patients who often are being "prayed for" by a priest, to say their own prayer, thus empowering them to express their struggles and needs on their own terms. Thus, interreligious spiritual care can at times introduce new practices that enrich the coping mechanisms and spiritual life of careseekers.

Both the Christian and the Muslim traditions have similar traditions of intercessory prayer. In Islam a du'a is a prayer that is not based in the Qu'ran but formulated for special concerns. A non-Muslim chaplain can offer a du'a, an intercessory prayer, as an expression of care and spiritual support for a Muslim patient, as long as it is directed to God and no mention is made of Jesus or Mary. A patient may be better helped through a person who shares their faith and can recite the Qu'ran and share a deeper spiritual connection, yet a du'a is a general intercessory prayer where Muslims and non-Muslims can connect. On the circle of interconnected spiritual practice, participants have an opportunity to acknowledge their differences and express their beliefs. At the same time, they find commonalities in their practices, and the pastoral encounter encourages mutuality.[31] Spiritual care interventions include some faith specific rituals, the use of sacred texts, and meditation. The primary role of the interfaith chaplain is that of *representative of the sacred*.

The Circle of Particular Spiritual Practice

This inner circle represents the core of the identity of a faith community, its formative symbols, rituals, and beliefs, such as baptism and communion for the Christian community. This circle is important because it nurtures and shapes the particular identity. Even these boundaries are not necessarily written in stone and persons who are not members of a particular community are often invited to participate. Often the most familiar ritual can offer the strongest support in a crisis. In our opening vignette, a Buddhist priest is called to offer particular chants that may connect powerfully with the family as they share the religious language and may be deeply familiar with its sounds. The spiritual care interven-

---

31. See also Griffith, "A Chaplain Reflects," 86.

tions offered in this circle of particular spiritual practice are faith specific rites that involve initiation into the community (such as baptism), rites of reconciliation (confession, Vidui), sacraments, as well as prayers and chants in the original language of the tradition, such as citations from sacred Hebrew texts or Qu'ran passages in Arabic.

The sacrament of the sick in the Roman Catholic tradition may only be administered by a Catholic priest. The Vidui, the final confession, a Jewish end-of-life ritual, most often is facilitated by a rabbi. Baptism is a spiritual practice at the core of Christian identity. Jewish chaplain Phyllis Brooks Toback expresses an additional concern a Jewish chaplain may experience with regard to baptism: "As a Jew I carry with me the history of centuries of persecution and attempts by Christians to get Jews to acknowledge the divinity of Jesus and to verbalize acceptance of Christianity."[32] She describes emergency situations when a Christian chaplain is not available and she may work together with Christian staff or when she as a Jewish chaplain can respond to the pastoral need for baptism and blessing by *declaring on behalf of* the parents that they desire to have their child baptized in the name of the triune God. Toback's reflections are very personal, and different chaplains may keep different boundaries when it comes to the participation in the particular spiritual practices of another tradition. At times, in situations of suffering and crisis, pastoral care givers may move into the terrain of a particular tradition, motivated by their care for the other persons as well as their faith in the presence of God in these moments.[33]

As mentioned previously, an interfaith chaplain's spiritual support can go a long way, but the primary role on the circle of particular spiritual practice is that of a *resource agent* who connects patients and families with their spiritual communities and resources. The spiritual care function is "*connecting*." In order to fulfill this function, interfaith chaplains need to develop relationships with diverse local religious communities, invite representatives to their setting for mutual education, set up procedures regarding how to notify them, and nurture such relationships.

32. Toback, "Theological Reflection on Baptism," 315–17.
33. Ibid., 317.

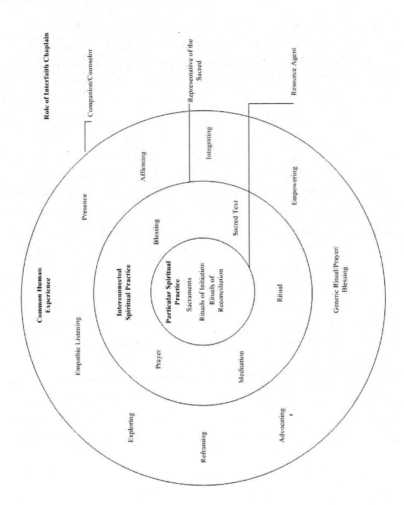

Figure 6.2.

Examples of Interfaith Spiritual Care Interventions

SUMMARY

Increasingly chaplains of diverse religious traditions offer spiritual care and counseling to persons of different cultures and faiths. It is part of the role and ethos of chaplains and spiritual counselors not to impose their own values but to assist counselees in tapping into their resources for coping and healing. Intercultural competency in spiritual care and counseling involves self-awareness, respect for difference, and empowerment. The same is true for interreligious spiritual care. A spiritual care function that is particularly pronounced in interreligious care is *connecting*: linking counselees to their faith specific resources and communities. Interfaith chaplains and counselors take on the role of resource agents who develop and nurture relationships to faith specific resources in their local communities.

Interreligious relationships of care can be envisioned along a continuum of three concentric circles: particular spiritual practice, interconnected spiritual practice, and common human experience. Each circle represents primary ways of interacting and primary spiritual care interventions. Together they signify a range of possibilities of interreligious interaction. This model of interreligious spiritual care takes into account boundaries and the particularity of religious practices. At the same time it reveals an encouraging potential for persons whose faiths differ to connect and be supported in times of crisis.

7

"There Was a Priest, a Rabbi, and a Minister"

Interreligious Issues in Clinical Supervision

UPDATING THE FAMILIAR JOKE to the twenty-first century would be a complex undertaking: "There was a priest, a rabbi, a minister, an imam, and a shaman . . ." We would have to clarify what kind of priest we are talking about, whether a Catholic, a Hindu, a Buddhist, and so on. Our religious landscape today is not a simple one. Not only are the titles of religious leaders distinct, so too is how their communities understand their roles and how those leaders prepare for their work. Yet, increasingly, religious leaders from different traditions come together in teams that provide and train others to give spiritual care in public institutions. In the following vignettes, chaplains and clinical supervisors in the Association for Clinical Pastoral Education, Inc. (ACPE) articulate their roles and practice in the emerging field of interfaith spiritual care and supervision.

Nina Davis is a Zen Buddhist who has trained with Christian supervisors in Australia. She writes about her experiences in the *Journal of Supervision and Training in Ministry,* followed by reflections of her supervisor David Larsen. Nina captures some of her experiences as follows: "As a CPE student, I needed to constantly translate Christian religious language so that I could communicate with my supervisors. . . . Throughout my CPE experience, as both a student and now as a supervisor, I have had the somewhat isolating experience of being the only non-Christian in every group in which I have participated. Had it not been through the skillful means of the three supervisors who intentionally acknowledged my faith and cultural differences, I wouldn't have written this paper."[1] Her supervisor, David Larsen, summarizes his sentiment: "It is not only possible but also enjoyable to supervise in the same arena as a Zen Buddhist."[2]

CPE supervisor Rabbi Bonita Taylor and Jewish chaplain Rabbi David Zucker have reflected on their own training in CPE. Their article "Nearly Everything We Wish Our Non-Jewish Supervisors Had Known about Us as Jewish Supervisees" introduces clinical pastoral supervisors to some of the key points of Jewish tradition and culture in order to help them to become more sensitive to their Jewish students. Recapping some of the issues they encountered, they say: "Most of us (Jews and Christians, alike) take for granted that when we use the same language, we mean the same thing. In actuality, sometimes we do, but often, we do not. . . . Often, the resulting conflict leaves Jewish students alienated from their CPE supervisors and peers—as though they are strangers in a strange land."[3]

George Tinker is professor of American Indian Cultures and Religious Tradition, a member of the Osage Nation, and ordained in the Evangelical Lutheran Church in America. In 1992 he raised some concerns about the dislocation Native American students experience in CPE. Whereas the dynamic group process in CPE often is shaped by Western values of self-knowledge through self-exposure and confrontation, Native Americans gain self-knowledge in their community through listening to traditional stories and particular rituals. He states: "To impose new cultural values, even with the best of intentions, is not only destructive to the old value system but can result in devastating cultural confusion."[4]

Looking back at her experience as a chaplain resident, Muslim chaplain Mary Lahaj states: "As a pioneer in the residency program, I felt I was carrying the future of the whole Muslim community on my shoulders."[5] Muslim chaplain S. E. Jihad Levine expresses a similar sentiment: "And Muslim chaplains, along with offering pastoral care, carry out another crucial function: they are unofficial ambassadors of their often misunderstood religion. . . . From shattering stereotypes to bridging

1. Davis, "Multicultural CPE Supervision Possible?" 62, 65.
2. Larsen, "Supervising in an Interfaith Environment," 58.
3. Taylor and Zucker, "Nearly Everything," 327, 328.
4. Tinker, "On Not Requiring CPE," 179.
5. Lahaj, "Making It Up," 151.

cultural differences, Muslim chaplains are obliged to carry heavy social responsibilities beyond those borne by chaplains of other faiths."[6]

Finally, Mike Monett, a Zen Buddhist chaplain, develops a model of health-care chaplaincy originating from a Buddhist perspective. He states: "The point is that as a professional chaplain I am not there to proselytize but to give support to the patients, staff, and families. *And it is through this interaction that I am expressing Buddhadharma, just as a minister in an Abrahamic tradition might feel that through the same interaction he [sic] was expressing God's love*" (original author's emphasis).[7]

These are a few voices that express the possibilities and the challenges of interreligious issues in the clinical supervision of spiritual care and counseling. Some articulate similar issues, such as representing a minority or having to communicate and translate their particular approaches in a field that has been established in a predominantly Christian context. Other struggles are unique to their faith tradition. For example, Muslim chaplains after 9/11 have had to confront an extra layer of stereotype and misunderstanding. I will refer to these different vignettes throughout the chapter. Together, they call attention to the unique dynamics of interfaith supervision and education for clergy.

The people who are in need of support in our hospital rooms, prisons, the military, and the counseling office are more culturally and religiously diverse than ever. Mental health professionals increasingly recognize that spirituality plays an important role in many persons' lives and that it needs to be acknowledged in a counseling relationship.[8]

While chaplain organizations and endorsement procedures for Christian and Jewish chaplains are well established, many chaplains from other traditions, such as Buddhism, Hinduism, and Islam, are trailblazers—in professional organizations of chaplains and clinical pastoral training as well as in their own faith communities.

Today, the majority of clinical supervisors of spiritual care and counseling continue to be Christian. Yet they must prepare the next generation of chaplains and spiritual counselors from diverse traditions. Engaging in interfaith issues in clinical supervision is increasingly a necessity—and yet also an opportunity welcomed by many.

---

6. Levine, "Muslim Chaplains in America," 143, 147.

7. Monett, "Developing a Buddhist Approach," 61.

8. Bernard and Goodyear, *Fundamentals of Clinical Supervision*, 146f.

In this chapter we reflect on some of the opportunities and challenges of clinical supervision of those who prepare for interfaith spiritual counseling. In particular, we explore three aspects of interreligious clinical supervision: the supervisory relationship, group supervision, and curriculum resources. Insights from intergroup relations theory again contribute to our understanding of issues in interfaith supervision. Although the primary milieu for this chapter is clinical supervision in clinical pastoral education, many concepts are applicable to other contexts of interreligious spiritual care and education.

INTERRELIGIOUS SUPERVISORY RELATIONSHIPS

Zen Buddhist Nina Davis credits her supervisors for their skill and intentionality in acknowledging her faith and cultural differences. Her statement points to the significance of the supervisory working alliance. I will explore interpersonal dynamics in the relationship between a supervisor and supervisee from different religious traditions with a focus on power dynamics, countertransference, the working alliance, and new learning.

Power Dynamics

While there is mutuality in caring and counseling relationships, they are marked by a power inequality as one person seeks support and counsel while the other's primary role is that of a care provider. Similarly, supervisory relationships are marked by mutuality and power inequality. Often supervisors learn from their supervisees and are affected by them. At the same time, power is inherent in the fact that the supervisor's role is to evaluate the student's professional growth.[9] Supervisees will feel the power inequality to a larger degree, and so supervisors do well to recognize power differences and handle them appropriately.[10] Because of the supervisor's evaluative function, a power surplus is inherent in the supervisory role.

When supervisee and supervisor represent different genders, cultural identities—and religious traditions, systemic power dynamics enter the supervisory relationship. In the terminology of intergroup relations theory, we say that in intercultural and interreligious relation-

9. Ibid., 185.
10. Ibid., 189.

ships supervisors and supervisees belong to different social groups. Some are members of dominant or majority groups; others are members of minority and less influential or less prestigious groups. The fact that they belong to different out-groups has an impact on the supervisory relationship. Those in the minority are often more attuned to differences of power, whereas members of majority or dominant groups may be oblivious to the power imbalance. When I represent a majority group I may assume sameness where in fact there is none. I may be blind to some of the differences between the groups because my own culture or religion is understood as normative in the wider social context. In their compendium on clinical supervision, Janine Bernard and Rodney Goodyear bring to our attention that the ignorance of cultural difference by the dominant culture brushed over much injustice experienced by nondominant cultures. They call on clinical supervisors to become aware of systemic issues of power.[11] Related to this idea of assimilation is James Poling's notion of cultural normativity and how it can influence pastoral caregiving.[12] Applying this notion to the context of interreligious relationships, we can speak of religious normativity: the dominant religious tradition is considered normative while minority perspectives are silenced, minimized, and overlooked.

As mentioned earlier, rabbis Bonita Taylor and David Zucker introduce in their article principles of Jewish tradition and culture in order to help non-Jewish supervisors develop cultural competency in their supervision of Jewish students. Their article illustrates the notion of religious normativity. Taylor and Zucker point out that Christian supervisors often assume that certain tenets and beliefs are the same in the Jewish and the Christian tradition when in fact they are not. Christian supervisors may speak of a shared Judeo-Christian tradition, assuming a common understanding of texts of the Hebrew Bible, of the role of belief or community, not realizing the clear differences in all those areas. At times, supervisors may misunderstand Jewish spirituality and conversational styles. As a result Jewish students in CPE have often felt like "strangers in a strange land."[13] Taylor's and Zucker's article reveals many Christian supervisors' blind spot: clinical pastoral education originated in the Christian tradition, and Christian paradigms and beliefs

11. Ibid., 127.

12. Poling, "Wahrnehmung kultureller Differenz," 70f.

13. Taylor and Zucker, "Nearly Everything," 327f.

continue to shape its philosophy. In addition, in much of our Western society Christian undertones predominate. A lack of knowledge and understanding of these dynamics places a burden on Jewish students, who have to translate beliefs and spiritual practices into their own belief systems. Nina Davis's statement echoes Taylor and Zucker's sentiment: "As a CPE student, I needed to constantly translate Christian religious language so that I could communicate with my supervisors."

In a similar fashion, Native American George Tinker invites us to reflect critically on cultural assumptions in clinical supervision that are shaped by the dominant Western culture, such as "instant intimacy" and "confrontation" in group processes. He hopes for creative collaboration that will generate new training models open to a variety of learning styles.[14]

Students from non-Christian traditions bring the experience of being a minority religion to CPE, where often they meet an otherwise all-Christian peer group. The peer and supervisory relationships are likely to mirror what they have encountered all along. Davis notes that throughout her CPE training as a chaplain and supervisory student she was the only non-Christian group member. In addition, non-Christian students work in institutions with a largely Christian patient population. They learn ways of caring for patients and families that are new to them, from spontaneous prayer to facilitating rituals. In many cases, as some of the quotations at the beginning of this chapter illustrate, such students do not have available to them established paradigms for chaplaincy in their tradition. They are trailblazers and in some cases have to confront heightened stereotypes regarding their faith tradition. Muslim chaplain Levine expresses the notion that Muslim chaplains are often unofficial ambassadors for their tradition.

In addition to these challenges, non-Christian students often work with supervisors who represent a tradition different from their own yet are responsible for evaluating the student's professional growth as a spiritual caregiver. The notion of religious normativity can help supervisors to become aware of systemic power differences, which add a layer of vulnerability as students from nondominant religious traditions experience the supervisory relationship. When cultural or religious difference becomes or remains a blind spot, however, then supervisees are left without adequate support and advocacy. Alternatively, supervisors can

14. Tinker, "On Not Requiring CPE," 177f., 179.

empower supervisees to articulate their religious beliefs and practices and discuss their differences to bring them to awareness.

Countertransference

A supervisor's countertransference involves unconscious and often exaggerated reactions to the supervisee. I limit myself here to emotional reactions to the supervisee that are based on cultural or religious difference. A supervisor's cultural countertransference can originate in limited experience with a student's culture. It may happen outside of the awareness of the supervisor and can manifest itself in bias, even in subtle forms.[15]

Circumscribed experience with the religious tradition of a supervisee can also cause a sense of insecurity, or, speaking in terms of intergroup relations theory, a supervisor may experience *intergroup anxiety*. Due to my lack of experience with a student's religious tradition I may feel unsure about the student's beliefs and practices and how to accommodate them. My inner monologue may go something like this: "How can I accommodate the religious observance of my student? Do I even know what kind of religious practices or holidays he or she observes? Shall I ask? What if I look ignorant? How can I engage in theological reflection on my student's spiritual care without knowing his or her theology well? How do I bring this all up without putting my foot in my mouth?" Intergroup anxiety is rooted in unfamiliarity; the fear of making a mistake may be amplified for a supervisor who is afraid to appear incompetent to the student.

Limited experience with the religion of a supervisee may also manifest itself as a blind spot for the student's experience. Muslim chaplain Bilal Ansari writes about his experience of praying with a Christian patient. He writes: "Although it was a simple interaction, I had taken a big leap inwardly in initiating this prayer. In Islamic doctrine as I had learned it, to perform personalized essential ritual worship, such as prayer, that is not prescribed by the legal sources, is grave sin. . . . However, if I, as a Muslim, don't pray with Christian patients, then I am less compassionate as a pastoral caregiver. . . . I came to understand that to perform an act of nonessential religious worship with an understanding of its

---

15. Bernard and Goodyear, *Fundamentals of Clinical Supervision*, 191f.

merit, while not believing it to be essential worship, is praiseworthy."[16] For an outside observer, the situation seems to be simple. An interfaith chaplain prays with a patient. But inside, the chaplain wrestles with difficult issues. His conscience is challenged because he has to confront boundaries of his faith tradition and negotiate them in the interests of patient care. He finds a way to integrate this challenging experience. His reflections illustrate how gut-wrenching some encounters can be as students experience inner conflicts in situations that may seem mundane to those observing them.

Interfaith spiritual care pushes the comfort zones of non-Christian as well as Christian chaplain interns. They have to articulate, evaluate, and negotiate principles of their traditions with the needs of the patient in the moment. A supervisor from a different faith tradition than the student may not be as in-tune with the particular struggles a student experiences. If these struggles and differences remain unconscious or unexpressed, the supervisor may actually be contributing to the sense of alienation.

For most of us who are currently supervisors and theological educators, our academic theological preparation did not include in-depth education about other religious traditions. Working as interfaith chaplains, we may have had exposure to other faiths in our clinical training, or we may have developed a rudimentary knowledge by reading and consulting informally on our own. The less we know about the tradition or culture another person represents, the more we respond to him or her based on the categories in our mind. At times, we use the little knowledge we have in categorical ways and miss a student.

Tim, a young man who converted from the Christian faith to Buddhism, has become a chaplain and entered supervisory education. In a group supervision session a senior supervisor, Henry, challenges him: "You mentioned earlier that you believe in a divine power. But Buddhists don't believe in a God. How do you integrate your Christian upbringing with your Buddhism?" Tim explains the diversity of beliefs and practices of Buddhist traditions, saying that there is room for deities in Buddhism. However, he leaves the meeting feeling that he has not "convinced" Henry. He has experienced the question as a challenge to his belief and feels that his identification with another faith has not been respected and, moreover, has been met with suspicion. It appears that the

16. Ansari, "Seeing with Bifocals," 173f.

Christian supervisor has some knowledge of Buddhism but is not aware how little he knows about the diversity of traditions within Buddhism.

When it comes to other traditions, we often do not know what we don't know. We do not have sufficient knowledge about particular branches within a tradition and treat them as if "they are all alike." In our minds they are more homogeneous than they really are.

The vignette raises an additional question. How does a supervisor respond to supervisees who have converted from the supervisor's faith tradition to another tradition? What feelings are triggered? In the terminology of social psychology, a supervisor may experience *symbolic threat* when a supervisee represents a challenge to the supervisor's faith. Another level of complexity arises when a supervisor has to evaluate a supervisee's work with a patient or student from the supervisee's tradition. How can the supervisor adequately evaluate the spiritual care offered by the supervisee when the supervisee has a more advanced knowledge of the spiritual practices and beliefs of a patient than does the supervisor? Also, how does a supervisor deal with feelings that he or she is the "outsider" in such a supervisory triad?

Interreligious supervision challenges supervisors to reflect on their bias and more fully explore their own religious identity. Christian supervisor David Larsen summarizes: "Supervising in an interfaith situation has brought to the surface some of my judgmental attitudes."[17] His openness in exploring his countertransference contributed to the strong working alliance his student, Nina, appreciates so much. Larsen also noticed a tendency to want to take more control in his supervision of students from his own tradition. As he gave Nina, his Buddhist student, space, he discovered opportunities in interfaith supervision: "There was objectivity about her supervision that did not include Christian baggage."[18]

My countertransference may manifest itself in bias, blind spots, insecurity, and maintaining distance in relation to a supervisee from another tradition. On the other hand, I may be keenly aware of my reactions and so overidentify with the supervisee that I become overprotective. Perhaps I am uncomfortable with the power inequality in our relationship and shy away from offering challenge when it is called for. Sometimes it is difficult to sort through these interreligious issues and

17. Larsen, "Supervising in an Interfaith Environment," 58.
18. Ibid.

our own emotional responses. German pastoral theologian Eberhard Hauschildt introduces a helpful notion when it comes to sorting through our emotional responses to those who are culturally different: typically we respond to what is foreign or other with ambivalence, with fear (xenophobia), or with xenophilia (meaning on principle considering the other as the better, or believing we cannot and are not supposed to find in the other anything that we dislike or find worthy of critique).[19]

A supervisee from another tradition may also represent a welcome escape for my dissatisfaction with my own faith tradition. I may idealize another tradition that I see as free from the disappointments I experience with my own faith community. Discomfort with our own complex feelings as well as fascination with the other may keep us from providing sound and balanced feedback for our supervisees from other traditions.

The Muslim chaplain Rabia Harris gives advice to supervisors working with Muslim students. Chaplaincy for Muslims is evolving, she says, and Muslim students may be hesitant to become active contributors to their traditions. Harris encourages supervisors to challenge Muslim students to engage in theological reflection: "Fire away: we need to stretch our theological muscles."[20] Recognizing our own bias and insecurity does not mean depriving supervisees of appropriate challenge.

Let us review the exchange between Tim (the Christian convert to Buddhism) and Henry once more, this time from a different perspective. Henry, the supervisor, may have articulated a question to the Buddhist supervisory student as follows: "Explain to me your belief in a divine power in the context of your Buddhist tradition. As a Christian I understand it in the context of your former Christian tradition. How do you understand it now? Also, does your conversion to Buddhism influence how Christian students experience you and how you work with them?" Such statements present an open inquiry rather than questioning Tim's religious tradition and conversion. At the same time they challenge Tim to reflect on the dynamics of supervising students from other faiths—a question with which all supervisors regardless of tradition should deal. Might Christian students feel threatened by being supervised by a clergy who has converted from their tradition? How does such a converted clergy person assist his students in developing a trusting working alliance with him? How does Tim feel toward his former religious tradition and

19. Hauschildt, "Interkulturelle Seelsorge," 242.
20. Harris, "Supporting Your Muslim Students," 158.

students who represent it? Is he aware of his feelings, and can he work with them constructively? Sorting through these questions requires a dialogue in which the Buddhist student and the Christian supervisor need to respect each other's viewpoint without letting go of any insights they might have.

How can supervisors work constructively with their cultural countertransference? The short answer is: through consultation, education, and a focus on the working alliance.

Supervisors need to learn about the religious tradition their students represent. To a certain degree our students can be our teachers about their traditions. At the same time, the student's primary role is not to teach their supervisor or peers but to grow in their professional development as chaplains, spiritual counselors, and clinical supervisors. Therefore, while I can bring up many questions directly with the student, I must protect them from using them for my own education by consulting with someone outside the supervisory relationship. For example, I regularly supervise rabbinical students. The director of their pastoral training program is part of the advisory board of our educational program. We cultivate conversations where questions and training issues can be addressed.

Literature addressing precisely such interreligious education is evolving. One example of education for supervisors is the ACPE Taskforce on Islam. That group has published helpful information about the experiences of Muslim chaplains and their supervision.[21] Yet while such education and consultation help develop supervisory cultural competencies, I suggest that the key for managing the complexities of interreligious supervision is the working alliance.

Working Alliance

A strong working relationship between supervisor and supervisee is a major ingredient for learning. The supervisory relationship fluctuates in quality and intensity, and conflict is always a part of it. The relational style of supervisor and supervisee, their sensitivity and flexibility in personality, and learning styles—all influence the relationship. A successful working rapport is not conflict-free but one where conflicts can

---

21. ACPE Taskforce, *Reflective Practice*, 141–86.

be worked through and used for professional growth.[22] Especially in multicultural supervisory relationships, "a strong working alliance is a prerequisite to productive multicultural supervision."[23] Interreligious supervision is a particular form of multicultural supervision and the supervisory alliance is instrumental in addressing its complexities.

The Buddhist supervisory student Nina Davis learns from her relationship with her supervisor that the foundation for a trusting relationship is the supervisor's ability to genuinely care for the supervisee and to address his or her own personal and spiritual issues.[24] Her supervisor David Larsen comments, "Nina sometimes jokes that she knows it is my wish to convert her to Christianity. In our associations, we have discussed this aspect and it is not an issue between us. . . . I think that one of the benefits about our supervisory relationship and the alliance we developed is in the fact that we each accept the differences between us."[25] Religious difference does not tend to become an obstacle when the supervisor can confront his or her own faith biases and cultural assumptions in order to facilitate the exploration of a student's faith beliefs and cultural expression.[26] As Davis and Larsen share how religious differences have been part of their supervisory discussions, the concept of mutual differentiation comes to mind. Individuals who find themselves in a common group or shared relationship can maintain their particular and differentiated identities. In other words, the open acknowledgement of cultural and faith differences by her supervisor helped Davis to feel less isolated.

Their reflections also illustrate that mutual trust can be developed through intentional self-disclosure. Self-disclosure involves openness about things we don't know. As a supervisor I can communicate to my students that I have limited knowledge about their faith tradition, invite them to let me know their needs of religious observance or to tell me when they feel that my feedback is inconsiderate of their religious beliefs.

Self-disclosure also involves the open communication of feelings. As I have mentioned in another chapter, when I began to supervise

22. Bernard and Goodyear, *Fundamentals of Clinical Supervision*, 167.
23. Ibid., 148.
24. Davis, "Multicultural CPE Supervision Possible?" 62.
25. Larsen, "Supervising in an Interfaith Environment," 56, 57.
26. Davis, "Multicultural CPE Supervision Possible?" 63.

Jewish students I found it helpful to share with my students that I was concerned how they experienced being supervised by a Christian from Germany. I communicated some of my complex feelings related to the Holocaust and the persecution of the Jewish people in Germany and how that history shapes me. My statements did not become a great concern for the group. I did not expect the students to take care of those complex feelings but wanted to open the door for dialogue. My sharing established trust and hopefully normalized and modeled ways to address the presence of intergroup anxiety in interreligious relationships.

Opportunities for Interfaith Supervision

Supervision in an interfaith milieu is not only complex but also incredibly enriching. Many supervisors appreciate the potential learning that occurs in culturally and religiously diverse groups. Working with non-Christian students can bring particular Christian paradigms of spiritual care and counseling to our awareness and introduce new paradigms. Supervisees of a different faith tradition expand our own understanding of the professional role of the chaplain or spiritual counselor.

For example, Judaism has a wealth of blessings throughout daily life and at transition points. A rabbinical student applied this rich tradition to her spiritual care in the hospital. She developed a ritual of thanksgiving and used it in her spiritual support of cancer patients to mark the remission of cancer and the release from the hospital. The ritual underscored the psychological and spiritual benefit of marking transition points and ritualizing thanksgiving. Her ritual has been adopted by other chaplains and integrated into their spiritual care.

Another rabbinical intern was called to be with the husband and adult son of a patient who had died. While most family members need many hours before they feel ready to leave the hospital, this husband and son felt a need to leave soon after the patient had passed on. The chaplain respected their need and thought of ways to support them. He applied to this pastoral situation a Jewish practice of washing hands after leaving the cemetery. The ritual of washing signifies the transition to the realm of the living. The student invited the husband and son to the bathroom where they washed hands. Then they entered the hospital garden and he offered a prayer supporting them as they faced the difficult situation of leaving the hospital without their loved one.

A Buddhist chaplain presented to our supervision group a workshop on Buddhist spiritual care. She taught our group a way to be present when verbal communication with a patient is impossible because the patient is unable to speak, dependent on a ventilator, or comatose. Chaplains still can communicate compassionate presence by staying with the patient and matching their breath to that of the patient. The Buddhist chaplain translated the meditation practice of awareness of breath into the hospital context.

These are just a few examples of spiritual care interventions that are informed by non-Christian traditions and in their spiritual and psychological wisdom can be practiced by chaplains of all faiths with patients of all faiths who are open to receive this kind of spiritual support. Interreligious clinical supervision and training offers many opportunities to expand our understanding of spiritual care and counseling, thus enriching our practice of interconnected spiritual care, discussed in chapter 6.

GROUP SUPERVISION

The second aspect of interreligious clinical supervision that can contribute to an understanding of issues in interfaith supervision is group supervision. We see this at work in a CPE group in large cultural urban medical center that experiences conflict on numerous levels throughout the training course. The group consists of eight members and a supervisor with equal representation of gender; one student is gay. The supervisor and four group members are Caucasian, the other four have been born and raised in Africa, Asia, and the Middle East. One group member is Muslim, another Unitarian Universalist, while the others represent different denominations within the Christian faith tradition. The CPE training course is conducted as an extended part-time course over a period of six months. The group meets for one whole day for group supervision and learning. The course begins not long after the terrorist attacks on the World Trade Center on September 11, 2001.

As the course progresses, the group works through interpersonal discord as well as cultural and religious conflict. The supervisor initiates a conversation with a Roman Catholic member about reference to the Trinity during a prayer in group interfaith reflection, raising the concern that the Christian prayer excludes the Muslim and Unitarian Universalist interns. The Roman Catholic member is upset with the supervisor and feels that her faith is not respected. The Muslim student feels vulnerable given the social climate of heightened stereotype towards Muslims; for her religious observance as a woman the student needs a private space for her prayers several times during the day, and yet there is no such space in the hospital; the interfaith meditation room does not provide enough privacy. She retreats to her car in order to pray several times a day. She uses breaks from the curriculum for her prayers and is unable to join her peers for the informal lunch breaks that contribute to group building. The gay student confronts the Muslim student several times during the course about Islam's "judgmental attitude" toward homosexuality. As conflicts erupt, the group does not always succeed in resolving them and does not reach its full potential to become a strong functioning team.

The majority of students report at the end of the CPE course that they feel they have developed a more appreciative view of the cultural and faith traditions of others. Two students keep an emotional distance from the Muslim intern throughout and label her as a "fundamentalist." Personality factors and the post 9/11 social context contribute to group tension. In addition, the Muslim group member, her gay peer, and those peers from different cultural contexts are keenly aware of their minority positions, which influences the conflict of the group.

Group experiences like these raise questions such as: How can cultural and religious differences in supervision groups be handled in such a way that intercultural and interreligious learning nonetheless takes place? How do we handle diverse groups so they contribute to growth rather than make things worse and further the alienation some members may feel when they join the group? With these questions in mind, next we explore three aspects of group supervision: the nature of supervision groups, group development, and group dynamics.

The Nature of Supervision Groups

Group supervision is a core element in CPE as well as other supervised learning of internships and counseling. Groups offer students possibilities to learn from each other. In addition to their own clinical experience, participants in supervision groups learn vicariously through observation and exposure to clinical material from peers. They not only receive feedback on their clinical practice from the supervisor but are exposed to more diverse perspectives through peers. Groups give members opportunities to experience themselves in the group context and learn about group dynamics through their own experience in a group.[27] Groups are important settings in the process of acquiring skills and self-awareness as professional spiritual caregivers and counselors. Working closely with peers from different religious traditions, students learn from their peers about their traditions and how to spiritually support patients and clients from that faith group.

Supervision groups are not intergroup contact groups whose primary goal is improving intercultural and interreligious relations. At the same time, insights from the field of intergroup relations can help us to facilitate supervision groups in ways that foster interreligious learning. In the following paragraphs I will trace how supervision groups are different from and similar to intergroup contact experiences.

Aside from the primary goal, the composition of supervision and intergroup contact groups differs. Intergroup contact experiences are often structured in a way that several members of social groups are represented. In supervision groups, often non-Christian group members are in the minority. Thus, one of the facilitating conditions, *equal status* in the group situations, is difficult to achieve. Group members are equal in that they are supervisees, but some group members represent a religious minority. In addition, the supervisor represents a particular tradition, in many cases that of the majority.

In most spiritual care and counseling supervision settings, *institutional support* of antiprejudicial norms is widely provided. The policies of the institutional settings, such as hospitals, hospices, and prisons, as well as organizational codes of ethics, establish norms of respect for the cultural and religious integrity of patients, families, staff members, and students.[28] This support by institutional authority underscores the appreciation of cultural and religious diversity.

Supervision groups do not work together to achieve *superordinate goals.* However, the members pursue a similar overall goal: graduating from their training and growing professionally as spiritual caregivers. Shared experiences contribute to a team spirit. While completing the

27. Bernard and Goodyear, *Fundamentals of Clinical Supervision,* 245f.

28. The ethics codes of the Association of Professional Chaplains, the Association of Pastoral Counselors, and the Association of Clinical Pastoral Education include respect for clients', patients', and students' religion. See also "Interdenominational Spiritual Care" in chapter 6.

numerous steps of orientation to a new setting, sharing the anxiety of being on call, confronting death and life issues for the first time and being "thrown into" serious clinical experience, students often reach out to each other for support.

Team projects, such as shared group presentations or team preparation of institutional interfaith services, encourage *cooperation*. In our center we meet every day for a fifteen- to thirty-minute "team huddle." Staff and students discuss patient situations, alert each other to possible on-call situations, and consult with each other. These short meetings have proven to be not only clinically helpful but also good teambuilding tools.

Group supervision can be a place for competition as well. Students want to impress their supervisor or peers with their pastoral skills. Some individuals may be more competitive than others and may seek to stand out, particularly during the storming phase of the group (a definition of which we turn to soon). Yet, as group cohesiveness is an important element in supervision, team spirit often develops over time and can be observed when the group has become a functioning working group. Even with different qualities of individual relationships or subgroups, there can be a sense of being one team; *recategorization* takes hold of group members who begin to see themselves as part of one group.

The fifth facilitating condition for intergroup contact is *friendship potential*. In supervision groups, supervisees meet often and over an extended period of time. They work closely together and get to know each other on a very personal level in the process of clinical work and group reflection. Group supervision, especially in the intensity of CPE, provides the opportunity for group members to become friends. Closely related is the potential for *decategorization*, which, we recall, has two components: First, we become aware that members of another social group are more differentiated than we originally thought. Second, we get to know them as persons, and as we relate to them this way categories become less important. Some supervision groups develop strong bonds and stay in touch even after their group experience is completed. In other groups some individuals have developed close friendships that endure beyond the experience. These friendships extend cultural and religious differences. I have observed close friendships develop between a Presbyterian and rabbinical student, a conservative Jew and a Palestinian Christian, a Buddhist and a Methodist. An evangelical student who entered CPE with some reservations about GLBT clergy attended her gay peer's ordination service long after the CPE unit had concluded. She stated that her close contact with her peer and the level of self-disclosure in the group had opened her mind not only to the particular gay peer but to gays and lesbians in general.

Group Development

While most groups do not follow a linear development pattern, group development stages can be helpful in understanding and facilitating complex dynamic group processes. A widely supported model of group development distinguishes five stages: Forming, Storming, Norming, Performing, and Adjourning.[29] During the forming stage members are concerned with belonging and affiliation. Storming is a stage with a focus on control, competition, and individual differentiation. Norming describes the conscious or unconscious development of group norms; supervisors have a special role in shaping these norms through modeling. Performing is the group's most productive phase when members address conflict constructively and work as a team. During the adjourning phase, group members work on closure of the supervisory experience.

In the context of CPE the forming stage is taken up by orientation to the hospital and often closes with a day set aside for group building. Students share their stories, discover commonalities and get to know each other as persons. This group phase provides opportunities for *decategorization* and *cross-categorization*. Storming and norming stages allow for *mutual differentiation*, as individual differences of group members come to the surface and their expression is encouraged. Mutual differentiation, maintaining an awareness of differences, can be helpful so that students of religious minorities do not become invisible and thus feel isolated. Supervisees have a chance to learn about the different denominations and movements of other religious traditions and get to know individual differences in spiritual beliefs and practices within one tradition. The content and assignments of the curriculum as well as communication norms and ground rules developed together at the beginning should reflect a diversity of cultures and religious traditions. While community is fostered, supervisors encourage the expression of differences and the active engagement of conflicts.

29. Bernard and Goodyear, *Fundamentals of Clinical Supervision*, 251.

The performing stage includes member's integration of theory and practice, the development of empathy and active listening skills in their clinical work as well as in the peer group. During the adjournment phase numerous CPE groups conduct a closing ritual, a ceremony of course completion, celebrating the accomplishments of each group member and the group as a whole, which emphasizes *recategorization*, or attaining a common group identity. The final evaluation allows room for a reflection on the meaning of encounters with peers and patients from other traditions and what they mean for the future clinical work of participants.

Summarizing, supervision groups are not intergroup contact groups with the primary goal of improving intergroup relations. However, they parallel intergroup contact groups in that they teach participants through experience how to engage peers from other religious traditions and how to support patients and clients of other faiths. They can and should be places of interreligious learning.

Group Dynamics

As important as the working alliance is for the counseling or supervisory process, so is group cohesiveness to therapy or the supervisory group. Insights from psychotherapist Irvin Yalom about group safety and group conflict shine light on the task of supervision of culturally and religiously diverse supervision groups.

Yalom understands group cohesiveness as encompassing participants' relationships to the group leader, to the other group members, and to the group as a whole.[30] In order for a group to be able to move to the performing stage, members need to feel connected and motivated to freely participate in the process and discussions of the group. Connectedness is achieved when members feel mutual respect and a sense of belonging.[31] The establishment of norms of inclusiveness and unconditional acceptance early on in the group's formation contributes to the development of engagement and cohesion, which form an essential foundation for the group to face more challenging work as conflict and discomfort arises.[32] Yalom expresses what we may call the "safety-

---

30. Yalom, *Group Psychotherapy*, 54.

31. Ibid., 55.

32. Ibid., 55f.

first-principle" of group facilitation as follows: "Before members feel free enough to express disagreement, they must feel safe enough and value the group highly enough to be willing to tolerate uncomfortable meetings."[33]

If safety is the foundation for any therapy or supervision group, we can assume that the safety-first-principle is even more important in highly heterogeneous groups with a diversity of culture and religious traditions. The Buddhist supervisory student Nina Davis sensed an "unspoken anxiety" from her students in each CPE unit she co-supervised as her students wondered whether she would understand them in their different belief systems.[34] Because of the power inequality inherent in supervisory relationships, this fear is to be assumed in supervisory relationships where student and supervisor represent different religious traditions.

Returning to our vignette, the concept of *intergroup anxiety* gives us insights in the dynamics of the peer group. Anxiety may well be at the root of some of the group conflicts. The presence of a number of members representing different cultures and religion may produce anxiety for the group. For group members who were born and raised on different continents, the medical center and the learning context represent a new culture. The Roman Catholic student may experience *symbolic threat*, a challenge to her religious values when she is asked to change her form of prayer. The Muslim and the gay student both may experience anxiety as they bring the experience of being negatively stereotyped in society to the group. Prejudice and physical violence toward Muslims after 9/11 has been on the rise. The fact that the Muslim student represents a religious minority in the group increases her sense of vulnerability. The gay student may feel vulnerable, because he has experienced discrimination from the religious community and because his peers from non-Western countries are even more unfamiliar with openly expressed different sexual orientations. Thus numerous threat categories may be experienced in the group, yet are never named as anxiety but materialize in mutual critique, assumptions, and prejudice. Intergroup anxiety is an integral emotion, in that it is directly related to the presence of members of different social groups in the group situation.

---

33. Ibid., 138.
34. Davis, "Multicultural CPE Supervision Possible?" 63.

In addition, first unit CPE students experience a significant incidental anxiety that is not related to the group situation but to other factors: many CPE students have to cope with a high level of stress because they are new to the role of a chaplain in an institutional setting and work daily with persons in crisis. They are expected to deal with intense issues, be with family members as their loved ones die or become critically ill, and make important decisions. In such a high stress environment, anxiety arises quickly. As explained in chapter 4, moderate levels of anxiety can provide motivation and engagement. However, when highly anxious, individuals cannot process information carefully and fall back on stereotypic responses.

Therefore, the supervisor needs to monitor the level of anxiety so that it does not become too high and exacerbate anxiety related to religious differences within the group. He or she needs to give special attention to creating the peer group as a safe space that encourages personal disclosure, normalizes anxiety, and allows group members to express their fears.

The development of group cohesiveness builds a foundation for deeper engagement that involves discomfort and conflict. Highly culturally and religiously diverse groups experience an additional layer of anxiety related to the intergroup relationships. Therefore it is important to create a sense of security, so that supervisees trust that the group can tolerate differences. Safety comes first.

Conflict, of course, may have an array of origins. It may be interpersonal in nature due to personality differences, rivalry, or projections. Intergroup relations may be another cause of conflict when prejudice or avoidance of someone from a different cultural or religious group stands between an open engagement of group members.

How can a group leader manage such conflict constructively? Once perceptions and feelings are brought out in the open, empathy can be one path by which to move through discord. Empathy can open communication without dismissing group members' feelings or opinions. Group members are encouraged to take the perspective of their peers. Imagine the group leader inviting the gay and the Muslim student to use their experience of being stereotyped to understand the situation of the other. The Catholic student might use her sense of being disrespected to sympathize with the alienation other non-Christian members might experience. Empathy can be taught and encouraged. When the group leader senses that a member might feel too exposed or isolated, she or he can ask the group: Has anyone experienced a similar situation? Can anyone relate to what Tom or Jenny is going through?

When conflict becomes so intense that it becomes toxic, it needs to be contained. A leader may restrict destructive arguments by referring back to norms of respect and acceptance the group has earlier agreed on. Another possibility is pausing to reflect and to understand the conflict. For example, a group leader may help members shed light upon their argument by introducing concepts of group dynamics or intergroup relations. Making sense of discord with the help of a theoretical frame-work can create some distance and cool the heat of a conflict that is threatening to become too intense to be constructive.

The presence of conflict and anxiety does not mean that the group is not cohesive. A functioning group will naturally experience conflict. Otherwise dissatisfaction, anger, and antagonism remain, smoldering under the surface. As open communication is maintained, discord is un-avoidable and needs to be permitted. In terms of intergroup relations, if conflicts are not worked through, members of different cultural and re-ligious groups relate only superficially to each other and will not expand their attitudes toward others. There may be times when the agreement and harmony between group members is suspiciously constant. Then the group leader may have to introduce an opportunity for differentiation in order to help members bring uncomfortable feelings to the surface.

During a CPE group session Roman Catholic student Jaime refers to his Jewish peer as his sister and points out that the two have the "Old Testament" in common. His statements sound simplistic to me and I wonder how his Jewish peer feels about the term "Old" Testament for the Hebrew Bible. She does not say anything. I am wondering if she doesn't mind Jaime's statement or if she does not feel comfortable to speak to her peer about the issue. I can move the conversation to a deeper level and invite differentiation: "Sarah, how do you hear Jaime's statement? Does it resonate with you? How would you describe the relationship between Christians and Jews?"

In describing conflict management Yalom introduces the metaphor of careful tritration: In order to use conflict in the service of growth one needs to find the right level. "Too much or too little conflict is counterproductive."[35]

---

35. Yalom, *Group Psychotherapy*, 370.

To summarize, supervision groups with religious diversity can and should be settings for interreligious learning. Participants can use their own experiences in diverse learning groups to develop intercultural and interreligious competency. When safety and group cohesiveness are established, conflict that is based in religious and cultural differences can be used for growth and learning. Such learning happens as a result of experience and an understanding of that experience. Therefore, I conclude this chapter with some thoughts on curriculum resources that integrate experiential and cognitive elements.

CURRICULUM

It is helpful to anchor interfaith resources in the educational program. Community religious leaders from different faith traditions can become members of the program's advisory board. They can be consultants to the supervisor as well as to students from non-Christian traditions so they feel less isolated and have support from their tradition. An increasing number of hospitals have departments for cultural services and conduct cultural competency programs, which can provide areas of cooperation for CPE programs. The admissions interview can be used to assess the openness of potential supervisees to engage religious diversity as well as provide clear and transparent information about the nature of the interfaith program from the beginning.

Some experiential approaches to intercultural and interreligious education are already common in clinical education, such as field trips to different houses of worship and cooperation in the facilitation of inclusive worship experiences, introducing participants to important celebrations and rituals of other communities. In many public institutions CPE students participate in the work of spiritual care departments by educating the institution about diverse religious observances and holidays. In their peer groups students from different religious traditions are experts of their culture and religion and are encouraged to share their perspective with their peers. They may share news from their religious communities and worship elements from their cultures and traditions.[36] Interfaith spiritual reflection in the group can be a place where students share spiritual practices that are not so particular to their faith that they exclude other participants. My students have introduced singing

36. Grace, "Thinking through Pastoral Education," 31.

nigguns (meditative songs without words from the Jewish tradition), meditation from the Buddhist tradition, contemplative prayer from the Christian tradition, reflection on sacred stories from different traditions, and walking the labyrinth, to only name a few examples. Most often rabbinical students invite their peer group to join them for a Sabbath meal, or students visit each other's houses of worship during the CPE unit.

Another experiential approach is working with spiritual and cultural narratives. I have modified the use of cultural autobiographies in a college setting for the small-group context of CPE.[37] Each student presents his or her personal cultural narrative to the peer group during one CPE course. This learning tool provides an opportunity for students to reflect on their memberships in particular religious, cultural, ethnic, and social groups and provides a window into the experiences of others. In a short essay, each group member writes about his or her family's membership in such social groups. They reflect on social events that have shaped them, and on their cultural and religious heritage and how they nurture it. They talk about their relationships with members of different social groups and how their experiences shape how they function as spiritual caregivers. These stories help students to learn about each other's social identities. They develop more differentiated understanding of the diversity of experiences within a particular culture and tradition, and develop skills in perspective taking.

These experiential approaches can be enhanced through theoretical frameworks. Interreligious and intercultural relations include issues of social group membership. An introduction to concepts of social identity, stereotype, and prejudice can provide a conceptual viewpoint that sheds light on psychological aspects of intercultural and interreligious relationships. Group members learn not only about personal but also about social tensions, ways in which they collude in and challenge social systems. They come to an understanding of power differences and develop skills of cultural analysis.

It becomes increasingly necessary to include in theological education basic teaching about world religions. CPE and other supervision groups need to help chaplains to become familiar with the beliefs and practices of other religious traditions. Guest speakers as well as group members who represent diverse traditions can be invited to teach. During a year-long CPE residency, one course unit can be set aside to

37. Schoem, "Teaching about Ethnic Identity," 20.

focus on intercultural and interreligious spiritual care. Didactic workshops along with reading assignments can help students to develop a basic knowledge of religious practices and beliefs they will encounter in their clinical work. Clergy working in interfaith settings also need to be able to articulate their own theological stance from which they approach the religious pluralism they encounter in their pastoral work and supervision groups. They benefit from an introduction to theologies of religious pluralism, which I address in the following chapter.

Some CPE programs have experimented with including didactic instruction about "isms" as part of the CPE curriculum. Students teach each other in didactic sessions on racism, sexism, and heterosexism in the context of spiritual care by utilizing their own experiences with these "isms" rather than having external information deposited.[38] As students share and face their own experiences, they promote a nonjudgmental attitude toward others.[39]

Intergroup contact theory developed in and is applied to group settings, but some of some of its concepts are also relevant for spiritual care and its supervision with individuals, as we can see in self-reports, co-visits, verbatims, and case conferences. I briefly present three clinical examples, in which the notions of decategorization, cross-categorization, and mutual differentiation can be used as heuristic concepts shedding light on intergroup dynamics.

When teaching about the introductory visit, the concept of *decategorization* illuminates aspects of the initial encounter between chaplain and patient or family in an interfaith setting. The first visit in a hospital leaves plenty of room for projection. Many patients or their family members are not familiar with the role of the chaplain and may think chaplains represent a particular religion. Often they expect a chaplain to be Christian. Therefore, many chaplains make a conscious choice to abstain from wearing clothes or symbols that identify them with a particular religious tradition. For other chaplains from different denominations, the wearing of a collar or the kippah is part of their religious identity. Whether they wear religious garment or not, as chaplains introduce themselves to patients and families for the first time, it is important for them to clearly describe their function and emphasize their role as interfaith chaplains who support people of all or no particular religious

38. Byrd, "Inclusiveness," 205f.
39. Ibid., 208f.

traditions. Because patients and families may attach categories of a particular faith to the word "chaplain," a chaplain should thus employ decategorization at the onset of the spiritual care relationship by clarifying his or her role as a health-care team member who cares about the spiritual well-being of the patient and family—regardless of his or her own faith affiliation.

Rhonda, a United Methodist chaplain intern, presents a case to her peer group. She has responded to a referral from a social worker to visit a Muslim American mother of Palestinian descent (Sabira) whose two-year-old daughter is hospitalized with cancer. Rhonda gathers information to help Sabira to connect to a Muslim faith community near the hospital. The initial visit develops to a long-term spiritual care relationship. Initially, Rhonda is nervous, as this is her first pastoral relationship with a Muslim family. She has had previous contact with the Muslim community through her local church and is open to engaging in interfaith spiritual care. She asks Sabira about her faith and asks her to teach Rhonda the special greeting for Ramadan, as Sabira's daughter is hospitalized during this holy month. Sabira is a devout Muslim who takes her ritual practice seriously. Rhonda summarizes for her peer group the topics of their conversations about Sabira's culture and her Muslim faith, the care for her child and family, and the meaning she makes of her child's illness. Rhonda characterizes her spiritual care as a presence that offers a nonjudgmental ear for Sabira to unburden her soul. When asked how she connects to Sabira, Rhonda describes commonalities she discovered with Sabira as women, mothers, and persons of faith. During supervision the group discusses that unconsciously Rhonda has used *cross-categorization* to establish points of connection, employing the categories of woman, mother, and religious person. Besides decategorization, cross-categorization is a strategy to connect with a person of a different religious tradition.

Rhonda talks to the group about differences as well. For example, she respects but cannot connect to how Sabira makes meaning out of her crisis, as she understands her daughter's illness as God's test for Sabira's faith. The group makes an interesting observation: When asked how Rhonda might have responded to a Christian mother who would understand her child's illness as God's test, Rhonda states that she would have respected this view but might have felt more defensive. The case demonstrates that ecumenical intergroup encounters can be just as or more challenging than interreligious encounters. It may be easier to connect with someone of a different tradition than with someone who represents a different set of beliefs within one's own tradition. Religious groups can function in ways similar to families. The familial faith relationships can be as complex as our relationships with siblings in our families of origin.

The following vignette from a CPE group in which all the students are Christian illustrates the importance of *mutual differentiation*. Stephen presents to his peers his social project. This assignment helps CPE interns to familiarize themselves with social system and cultural issues as they are relevant to hospital chaplaincy and spiritual care. Stephen has gathered information about the Muslim community in the United States. He talks about the increase of stereotypes toward Muslims after 9/11, stereotypes that make some patients and families fearful to identify themselves as Muslims when they are admitted to the hospital. Michelle and Peter express sympathy for the development of stereotypes in the United States because of the attacks on 9/11. Stephen challenges their perceptions, reminding them of the Muslim physician, Salama, who is actively involved in the CPE program and teaches students about the Muslim faith. Michelle states: "Not everyone is like Salama." During her internship Michelle has had several encounters with the physician and respects her. Yet, she does not see Salama as representative of the Muslim community, but rather as a special person, an exception. During the course of the discussion Michelle expresses that she is "sick of the critique of Americans and the demands for political correctness," which she projects onto Stephen, who has challenged her stereotype of Muslims as primarily fundamentalist and anti-Western. In spite of her respect for a Muslim individual, Michelle's response comes across as defensive and reveals a need for her to maintain her position. The interaction can be employed as a teaching moment in which the supervisor might introduce the common defense mechanism of the exception to the rule: we tend to consider stereotype-disconfirming information as the exception to the rule rather than changing our mental images about another social group. The supervisor then can invite the group to explore how Salama might be a representative of her faith tradition.

SUMMARY

Table 7.1 illustrates how key concepts from the field intergroup relations can be applied to the supervision of religiously diverse groups.

Group Development Stage	Intergroup Contact Facilitating Conditions	Facilitating Methods	Curriculum
Structuring of Group/Project	Group size allows for the development of friendly bonds.	Admissions interview assesses supervisees' openness to religious diversity.	Group experience is structured over an extended period of time. Peer group ideally does not extend beyond 8 members.
	Institutional support	Interfaith representation in the program's advisory board.	Code of Ethics and institutional policies express respect for diversity.
Forming	Common goals	Decategorization Cross-categorization Creating safety	Group building exercises Personal stories Expression of feelings is normalized.
Storming		Mutual differentiation Working through conflict (titration) Normalizing and monitoring anxiety	Differences and particular religious identities are acknowledged. Students teach each other about their cultural and faith traditions.
Norming		Perspective-taking	Experiential and cognitive elements: Cultural autobiographies Theories of social identity and prejudice Development of group norms and communication skills (active listening and empathy)
Performing	Cooperation	Group cohesiveness	Shared projects/teamwork
Adjourning		Recategorization Group affirmation	Final evaluation Shared processing of what group members have learned about other religious traditions

Table 7.1: Facilitating Intergroup Contact in a Clinical Supervision Group

Religious diversity adds new layers to the work of clinical supervision. It challenges us to rethink curriculum, group dynamics, and the supervisory relationship. The theories of intergroup relations employed in this book provide us with concepts and tools that equip us to facilitate increasingly religiously diverse learning groups. They help us to use the potential of these groups to become milieus for interreligious learning.

8

Why Engage Religious Diversity?

Interreligious Encounters through a Theological Lens

IN THE PRECEDING CHAPTERS we have met spiritual counselors and chaplains in public settings who work with people from all walks of life and religious persuasions. We have heard voices of community leaders who engage interfaith youth in shared service, organize interfaith travel to Israel and Palestine, take parishioners on bus tours to houses of worship of different faiths, and develop interfaith community partnerships. However, we have learned that many religious communities exist in isolation and keep contact with each other at a minimum. We introduced tools that help persons to overcome fears of the other, reduce bias, and facilitate interreligious connections. In this last chapter I address the role of theology in interreligious encounters. What are the beliefs that motivate some to engage religious diversity and others to avoid or resist it?

Religious leaders, chaplains, counselors, and theological educators have to sort out what the new pluralist context means for their faith and their work. They need a vision, a compass, to guide their work. This compass is different for people of diverse faith traditions, and, as we shall see, looks very different even within Christianity. In this chapter I share my own compass and guiding vision, which is clearly shaped by my own faith and social location. I write as an ordained Christian female minister living in the United States and working as a chaplain in a secular public health-care organization. My reflections tell the reader why I believe that interreligious work is important, why I devote so many pages to understanding social and interpersonal dynamics in interreligious relations, and why these dynamics matter theologically. My reflections account for my hope that we can create an alternative to pervasive divisive and ignorant voices that may discourage us from engaging the religiously other. It is my hope that this final chapter will spark ideas and thoughts that take readers on their own theological journeys. My compass developed in conversation with different theological approaches to religious pluralism, and so I begin by providing a brief overview of this conversation and some issues that it raises.

DIFFERENT PATHS

Religions have been compared with different paths that lead up the same mountain. "It is possible to climb life's mountain from any side, but when the top is reached the trails converge. At base, in the foothills of theology, ritual, and organizational structure, the religions are distinct. Differences in culture, history, geography, and collective temperament all make for diverse starting points. . . . But beyond these differences, the same goal beckons."[1] This metaphor developed by religious studies scholar Huston Smith has become a popular way to describe the relationships of the religions, but it is not without controversy. Most recently, professor of religion Stephen Prothero has taken issue with Smith's view. He represents a growing group of scholars who look for a new approach in understanding the diversity of religious paths. In his book *God Is Not One* Prothero challenges: "For more than a generation we have followed scholars and sages down the rabbit hole into a fantasy world in which all gods are one."[2] He warns that the idea of religious unity is naïve and unrealistic because it obscures the dangerous clashes of religions worldwide. It is important to look not only at religion's "awe-inspiring architecture and gentle mystics but also their bigots and suicide bombers,"[3] he reminds us.

Smith and Prothero represent two poles of a spectrum, one emphasizing the universality of religions, the other their particularities. Different theological approaches can be placed somewhere along this spectrum. Paul Knitter's book *Introducing Theologies of Religion* lays out the major theological positions on the relation of Christianity to other

1. Smith, World's Religions, 73.
2. Prothero, *God Is Not One*, 3.
3. Ibid., 3, 7.

religious ways. He sorts through the diversity and controversy of numerous Christian approaches to religious pluralism and distinguishes four models, within which there is much variety. Relying heavily on Knitter's description and analysis, I present a rough sketch of major positions for a brief orientation. For a detailed overview of theological approaches to religious pluralism I refer the reader to Knitter's introduction.

Replacement Model

This approach to other religions has also been called exclusivist and has been the primary way Christianity has understood other religious traditions throughout much of history. Today the majority of fundamentalists, evangelicals, and Pentecostals hold this view.[4] Its core concern is salvation understood as a gift from God through Jesus Christ. Because salvation is not a human achievement but a gift, followers of this approach want to share this gift with others with the goal of conversion.[5] Some hold that while there is no salvation outside of Christ, God is revealed in other traditions. They seek collaboration with other religionists in service and social concerns. The dialogue with other traditions is done with respect but coming from the conviction of the supremacy of Christ, that Christianity is meant to replace other traditions.[6] I suspect evangelicals might hold the view that the only path that leads to the mountaintop is a personal relationship with Christ.

Fulfillment Model

This model is also known as an inclusivist approach and represented in many mainline Protestant, Orthodox, and Roman Catholic churches.[7] The document Nostra Aetate of the Second Vatican Council (1962–1964) has prepared the ground for this approach. While the document affirms Christ as the way, the truth, and the life in whom all find the fullness of religious life, it discovers in other religious beliefs and practices rays of truth and enlightenment. It goes on to "exhort" church members to dialogue and collaboration to witness to the Christian faith while pro-

---

4. Knitter, *Introducing Theologies of Religion*, 19–21.

5. Ibid., 28, 22.

6. Ibid., 36, 40f., 21.

7. Ibid., 63.

moting the good in other religious and cultural expressions.[8] Vatican II laid the groundwork for the kind of dialogue and cooperation that the Roman Catholic Church in Los Angeles and elsewhere engages in, as described in chapter 5.

The thinking of the Catholic theologian Karl Rahner particularly influenced the Second Vatican Council's understanding of the church's relationship to other faiths.[9] He argues that God's grace must be active in the religions because God's grace penetrates our very beings.[10] God has given the assurance of God's grace most clearly in Christ, in whom all religious paths find their final fulfillment. Those who do not know Jesus can still experience the saving power of God; they just do not fully realize it yet. Rahner coined the term "anonymous Christians" for those who follow other religious paths.[11] According to this model, different paths lead up the same mountain and find their final destination in Christ.

Mutuality Model

In the 1970s and early 1980s new viewpoints emerged that have been summarized as pluralist approaches. They avoid claims that one religion surpasses others. While they envision the relationship between religions from different perspectives, they are unified in the attempt to create a real and mutual dialogue situation where partners are equal. They assume that the conversation partners from the different religions need to listen to each other and learn from each other.[12] Therefore Paul Knitter summarizes these approaches under the term Mutuality Model. Proponents of this model feel that dialogue is not possible if there is no common basis for it, and so without brushing over differences among the religions they seek to formulate some common ground between them, without which no conversation can take place.[13] This common ground, which forms a bridge on which Christians can cross over into the new terrain of interreligious dialogue, is situated differently. Knitter distinguishes

8. Vatican, "Declaration."

9. Knitter, *Introducing Theologies of Religion*, 75.

10. Ibid., 69, 70.

11. Ibid., 72–74.

12. Ibid., 110.

13. Ibid., 111.

three bridges: a philosophical-historical bridge, a religious-mystical bridge, and an ethical-practical bridge.[14]

A pronounced proponent of the philosophical-historical bridge is John Hick. The philosophy of Immanuel Kant forms the basis of his approach: We can never experience an object as it is but only as an image that has gone through the process of our perception. Our experience is shaped by our cognitive categories, our particular psychological and historical situations. Hick calls the object of religious experience the Real-in-itself, which we cannot perceive directly. The Real-in-itself is one, but the symbols through which it is expressed are different. The different religious traditions represent human responses to this ultimate transcendent Reality. Thus, human religious experience always involves some projection.[15] Hick claims that the great world religions have a core concern in common: in different ways the religious traditions call human beings to transform their ego-centeredness to Reality-centeredness, promoting love and compassion. From the Greek word *soteria* for salvation or deliverance, this soteriological central concern in all world religions is called salvation, liberation, enlightenment, or awakening, depending on the particular tradition.[16] Because Hick wants to avoid the absolutism of any particular religion, he turns his eyes—like Huston Smith—to the mountaintop. He seeks a global interpretation, a comprehensive view of religions.[17] This approach has been critiqued as just another form of inclusivism, only with a Western Enlightenment philosophical viewpoint rather than Christianity encompassing and appropriating the different religions under one roof.

Would Hick say that all religious paths lead to the same mountaintop? According to Knitter's assessment, Hick does not deny real differences among the religions. History is witness to religions' helpful and destructive forces and documents that not all religious practices and beliefs are of equal value. Not all religious paths are equal and lead up the mountain. The religious paths can be evaluated by concern they all have in common, promoting Reality-centeredness instead of self-centeredness.[18]

14. See ibid., 112f.

15. Hick, *Christian Theology*, 28.

16. Ibid., 17f., 76.

17. Ibid., 47f.

18. Knitter, *Introducing Theologies of Religion*, 118.

In the perspective of the historian the common ground among religions does not lie in a shared core concern but in their interconnectedness. Wilfred Cantwell Smith argues that throughout history, people have traded, traveled, and migrated. Religions have been historically interconnected and have influenced each other. We are connected through a common history of religious processes, our own as well as those of our neighboring communities.[19] Our common ground for interreligious interaction is situated in our interconnected history and solidarity as human beings, which "precedes our particularity."[20]

Raimundo Panikkar, son of a Spanish Roman Catholic mother and a Hindu Indian father, has been nurtured by both traditions. He was a Roman Catholic priest and an accredited scholar of Hinduism and perhaps personified the mutual influence of religions that W. C. Smith talks about. He represents the religious-mystical bridge and seeks to hold the tension of both the universal and the particular in his approach to interreligious dialogue. Having lived in Asia, he is critical of a comprehensive or comparative theory of religion that imposes its own frame of reference on the relationship of different religions. Instead he proposes a "dialogical theology" the agenda of which is developed in the dialogue itself.[21]

For Panikkar Christian identity means living a personal religiousness rather than merely belonging to an institutionalized religion or defending a particular culture. This Christianness or Christlike attitude represents the mystical core. The universal that makes interreligious dialogue possible is mystical-spiritual. Panikkar introduces a new metaphor to describe the relationship of Christianity to other religions, that of the rivers of the earth, which are distinct from each other. Christianity began at the Jordan where Jesus was baptized. Spiritually, it cannot be understood apart from Judaism. Intellectually it was fed by the Tiber, by Greek-Roman-Gothic elements, the mentality of the West. Today, the question is whether these two rivers define the boundary of Christianity or whether it can peacefully meet the Ganges, a metaphor for the many non-Abrahamic traditions of the world.[22] Panikkar suggests that the rivers of the earth, symbolizing the religions, do not meet as water on earth but in the sky in the form of clouds having "transformed into vapor,

---

19. Smith, *Towards a World Theology*, 38, 42, 44.

20. Ibid., 79.

21. Panikkar, "Jordan, Tiber, and Ganges," 102.

22. Ibid., 89f.

metamorphized into Spirit, which then is poured down in innumerable tongues."[23] No religious tradition has a "monopoly on the living waters of the rivers (salvation)."[24] At the same time we should not "water down" particular religious beliefs for the sake of reaching agreement.[25] In order to engage other religions we do not have to move outside our particular tradition to a quasi-neutral standpoint, but we do have to be at home in our own tradition, which includes an openness to learn from other traditions.[26]

Panikkar draws on the teaching of the Trinity to hold the tension of the universal and the particular or concrete. The Divine is incredibly diverse and cannot be boxed in or reduced to one thing.[27] In the Trinitarian vision there is unity between the divine-human-cosmic reality. "There is no absolute center."[28] Reality is concentric, and different traditions complement, correct, and challenge each other. The human dimension of religion includes the possibility of mutual conflict, of common as well as irreconcilable views.[29]

The concepts within the mutuality model do not negate differences between the religions but put more emphasis on the universal. Proponents of the mutuality model see two major driving forces as creating a new way of relating to other religious paths. First, the world has become a global village and we are more aware of our neighbors of different cultural and religious traditions. Second, the environmental, social, and political problems on a global scale call for collaboration of people from all over the world and from many traditions.[30] For some the social and ecological problems that threaten our survival press themselves on us with such urgency that ethical-practical concerns are the pillars of the bridge to the religiously other.[31] These ethical issues

23. Ibid., 92.

24. Ibid.

25. Ibid.

26. Ibid., 97.

27. Knitter, *Introducing Theologies of Religion*, 129.

28. Panikkar, "Jordan, Tiber, and Ganges," 109.

29. Ibid., 109, 112.

30. Hick speaks to globalization as a factor in how Christians experience plurality of religions today (*Christian Theology*, 12f.). Smith and Panikkar talk about the need to collaborate in facing global social and ecological problems (Smith, *Towards a World Theology*, 193; Panikkar, "Jordan, Tiber, and Ganges," 102).

31. Knitter, *One Earth*, 22, 57.

form a common context of cooperation and of interreligious exchange, such as in the work of the Parliament of the World's Religions, which was described in chapter 5. Liberation and feminist theologians choose this bridge, which has been articulated by Paul Knitter as a "globally responsible, correlational dialogue among religions" that is concerned with the well-being of human beings and the earth.[32] Knitter's model addresses concerns that I have summarized in the first chapter under the term "glocal responsibility." Glocal responsibility means an attitude that allows people to be committed to their cultural, religious identity while living in connection with the earth and the global community. This sense of interdependence is expressed in concrete actions of responsibility to the earth and fellow human beings. This correlational dialogue is first and foremost collaborative action, followed by a dialogue of belief. While action is a primary and first step, Knitter points out that it needs to be accompanied by study and prayer in order to survive.[33]

The reality of suffering we all face forms a common context and starting point for collaboration. Knitter describes the challenge of suffering more concretely in four ways:[34] First, there is physical suffering rooted in poverty. The gap between poor and rich in the North and the South as well as increasingly within wealthier nations is ever widening. Second, the earth is suffering abuse. Rosemary Radford Ruether provides a sobering assessment of how many religious traditions, valuing the spiritual over material, male over female, individual salvation over communal salvation, have contributed to the exploitation of the earth. She sees the potential in these same religious traditions to retrieve ecological values that cultivate reverence for the nonhuman world. Religious communities can use their moral authority and their constituencies to promote an individual and communal lifestyle of ecological sustainability.[35]

Third, victimization harms the spirit. Throughout the world people are underprivileged and shut out from political and social processes because they are poor or because of their race and gender. Maura O'Neill underlines that for women, similar to minorities and the poor, concerns

---

32. Ibid., 15.
33. Ibid., 154.
34. Ibid., 58–67.
35. Ruether, *Integrating Ecofeminism*, 47ff., 81.

for justice already form a common starting point for action and dialogue, as religion is not apart from practical social aspects of life.[36]

Fourth, there is "suffering due to violence."[37] The threat to survival due to armed conflict is unprecedented given the vast and destructive potential of the weaponry we have created.[38]

As these forms of suffering form a challenge and common context, the reign of God represents the guiding symbol for Christians for interreligious collaboration. Jesus lived and died for the reign, the vision, and the presence of a God of justice and compassion. Christians pray and work for God's kingdom to come and God's will to be done on earth as it is in heaven.[39]

The ethical-practical approach has been criticized as introducing a new inclusivism of the all-encompassing value of justice and social action at its core. Critics point out that what is "just" is defined differently in different communities. Are tolerance, justice, and eco-human well-being really universal concerns or do they reflect Western values? In considering the warnings of his critics, Knitter points out that the search for eco-human well-being is not a common essence of religions but a common agenda that needs to be continuously discussed and reexamined in the dialogue.[40] Knitter feels that if we cannot find any common agenda or commitment to what is true or right, we open ourselves up to a dangerous ethical relativism and leave the pursuit of truth up to those who have power—meaning the power of weaponry or money.[41] The world as it is does not give us another moral choice than to seek collaboration in addressing its problems. For Knitter the experience of suffering urges the involvement of religions, and makes new interreligious encounters both necessary and possible.

How does the metaphor of the religious paths play out in the ethical-practical approach? This approach turns our attention away from the mountaintop to the mountain terrain. Here, traveling is a struggle, and the terrain itself is endangered. I imagine it looks like the scene Jesus depicted in the parable of the Good Samaritan. Like a man who was robbed,

36. O'Neill, *Women Speaking, Women Listening*, 54.

37. Knitter, *One Earth*, 65.

38. Ibid., 66.

39. Knitter, *Introducing Theologies of Religion*, 143.

40. Knitter, *One Earth*, 76.

41. Ibid., 56.

beaten, and left to die on the dangerous road from Jerusalem to Jericho, there are many people in the foothills who are hurting and suffering. The ethical-practical bridge calls on travelers to cross purity laws and boundaries between the paths and act as neighbors. The mountaintop is not irrelevant, the paths are indeed different, but the primary concern is the threatened terrain and the hurting neighbor by the roadside.

Acceptance Model

Coming from a postmodern perspective, proponents of this approach point out that it is impossible to find a common value system or perspective on truth, or better truths. For them the mutuality model emphasizes the universal at the cost of the particular, and they seek to accept the real differences between religious paths. The acceptance model contributes to the debate a healthy skepticism. Proponents of this model are suspicious of grand narratives that encompass the different religions in a neat package that thus miss their unique differences. Some propose more modest steps in interreligious dialogue; others emphasize differences and boundaries to a degree that mutual respect but not mutual engagement is encouraged.

Theologian Mark Heim critiques pluralist approaches for not taking differences seriously enough, in other words, for not being pluralist enough.[42] Heim does not only suggest that the religions understand reality differently. He proposes the existence of a real diversity of salvations, of actual religious ends.[43] Based on the doctrine of the Trinity, which conceptualizes differences in communion with each other within God, he imagines multiple salvations as ends for different religious ways.[44] Holding both the "finality of Christ and the independent validity of other ways," he sees different religious paths leading up different mountains, yet linked to the Christian mountain, reflecting the diversity fully manifested in Christ.[45] Postliberal theologians understand religion as a cultural and linguistic framework that shapes the way we experience the world.[46] We can see the world only within one particular viewpoint. Therefore it

---

42. Heim, *Salvations*, 7.

43. Ibid., 6.

44. Ibid., 158ff.

45. Ibid., 3; Knitter, *Introducing Theologies of Religion*, 202.

46. Lindbeck, *Nature of Doctrine*, 33.

is very difficult or even impossible to have a single universal experience or common ground among the different religions.[47] Postliberal theology accentuates the differences of the various religious traditions and wants to protect the integrity of the Christian community and its teachings. It underscores the boundaries within a dialogue situation.

Another approach to religious diversity is represented in comparative theology, as developed by Catholic theologian James Fredericks. It is not to be confused with comparative religion because it does not study religion from an outside perspective.[48] It is also not to be confused with a theology of religions where Christian theologians talk amongst themselves about how to understand other traditions. It begins in concrete and practical dialogue situations, like the Buddhist-Catholic dialogue described in chapter 5. Comparative theology is committed to the Christian tradition *and* open to the truth that may lie beyond our particular understanding. It studies other religious traditions on their own terms and resists the temptation to domesticate the other and fit the tradition neatly into Christian presuppositions.[49] Why engage in dialogue? Because the other is my neighbor. Comparative theology is a critical reflection of the engaged dialogue with others.[50]

Comparative theologians do not want to reflect in abstraction about the other. Therefore, they don't speculate about the mountaintop and do not find it helpful to develop a topography of the mountain terrain. Instead, they propose that travelers of the different paths walk together for a bit, learn from each other, and in the process learn about themselves.

DIFFERENT TRAVELERS

So far, we have looked at different ways in which Christian theologians conceptualize the relationship of the religious paths. Voices from minorities and women have brought to our attention that we cannot understand the paths aside from the travelers. We cannot make sense of religious difference without attention to difference of social location, gender, and historical and present power relationships.

47. Knitter, *Introducing Theologies of Religion*, 181. For more details about the postliberal approach see Knitter's analysis, 173ff.

48. Fredericks, *Buddhists and Christians*, 97.

49. Ibid., 98.

50. Ibid., 103.

The history of Christian imperialism and anti-Judaism present a special obligation for Christians to rethink our relationship to other faiths. Historically, Christianity has come to countries in the southern hemisphere in connection with secular colonial control and the exploitation of other cultures. In recent decades many Christians have initiated dialogue with people of other faiths. Yet members of other faiths approach Christian invitations to dialogue with caution and suspicion because these dialogue situations are shaped by this history.[51] Participants in interreligious dialogue bring a complex history to the conversation. Historical relations may be shaped by oppression, hurt, and suffering caused by believers of one path toward those of another. These histories need to be faced for the dialogue to be authentic.

Until the present day, the North and West, nominally primarily Christian, has represented economic power. Malaysian theologian Kenneth Surin urges a discourse that is not so much focused on doctrinal issues but carried out with an understanding of the social locations of those who participate in the dialogue. He warns that a global theology of religions is blind to the dominance of the West and makes invisible the local situation of persons in the southern hemisphere who struggle with poverty.[52]

Maura O'Neill's book *Women Speaking, Women Listening* responds to the void of the female voice in interreligious dialogue. She sees the pluralistic approaches to interreligious dialogue as insufficiently plural when the difference and particularity of gender goes unacknowledged.[53] Ways of knowing and thinking as well as ethical deliberations are different, not only among religions, but also among men and women; these differences need to receive conscious attention in interreligious dialogue.[54]

These voices mentioned so far point out that sociocultural, gender, and power differences shape relationships between people. Their analysis parallels that of social psychologists mentioned in chapter 2. Realistic conflict theory states that many intergroup conflicts, aside from differ-

---

51. Samartha provides a few glimpses of how these dialogues are experienced by members of other faith traditions as well as initiatives of dialogue in other religious traditions. See Samartha, *One Christ*, 22–31.

52. Surin, "A Politics of Speech," 196, 200.

53. O'Neill, *Women Speaking, Women Listening*, ix.

54. Ibid., 29.

ences in values and beliefs, are rooted in real differences in access to power, land, or money. Doctrinal differences today are less divisive than the social inequalities that cut across religious divisions. Therefore, feminist and liberation theologians call attention from particularities of religious traditions to particularities of gender and social context. Religious paths differ. Sociocultural differences can heighten the conflicts between religious paths. At the same time, the shared living situation and social context provides links and bridges between persons of different faiths. Christians, Hindus, and Muslims in Asia, for example, join hands to address their common social problems. Women across religious traditions collaborate in the struggle for women's rights in their societies and religious traditions. We miss an important dimension of the dialogue situation if we leave out the consideration of the participants, their social locations, and their historical and present relationships. Therefore, it is important to integrate theology with the social-psychological considerations that have played such an important role in this the book so far.

A RELATIONAL-ETHICAL APPROACH
TO INTERRELIGIOUS ENCOUNTERS

The ecumenical movement has been dealing for a long time with issues of dialogue, community, and difference in the search to realize the unity of the church. In the twentieth century the issues of unity were shaped anew by the growing relationships between churches from different continents, social and cultural locations, and an increasing awareness of our global interdependence. In his 1972 publication *And Yet It Moves: Dream and Reality of the Ecumenical Movement*, German theologian Ernst Lange claims that the church needs to be involved in today's urgent need for peace. Ecumenism is an expression of peace and the only way for the church to be one, holy, catholic, and apostolic.[55] Lange notes that ecumenical consultation has been often conducted without attention to factors such as group dynamics, participants' intercultural anxieties, and prejudice levels.[56] But these "non-theological" sociocultural, and psychological factors permeate even development of doctrine and statements of faith. Not only the content of beliefs but also deeply rooted

---

55. Lange, *And Yet It Moves*, 148.

56. Ibid., 125f.

attitudes and patterns of behaviors need attention.[57] Not only doctrinal differences, but also sociocultural psychological factors cause divisions in the life of the churches. Lange argues that ecumenical theology needs to be interdisciplinary. "If theology is concerned with the truth about reality, then all man's [sic] knowledge and experience of reality must be brought into the reflection process and exposed to the test of truth."[58] He proposes the development of a social ecumenical didactic. Such a didactic is a theory and method that assists persons to develop an ecumenical and universal commitment, meaning an ability to connect with others near and far while maintaining their commitments to their denominational, cultural, and social context.[59] Churches and their members need to overcome their provincialism and understand themselves as having a sense of responsibility to the whole world, or as we might paraphrase, to develop a glocal responsibility.[60] They need assistance in the process to help them to enter conscientiously into these new levels of engagement without being "automatically shut out from them for fear of losing their own integrity and identity."[61]

The relationships with other religious traditions were not at the forefront of his reflection in 1972. Since then, our social context has become more globalized and pluralistic. Lange argued that is an essential task of the church to work as an agent for peace in the world. Today the fulfillment of that role involves the active and open engagement of our neighbors of different religious traditions. Lange's suggestion to give attention to theological *and* nontheological factors in ecumenical theology rings true for this broader context as well. I see my own attempts to integrate theological considerations of interreligious dialogue with insights from intergroup relations theory as one aspect of this broader interdisciplinary enterprise. If we want to help religious communities, their members, and their leaders to constructively engage the pluralistic context, we need to develop ways to understand and nurture relationships, not just to exchange beliefs. As Lange notes, even the development of our beliefs is shaped by social context, cultural location, and intergroup relationships. My own theological perspective is shaped primarily

---

57. Ibid., 75.

58. Ibid., 127.

59. Becker, "Ecumenical Learning," 342.

60. Lange, *And Yet It Moves*, 135.

61. Ibid., 139.

by Paul Knitter's approach and integrates social psychological aspects. Therefore I call my approach to interreligious encounters a relational-ethical bridge. I delineate this approach with the help of three theses: (1) Religion does not equal God. (2) Christian commitments lead to the religiously other. (3) We are social animals.

Religion does not equal God.

I arrive at this statement that "Religion does not equal God" from two directions: first, from an understanding of the process of human cognition, and second, from a theological perspective.

Religious symbols, beliefs, and practices, such as worship or meditation, embody and convey intangible encounters with the Sacred. In that sense religion enables experience of what we call God. Religions give concrete form to human understandings and experiences of God. Religious communities nurture and interpret these experiences over time and give their members a sense of belonging and identity. Because religious expression is embodied, it is always limited by our language, our culture, and our historical context. John Hick underscores that we cannot access reality unfiltered but that everything we perceive passes through the lens of our human cognition. Religious experience seeks to express something that cannot be seen. It points and responds to an ultimate reality, which we cannot access directly and which is incomparable to what we know. Religion, while pointing and responding to the Sacred, is deeply human with all its limitations.

The story of Moses at the burning bush illustrates the theological perspective.[62] While herding sheep one day Moses finds himself in front of a bush that burns but is not consumed by the fire. He hears a voice asking him to take off his sandals, as he stands on holy ground. Moses is afraid to look at God, who speaks to him from the fire. God identifies God's self in concrete historical terms as the God of Abraham, Isaac, and Jacob, and as a God of compassion for the suffering of the Israelites. But when Moses asks God's name, the response is: "I am who I am." God makes God's self known while at the same time eluding our attempts to know God. As the ground of being, God is always Mystery that cannot be grasped. Religions exist in this tension between the embodied experience of the Divine and the inaccessibility and transcendence of God. If

---

62. Exod 3:1–12.

we wanted to confine God to our concepts, we would limit the freedom of God. Our understanding of God cannot be absolute and objective but emerges in the context of faith. A religious community that claims to have an exclusive or ultimate knowledge of God seeks to capture God and escape the Mystery.

Our expressions of religious experience are human, conditioned, and limited. They can become self-serving and distort the Sacred. Therefore, prophets, reformers, and often heretics provide critical correctives for religious traditions. A faith that is alive needs critical evaluation of its religious expression and continuous reform. Religion, while pointing to God, is not to be confused with God.

In our postmodern, postenlightenment time, religion continues to be a powerful force in personal and social lives. At the same time, many feel ambivalent toward institutional religion. The most extreme and divisive religious voices seem to be heard the most, either because fundamentalist religious organizations are media savvy or because extreme positions attract media reports more easily than voices of moderation and reconciliation. Over the years as a chaplain I have met many people who have told me, "I am not religious but spiritual." In so doing, some communicate to me that they are not attached to a religious community but still feel a strong connection to their faith and spirituality. Others communicate their disillusionment with religion. They may have had disappointing experiences of religion or belonging to a religious community does not seem meaningful to them. Some see institutional religion as too concerned with its own self-preservation or too entangled with the question of which religious path is the right one. To them it seems that leaving religion and its quarrels behind and focusing on the spiritual—however nebulous that may be—is a more sensible approach to find meaning in their lives. At the bedside it is my role to listen and explore with them how their personal spirituality can support them in what they are going through. Often I can empathize and sympathize with many of the critical statements I hear about organized religion.

Yet I feel that it is impossible to move beyond my particular religious tradition, however flawed it may be. Just as I cannot crawl into a time capsule that would transport me out of my historical, cultural, or social context, so also I cannot move beyond my particular faith and practice spirituality void of concrete expression. My particular religious tradition and community nurtures and shapes my relationship with the

Divine. I could not live a life of faith without the community of others. The best I can do is to be at home in my religious tradition while giving it its right place. Being part of a community involves commitment and a willingness to struggle with its shadows. Moving beyond a particular faith is also not a viable option that would enable me to more easily embrace religious pluralism. A comprehensive bird's-eye view of religion is impossible. I believe that we are not better off in our relationship to other religious faiths by leaving particular beliefs out of the conversation. I can start the conversation by realizing that my understanding of God is always limited. I can be open to the experiences of other co-religionists so I might be enriched in my understanding and learn something new.

Religion does not equal God. If we claim absoluteness for our own faith community, we turn God into a tribal God. If we confuse religion with the Sacred itself, we run into the danger of idolatry: we cling to our own image of God rather than letting the spirit of the living and indescribable God guide us. The best approach to our own faith and the faith of our neighbor is a stance of realistic humility. The stance is realistic because we recognize the limitations of our human mind and cognition. It is a stance of humility because this is the only appropriate response to the mystery of God.

Christian commitments lead to the religiously other.

This section does not answer the question of when and how we bring core Christian beliefs to the conversation table in our dialogue with Buddhist, Jewish, Muslim, and Hindu friends. It also is not an attempt to fit other religious traditions into a Christian worldview. Instead, in this section I ask how as a Christian I understand reality and what my faith tells me about how to relate to this reality, the Divine, the world, and my fellow human beings. I ask what implications this Christian worldview has for my encounters with those who have different worldviews. In a very rough sketch I explore Christian teachings about Jesus' ministry, Christology, and the Trinity in how they might guide my encounter with the religiously other.

Jesus' life in his words and actions was centered on the reign of God. His ministry realized the reign of God and he invited everyone to join. Its shape and form is that of a radically inclusive community where there is no longer Jew or Greek, there is no longer slave or free, there is no longer male or female; for all are one in Christ.[63] Jesus tended to the suffering, reaching out and welcoming those whom society expelled to the margins—the dispossessed and poor, the sick, women and children. Not the hierarchical and patriarchal structures of ancient society, but solidarity and compassion shape relationships in God's reign.

The Christian community prays for the coming of this reign and is called to express its reality by living in the patterns Jesus has provided, as an inclusive community of compassion and solidarity. Christian life is primarily concerned not with the right belief (orthodoxy) but right living, following in Jesus' footsteps (orthopraxis), although it would be problematic to separate belief and praxis from each other.

With Knitter I see the concern for the well-being of humans and the earth as a faithful response to Jesus' ministry. With him I also see in this ethical bridge connection points to believers of other religious paths. Tending to the suffering and working for personal, social, and ecological healing are values shared by many other traditions. While they do not represent a catalogue of consensus, they provide modest goals and can be places of collaboration, entry points of interreligious connection. While the religious traditions have real differences, our common ground is in our common humanity and the shared problems we face as human beings.

The experience of suffering is universal. We may interpret it differently, we may disagree on how to alleviate suffering, but it does lay a claim on us with immediacy to engage in repair work. As Knitter puts it: "Suffering has a universality and immediacy that makes it the most suitable, and necessary, site for establishing common ground for interreligious encounter."[64]

When as a chaplain I am with persons from a different tradition who are sick or in crisis, I have to find ways to reach out and enter their world. I am not so naïve to think that I can fully understand their spiritual beliefs and practices, but I have to do all I can to support them in their faith as it helps them through the crisis. This may mean reaching out to someone else from that tradition for help, but often I do not have that luxury. As I have demonstrated in chapter 6, it is possible for spiritual caregivers to be meaningfully present with persons of a different

---

63. Gal 3:28.

64. Knitter, *One Earth*, 89.

religious tradition. Interreligious spiritual care and counseling addresses human suffering, such as illness, crisis, and death, on a personal level.

When as a parish pastor I hear that the mosque in my part of town has been vandalized, my congregation can visit the mosque to express support, write a letter to the local newspaper, and organize a vigil. We respond to the hurt. We can repair and heal suffering in interreligious relations.

The poor in my neighborhood or in a country far away, the destruction of plant and animal species, and the danger of the survival of the earth call for a response from the Christian church. In the first chapter I pointed out that many problems in the global village are so vast that we need to join hands with other co-religionists to respond effectively and address suffering on a broader social and global level. Collaborating with people of all walks of life and different religious paths in the work for healing is living a life patterned by Jesus' ministry and the reign of God.

The central Christian belief that distinguishes us from our co-religionists of other religious paths is the belief that Christ is both human and divine. In the life, crucifixion, and resurrection of Jesus, God has become human, joined our plight even unto death, and brings new life to us. While believers of other traditions can affirm Jesus as a prophet or the founder of a religion, the confession of Christ as God incarnate is unique to Christianity. Is this Christian commitment an obstacle in the dialogue with other faiths?

Confessing Christ has been used in a way that suggests the supremacy of Christianity over other religious paths. Throughout history it has often been connected with the political powers of imperialism. It has robbed others of their religious freedom and shut the door to a conversation open to the truth in other traditions. We need to face and transform this abuse of Christian teachings. But it does not mean that we have to abandon central Christian commitments altogether.

The new context of religious pluralism poses for us the question of how we understand Christ in relationship to other religious paths. In order to develop a Christology in this new context, Indian theologian Stanley Samartha returns to the context of the first Christian communities and looks anew at their expressions of faith. He notes that statements about Christ in the Second Testament have a confessional character, which need to be understood in the life of the worship of the

Christian community. Creeds are not statements about other faith traditions but affirmations of the community's faith in Christ and should be understood within the boundaries of the community.[65] Samartha also emphasizes that the biblical testimonies of the crucified and risen Christ reveal the meaning of these events but the "*being* [emphasis by author] (or truth) of Jesus behind them remains unknown to us."[66] If we truly believe that Christ is human *and* divine, we will realize that we never fully understand Christ. The gospels and other accounts of Jesus' person and ministry in the New Testament are diverse. They elude a definitive understanding, and the mystery of the living Christ remains. That Jesus evades the full comprehension of those who encounter him forms a thread through the Gospel of Mark. Those who listen to Jesus' parables are often confused. The closing scene of that Gospel depicts an empty tomb and some women and men who lack understanding, who are scared and asked to go back to Galilee where their journey with Jesus had begun. The ending of the Gospel leaves the early Christian community with a call to discipleship, understanding themselves as being on the way rather than having already arrived.[67] Creeds and stories about Christ are to be read in the context of discipleship. They are not objective definitions but testimonies that call for a response and want to be interpreted through our lives.

What is the content of these testimonies and what do we mean when we understand the historical person Jesus of Nazareth as Christ, the Word of God incarnate?

In his book *Ethics* German theologian Dietrich Bonhoeffer articulates that in Christ God enters human life to the fullest and affirms the human person in compassion.[68] The Christ event means that God's love to the world is not a general idea but "really *lived* love of God in Jesus Christ." The human and suffering Christ is the affirmation that God loves humanity and the world, not in an ideal state but as they are. As we try to grow beyond our humanity, as we leave humanity behind us, God becomes a human being and wishes us to be real human beings: "what we shrink back from with pain and hostility . . . is for God the

---

65. Samartha, *One Christ*, 133.

66. Ibid., 140.

67. Note that it is widely considered that Mark 16:9ff are later additions to the original text.

68. For the following, see Bonhoeffer, *Ethics*, 9f.

ground of unfathomable love." God loves the real human being without distinction. God's outgoing love is not based on sameness or likeness but God unites God's self with that which is different and unlovable in our eyes. This means we cannot put boundaries on the dignity and worth of any human person. Dignity does not depend on race, ethnicity, age, ability, gender, sexual orientation, or social location. It does not depend on what persons believe. Respecting a person's dignity involves regard for the other's freedom and striving to understand them not in our image but as they understand themselves.

The notion of God as outgoing love has been further developed in the symbol of the Trinity. For feminist theologian Catherine Mowry LaCugna the doctrine of the Trinity preserves the notion of a relational God that the biblical Jewish and Christian traditions convey.[69] The understanding of God as triune, as one in three persons, is also uniquely different from other religious paths. In the fourth century the Cappadocian Christian philosophers developed the first complete trinitarian doctrine of God.[70] They conceptualized oneness in three persons because they thought of God primarily not in terms of a substance, a thing, but in terms of relationship. The three persons of the Trinity relate to each other in a mutual and reciprocal relationship. The ultimate originating principle of reality is understood as being-in-relation-to-another.[71] Not self-containment and autonomy but mutuality and relationship are the basic principles of life.[72] Because Christian theology understands the human being as created in the image of God, LaCugna underscores that the teaching of the Trinity conceptualizes God as essentially related, the human person as relational, and our being in and with the world as interdependent.[73] When we understand our being and our world primarily in terms of substance, we tend to see beings as self-contained and reality as static. Unity means being of the same substance. However, comprehending reality as relatedness is dynamic. Uniqueness and difference are appreciated and unity is not sameness or conformity but community. On the one hand, this dynamic understanding of reality corresponds to the understanding of culture put forth in the first chapter: hybrid culture

69. LaCugna, *God for Us*, 289.

70. LaCugna, "God in Communion with Us," 86.

71. Ibid., 86f.

72. Ibid., 86.

73. LaCugna, *God for Us*, 289.

is in flux and interconnected, not separate from other cultures. On the other hand, understanding life first in terms of relatedness has parallels in contemporary psychological concepts.

We are social animals.

In his book *Relational Concepts in Psychoanalysis*, the psychoanalyst Stephen Mitchell observes that relational-model theories have dominated contemporary psychoanalytic thinking for the last decades. They share the notion that relations with others are "the basic stuff of mental life."[74] While we experience ourselves as having an identity that is somewhat constant, we partially construct ourselves depending on the interpersonal context we find ourselves in. We are not self-contained and separate entities that engage others or the world as external self-contained entities, putting parts together like a jigsaw puzzle. A relational view is dynamic and sees the person in a field with the world it relates to and the space between the two. The person is multiple, in flux.[75] Mitchell suggests: "The most useful way to view psychological reality is as operating within a relational matrix which encompasses both intrapsychic and interpersonal realms."[76]

We are social animals. Our bodies and their physiological processes fundamentally shape us. A relational understanding of the person allows for interdependence. We realize our reliance and connection not just with other people but our physical environment. It thus forms a strong basis for ecological ethics. Physiological processes are core to our being, but our mind interprets them and gives them meaning through our relational patterns.[77] In other words: We are wired for relationship. We seek to connect to others in attachment, love, and friendship. We seek resonance with others and are formed by our interactions with other persons. We find joy in our connections, and are angered and saddened by them. Our conflicts and disconnections can cause great pain. Even our animosities are expressions of our fundamental connectedness.

Throughout this book, intergroup relations theory plays an important role in understanding our relationships to others, especially other

74. Mitchell, *Relational Concepts*, 2.

75. Ibid., 3, 33.

76. Ibid., 9.

77. Ibid., 4.

religious groups. Intergroup relations theory differs from relational psychoanalysis in its focus on relationships between social groups. When it comes to the importance of relatedness for our identity, both schools of thought seem to be compatible. Especially social identity theory explains how much we are influenced by others. We not only construct a sense of personal identity, our identity has social aspects that are connected to our membership in social groups. We desire to belong to groups that enjoy distinct and positive identities. Our membership in social groups has a powerful influence on our sense of self and worth.

"COOPERATE!" INTEGRATING A RELATIONAL AND ETHICAL APPROACH TO INTERRELIGIOUS ENCOUNTERS

To sum up, Christian beliefs about the reign of God, Christ, and the triune God emphasize Christian identity as a journey. We are underway in this faith journey, following the path Jesus has patterned and finding ourselves embraced by God's unconditional love. We are created in God's image, are not separate but exist within an interdependent web of life. Our personal, social, and religious identities are not self-contained static entities that get lost in contact with the other. They are shaped by our relationships. Healthy relationships need boundaries. We need articulated beliefs that guide and shape us. Yet our faith is not a static possession but in flux and in relationship. I see myself not as "having" a religion but as a participant, a disciple, who needs spiritual practices and beliefs to grow. My faith is affected by my community and grows in my encounters with those on other religious paths.

Uniquely Christian beliefs define our faith. I believe their very content moves us to reach out to our neighbor. In Christ God has revealed God's unconditional love, uniting those who are unlike each other. This good news impels us to reach out to the others independently of their social, cultural, or religious group. The mystery of God keeps us humble and aware that we cannot understand God. God's unconditional love lived out in Christ gives us confidence and trust to engage the other.

Jesus lived this love in his actions and his words, which were centered on the reign of God: an inclusive community of those who are not alike but united through God's love. The hurt of persons we meet in the hospital bed, prison, or on campus; the poverty of our neighbors close and far away; the suffering of the earth—all have an immediacy that impels a response of healing and repair. The more we cooperate with people from different nations and religious traditions, the more effective we can be in tending to the suffering. We do not have to find a single grand approach in our understanding of the different religions; modest and flexible points of collaboration will suffice. The suffering we experience is indeed a starting point for the interreligious encounter and place of dialogue about shared and differing beliefs.

Aside from this ethical bridge, the relation to the other itself is the pathway. Relationship as a unifying agent can hold both—commonality and distinctiveness.

An inclusive community of those who are different and unlike each other is not a harmonious community. It is conflict-laden and involves differences and disagreements. Unity is not sameness but comm-unity. More important than agreements are resonance and mutual understanding between people.

The bumper sticker "COEXIST," consisting of letters shaped by diverse religious symbols, has become a popular statement calling for tolerance in our religiously plural society. We are facing urgent social and ecological problems locally and globally. The relationships between religious groups are fragile and conflicted. Our Christian faith provides us with the vision of a God who is outgoing love and of God's reign as ruled by solidarity and compassion. Our faith impels us to go beyond tolerant coexistence. It moves us to reach out beyond our particular community and engage the problems we face together. It calls us to cooperate.

9

Conclusion

THROUGHOUT THE BOOK I have spelled out the spiritual practice of developing relationships between communities and individuals of different religious groups. I have done so in an interdisciplinary exploration, weaving together ideas from social psychology and theology, because it is not belief systems but people with different beliefs and identities who meet in interfaith encounters.

People of different faiths face urgent problems together, globally as well as in their local communities. These problems call for cooperation. In the global village, the local place is less significant for our sense of identity and belonging than it used to be. I have suggested that persons' cultural and religious identities are becoming more important in providing a sense of belonging. Social identity theory assists in understanding the significance of our membership in social groups for our sense of self. It also aids in understanding why relationships between different groups are often conflictual.

While there are many examples of peaceful and constructive relations between different religious groups, religious difference can contribute to isolation and division. Just like other social groups, religious communities are vulnerable to the dynamics of intergroup relations. Rather than actively engaging the increasing religious diversity in our society, many religious communities keep contact with other religious traditions at a minimum. Interreligious relationships remain strained and distant, with some religious groups asserting their own particular identity over others. It is not just different beliefs but also social inequalities and power imbalances, as well as fears, stereotypes, and prejudices that divide and isolate persons of different faiths from each other. Intergroup relations theory has developed tools that assist in the repair of relationships. Especially if we want to move interfaith work beyond academia and religious leadership to grassroots levels, we need to take relational factors seriously. In order to empower different religious communities to constructively engage each other, we need to understand and nurture relational dynamics.

Bringing people of different religious communities together in cooperation has promise for the development of constructive relationships between them. When these religious communities have intergroup contact, enjoy authority support, and experience equal status in their group encounter, when they work together toward shared goals and can develop friendships, there is a potential that bias is reduced. I have introduced strategies for the facilitation of such cooperative interfaith projects that can change how people perceive, feel about, and act toward each other.

Social psychologists have developed and tested strategies of decategorization, cross-categorization, mutual differentiation, and recategorization. Together they acknowledge both what people of different groups have in common as well as their particularities and differences. Cooperation does not aim for agreement and sameness but for resonance and openness toward the other. It has been noted that theories of intergroup relations focus heavily on cognitive processes of perception and that future research needs to give stronger attention to the role of emotions in intergroup relations.[1] I have explored the role of two emotions in interreligious encounters: anxiety and empathy. Yet, a further investigation of the dynamic interplay between perceptions, feelings, and behavior will deepen our understanding of the relationships between religious communities. An additional area that is beyond the scope of this book is the role of social structures and media in fostering or reducing bias between different religious groups.

Not only community religious leaders but also chaplains and counselors encounter religious diversity in their work. In spiritual care and its supervision, cooperation means actively engaging the spiritual beliefs and practices of those who seek care and connecting them with spiritual resources that are meaningful to them. Caregivers and careseekers of different religious traditions can connect along a continuum of common human experiences, interconnected and particular spiritual practice. In

---

1. Pettigrew, "Intergroup Contact Hypothesis Reconsidered," 192.

spiritual care and its clinical supervision, attention to what we have in common needs to be balanced by a respect for where we differ.

We hear religious leaders who are engaged in interfaith work. They generally do not feel they have to abandon core beliefs that are important to them. Moreover, interreligious dialogue requires that partners can be authentic and committed to their faith to credibly enter the dialogue. They speak with deep appreciation about the friendships they have developed with people of other religious paths.

The religious diversity we encounter globally and locally—in our neighborhoods, in the hospital room, or in the counseling office—calls us to care for individuals and communities by working together. Speaking from the context of my own Christian faith, cooperating with persons across religious traditions in the work of healing is a spiritual practice rooted in core Christian beliefs. Collaborative action provides modest goals, entry points, and a low threshold where participants do not feel threatened in their religious identity. Cooperation starts with a common ground but does not intend to dissolve differences. As we work together and get to know each other, we are changed in the process. Interfaith cooperation involves head, heart, and hands. We begin to feel differently and perceive the religiously other more realistically. In the process of caring for our community and each other, we can repair strained and distant interreligious relationships.

Interfaith work is not without struggles, and challenges us to ongoing learning. I share the experiences of other religious workers whose voices are heard in the book: interreligious encounters can expand and deepen the understanding not only of another faith but of our own tradition. Moreover, the discovery of connections and development of friendships encourage and nurture our work. I hope I have been able to demonstrate throughout this book that cooperation makes sense, theologically *and* psychologically.

Bibliography

ACPE Taskforce on Islam. "Section 3: Islamic Perspectives for Supervision." *Reflective Practice: Formation and Supervision in Ministry* 29 (2009) 141–86, http://journals .sfu.ca/rpfs/index.php/rpfs/article/viewFile/35/36, accessed 7/6/11.

Adorno, Theodor W., et al. *The Authoritarian Personality: Studies in Prejudice.* Norton Library, N492. New York: Norton, 1969.

Allport, Gordon W. *The Nature of Prejudice.* 25th Anniversary Edition. New York: Basic Books, 1979.

Ansari, Bilal. "Seeing with Bifocals: The Evolution of a Muslim Chaplain." *Reflective Practice: Formation and Supervision in Ministry* 29 (2009) 170–77.

Arai, Tosh, and S. Wesley Ariarajah, eds. *Spirituality in Interfaith Dialogue.* Geneva: WCC Publications, 1989.

Ariarajah, S. Wesley. "Interfaith Dialogue." In *Dictionary of the Ecumenical Movement,* edited by Nicholas Lossky, José Miguez Bonino, John Pobee, Tom Stransky, Geoffrey Wainwright, and Pauline Webb, 281–87. Geneva: WCC Publications, 1991.

———. *Not without My Neighbor: Issues in Interfaith Relations.* Geneva: WCC Publications, 1999.

Association of Clinical Pastoral Education. "Standard 100 Code of Professional Ethics." In *ACPE Standards and Manuals: 2010 Standards,* www.acpe.edu/NewPDF/2010%20 Manuals/2010%20Standards.pdf, accessed 1/11/09.

Association of Professional Chaplains. "Code of Ethics." Standard 130.13, http://www. professionalchaplains.org/uploadedFiles/pdf/code_of_ethics_2003.pdf, accessed 1/11/09.

Augsburger, David W. *Conflict Mediation across Cultures, Pathways, and Patterns.* Louisville: Westminster John Knox Press, 1992.

———. *Pastoral Counseling across Cultures.* Philadelphia: Westminster Press, 1986.

Avlon, John P. "Anti-government hate militias on the rise." CNN Opinion, http://www .cnn.com/2010/OPINION/03/30/avlon.hatriots.militia/index.html, accessed 4/7/2009.

Batson, C. Daniel, Marina P. Polycarpou, Eddie Harmon-Jones, Heidi J. Imhoff, Erwin C. Mitchener, Lori L. Bednar, Tricia R. Klein, and Lori Highberger. "Empathy and Attitudes: Can Feeling for a Member of a Stigmatized Group Improve Feelings Toward the Group?" *Journal of Personality and Social Psychology* 72/1 (1997) 105–18.

Batson, C. Daniel, and E. L. Stocks. "Religion and Prejudice." In *On the Nature of Prejudice: Fifty Years after Allport,* edited by John F. Dovidio, Peter Glick, and Laurie Rudman, 413–27. Malden, MA: Blackwell Publishing, 2005.

Becker, Ulrich. "Ecumenical Learning." In *Dictionary of the Ecumenical Movement,* edited by Nicholas Lossky, José Miguez Bonino, John Pobee, Tom Stransky, Geoffrey Wainwright, and Pauline Webb, 341–42. Geneva: WCC Publications, 1991.

Beek, Aart M. van. *Cross-Cultural Counseling*. Creative Pastoral Care and Counseling Series, edited by Howard W. Stone and Howard Clinebell. Minneapolis: Fortress Press, 1996.

Bernard, Janine M., and Rodney K. Goodyear. *Fundamentals of Clinical Supervision*. 4th ed. Upper Saddle River, NJ: Pearson Education, 2009.

Beyer, Peter. *Religion and Globalization*. London: Sage Publications, 1994.

Bodenhausen, Galen V. "Emotions, Arousal, and Stereotypic Judgments: A Heuristic Model of Affect and Stereotyping." In *Affect, Cognition, and Stereotyping: Interactive Processes in Group Perception,* edited by Diane M. Mackie and David L. Hamilton, 13–37. San Diego: Academic Press, 1993.

Bonhoeffer, Dietrich. *Ethics*, edited by Eberhard Bethge. The Library of Philosophy and Theology. New York: MacMillan, 1955.

Brewer, Marilyn. "Reducing Prejudice through Cross-Categorization: Effects of Multiple Social Identities." In *Reducing Prejudice and Discrimination,* edited by Stuart Oskamp, 165–84. Mahwah, NJ: Lawrence Erlbaum, 2000.

Brewer, Marilynn B., and Norman Miller. "Beyond the Contact Hypothesis: Theoretical Perspectives on Desegregation." In *Groups in Contact: The Psychology of Desegregation,* edited by Marilynn B. Brewer and Norman Miller, 281–302. Orlando: Academic Press, 1984.

———, eds. *Groups in Contact: The Psychology of Desegregation*. Orlando: Academic Press, 1984.

Brodeur, Patrice. "Towards a Transnational Interfaith Youth Network in Higher Education." In *Building the Interfaith Youth Movement: Beyond Dialogue to Action,* edited by Eboo Patel and Patrice Brodeur, 51–64. Lanham, MD: Rowman and Littlefield, 2006.

Buddhist Sangha Council and the Archdiocese of Los Angeles, Buddhist-Catholic Dialogue, Los Angeles, http://www.urbandharma.org/bcdialog/index.html, accessed 1/26/2011.

Bueckert, Leah Dawn. "Stepping into the Borderlands: Prayer with People of Different Faiths." In *Interfaith Spiritual Care: Understandings and Practices,* edited by Daniel S. Schipani and Leah Dawn Bueckert, 29–49. Kitchener, ON: Pandora Press. In collaboration with the SIPCC, Society for Intercultural Pastoral Care and Counseling, Gesellschaft für interkulturelle Seelsorge und Beratung, Düsselfort, Germany, 2009.

Butt, Gerald. "Muslims' Support Makes It a Quiet Coptic Christmas." *Church Times* 7713 (14 January 2011), http://www.churchtimes.co.uk/content.asp?id=106595, accessed 1/22/11.

Byrd, Cameron W. "Inclusiveness in a Basic Unit of Clinical Pastoral Education: A Story of Struggle, Risk, and Commitment." *Journal of Supervision and Training in Ministry* 14 (1992/1993) 201–11.

The Christian Education Movement, *Praying Their Faith. An Insight into Six World Religions through the Prayers of their Members*. 2nd ed. Birmingham: Christian Education Movement, 1999.

Clinebell, Howard. *Basic Types of Pastoral Care and Counseling: Resources for the Ministry of Healing and Growth*. Nashville: Abingdon Press, 1992.

Commission on Global Governance. *Our Global Neighbourhood: The Report of the Commission on Global Governance*. New York: Oxford University Press, 1995.

Council for a World Parliament of Religions, http://www.parliamentofreligions.org/, accessed 2/20/2011.

Davis, Nina C. "Is Multifaith and Multicultural CPE Supervision Possible?" *Journal of Supervision and Training in Ministry* 23 (2003) 60–65.

Dollard, John, Leonard W. Doob, Neal Elger Miller, Orwal H. Mower, and Robert R. Sears. *Frustration and Aggression.* New Haven, CT: Yale University Press. Published for Institute of Human Relations, 1939.

Dovidio, John F., and Samuel L. Gaertner, eds. *Prejudice, Discrimination, and Racism.* Orlando: Academic Press, 1986.

Dovidio, John F., Samuel L. Gaertner, Alice M. Isen, Mary Rust, and Paula Guerra. "Positive Affect, Cognition, and the Reduction of Intergroup Bias." In *Intergroup Cognition and Intergroup Behavior,* edited by Constantine Sedikides, John Schopler, and Chester A. Insko, 337–66. Mahwah, NJ: Lawrence Erlbaum, 1998.

Dovidio, John F., Samuel L. Gaertner, Tracie L. Stewart, Victoria M. Esses, Marleen ten Vergert, and Gordon Hodson. "From Intervention to Outcome: Processes in the Reduction of Bias." In *Education Programs for Improving Intergroup Relations: Theory, Research, and Practice,* edited by Walter G. Stephan and W. Paul Vogt, 243–65. Multicultural Education Series. New York: Teachers College Press, 2004.

Dovidio, John F., Peter Glick, and Laurie A. Rudman, eds. *On the Nature of Prejudice: Fifty Years after Allport.* Malden, MA: Blackwell, 2005.

Dovidio, John F., Kerry Kawakami, and Samuel L. Gaertner. "Reducing Contemporary Prejudice: Combating Explicit and Implicit Bias at the Individual and Intergroup Level." In *Reducing Prejudice and Discrimination,* edited by Stuart Oskamp, 137–63. Mahwah, NJ: Lawrence Erlbaum, 2000.

Eck, Diana L. *Encountering God. A Spiritual Journey from Bozeman to Banaras.* Boston: Beacon Press, 1993.

———. *A New Religious America: How a "Christian Country" Has Now Become the World's Most Religiously Diverse Nation.* New York: HarperOne, 2001.

Eck, Diana L., and Devaki Jain, eds. *Speaking of Faith: Cross-Cultural Perspectives on Women, Religion, and Social Change.* London: Women's Press, 1986.

Esses, Victoria, Geoffrey Haddock, and Mark P. Zanna. "Values, Stereotypes, and Emotions as Determinants of Intergroup Attitudes." In *Affect, Cognition, and Stereotyping: Interactive Processes in Group Perception,* edited by Diane M. Mackie and David L. Hamilton, 137–65. San Diego: Academic Press, 1993.

Falk, Richard. *Religion and Human Global Governance.* New York: Palgrave, 2001.

Featherstone, Mike, ed. *Global Culture: Nationalism, Globalization, and Modernity.* London: Sage Publications, 1990.

Featherstone, Mike. "An Introduction." In *Global Culture: Nationalism, Globalization, and Modernity,* edited by Mike Featherstone. London: Sage Publications, 1990.

Federschmidt, Karl, Eberhard Hauschildt, Christoph Schneider-Harpprecht, Klaus Temme, and Helmut Weiß, eds. *Handbuch Interkulturelle Seelsorge.* Neukirchen-Vluyn: Neukirchner Verlag, 2002.

Fistarol, Corina. "Der Himmel ist gross genug für alle—Neue Abstimmungsstrategie lanciert." In Das Portal der Reformierten, 16.10.09, http://www.ref.ch/index.php?id=127&tx_ttnews[tt_news]=362&tx_ttnews[backPid]=21, accessed 6/14/11.

Fredericks, James L. *Buddhists and Christians: Through Comparative Theology to Solidarity.* Faith Meets Faith Series. Maryknoll, NY: Orbis Books, 2004.

Friedman, Dayle A., ed. *Jewish Pastoral Care: A Practical Handbook from Traditional and Contemporary Sources.* 2nd ed. Woodstock: Jewish Lights, 2005.

Gaddy, Welton. "Great Irony in Outcry over Ground Zero Mosque." *The Washington Post* online, July 22, 2010, http://newsweek.washingtonpost.com/onfaith/panelists/c _welton_gaddy/2010/07/great_irony_in_outcry_over_ground_zero_mosque.html.

Gaertner, Samuel L., and John F. Dovidio. "Prejudice, Discrimination, and Racism: Problems, Progress, and Promise." In *Prejudice, Discrimination, and Racism*, edited by John F. Dovidio and Samuel Gaertner, 315–32. Orlando: Academic Press, 1986.

———, eds. *Reducing Intergroup Bias: The Common Group Identity Model.* Essays in Social Psychology. Philadelphia: Psychology Press, 2000.

Gaertner, Samuel L., John F. Dovidio, Jason A. Nier, Christine M. Ward, and Brenda S. Banker. "Across Cultural Divides: The Value of a Superordinate Identity." In *Cultural Divides: Understanding and Overcoming Group Conflict*, edited by Deborah A. Prentice and Dale T. Miller, 173–212. New York: Russell Sage Foundation, 1999.

Galinsky, Adam D., and Gordon B. Moskowitz. "Perspective-Taking: Decreasing Stereotype Expression, Stereotype Accessibility, and In-Group Favoritism." *Journal of Personality and Social Psychology* 78/4 (2000) 708–24.

Goggin, Michael. "The High School Youth Program of the InterFaith Conference of Metropolitan Washington." In *Building the Interfaith Youth Movement: Beyond Dialogue to Action*, edited by Eboo Patel and Patrice Brodeur, 185–97. Lanham, MD: Rowman and Littlefield, 2006.

Goleman, Daniel. *Social Intelligence: The New Science of Human Relationships.* New York: Bantam Books, 2007.

Grace, Mark. "Thinking through Pastoral Education with Culturally Diverse Peer Groups." *Journal of Supervision and Training in Ministry* 22 (2002) 21–39.

Grefe, Dagmar. "What Chaplains and Clergy Need to Know about Cultural Self-Awareness." Online Healthcare Chaplaincy course, http://www.healthcarechaplaincy.org.

Grew, Raymond. "On Seeking the Cultural Context of Fundamentalism." In *Religion, Ethnicity, and Self-Identity: Nations in Turmoil*, edited by Martin E. Marty and Scott Appleby, 19–34. Hanover, NH: University Press of New England, 1997.

Griffith, William H. "A Chaplain Reflects on Caring for a Jewish Family." In *Interfaith Spiritual Care: Understandings and Practices*, edited by Daniel S. Schipani and Leah Dawn Bueckert, 81–87. Kitchener, ON: Pandora Press. In collaboration with the SIPCC, Society for Intercultural Pastoral Care and Counseling, Gesellschaft für interkulturelle Seelsorge und Beratung, Düsseldorf, Germany, 2009.

Harris, Grove. "Youth and the Pluralism Project." In *Building the Interfaith Youth Movement: Beyond Dialogue to Action*, edited by Eboo Patel and Patrice Brodeur, 91–100. Lanham, MD: Rowman and Littlefield, 2006.

Harris, Rabia Terri. "Supporting Your Muslim Students: A Guide for Clinical Pastoral Supervisors." *Reflective Practice: Formation and Supervision in Ministry* 29 (2009) 154–69.

Hauschildt, Eberhard. "Interkulturelle Seelsorge als Musterfall für eine Theorie Radikal Interaktiver Seelsorge." In *Handbuch Interkulturelle Seelsorge*, edited by Karl Federschmidt, Eberhard Hausschildt, Christoph Schneider-Harpprecht, Klaus Temme, and Helmut Weiß, 241–61. Neukirchen-Vluyn: Neukirchner Verlag, 2002.

Heckman, Bud, and Rori Picker Neiss, eds. *Interactive Faith: The Essential Interreligious Community-Building Handbook.* Woodstock, VT: Skylight Paths, 2008.

Heim, S. Mark. *Salvations: Truth and Difference in Religion*. Maryknoll, NY: Orbis Books, 1995.

Hewstone, Miles, and Rupert Brown, eds. *Contact and Conflict in Intergroup Encounters*. New York: Basil Blackwell, 1986.

Hewstone, Miles, and Rupert Brown. "Contact Is Not Enough: An Intergroup Perspective on the 'Contact Hypothesis.'" In *Contact and Conflict in Intergroup Encounters*, edited by Miles Hewstone and Rupert Brown, 1–44. New York: Basil Blackwell, 1986.

Hewstone, Miles, and Charles G. Lord. "Changing Intergroup Cognitions and Intergroup Behavior: The Role of Typicality." In *Intergroup Cognition and Intergroup Behavior*, edited by Constantine Sedikides, John Schopler, and Chester A. Insko, 367–92. Mahwah, NJ: Lawrence Erlbaum, 1998.

Hick, John. *A Christian Theology of Religions: The Rainbow of Faiths*. Louisville: Westminster John Knox Press, 1995.

Hogue, David A. *Remembering the Future, Imagining the Past: Story, Ritual, and the Human Brain*. Cleveland: Pilgrim Press, 2003.

Howe, Edith, and Mark Heim. "The Next Thing to Dialogue." In *Interfaith Dialogue at the Grass Roots*, edited by Rebecca Kratz Mays, 47–60. Philadelphia: Ecumenical Press, Temple University, 2008.

Hunter, Rodney, ed. *Dictionary of Pastoral Care and Counseling*. Nashville: Abingdon Press, 1990.

Huntington, Samuel P. *The Clash of Civilizations and the Remaking of World Order*. New York: Simon and Schuster, 1996.

Islamic Society of North America, Chaplain Services, www.isna.net/Leadership/pages /Chaplain-Services.aspx, accessed 07/05/09.

Institute for Christian and Jewish Studies, http://www.icjs.org, accessed 1/22/2011.

Interfaith Alliance, http://www.interfaithalliance.org/about/our-new-identity, accessed 2/27/2011.

Jackson, Lynne M., and Bruce Hunsberger. "An Intergroup Perspective on Religion and Prejudice." *Journal for the Scientific Study of Religion* 38/4 (1999) 509–23.

The Joint Commission. Standard RI.2.10 EP4, www.jointcommission.org, accessed 07/05/09.

Keen, James P. "Young Adult Development, Religious Identity, and Interreligious Solidarity in an Interfaith Learning Community." In *Building the Interfaith Youth Movement: Beyond Dialogue to Action*, edited by Eboo Patel and Patrice Brodeur, 25–41. Lanham, MD: Rowman and Littlefield, 2006.

Kenworthy, Jared B., Rhiannon N. Turner, Miles Hewstone, and Alberto Voci. "Intergroup Contact: When Does It Work, and Why?" In *On the Nature of Prejudice: Fifty Years after Allport*, edited by John F. Dovidio, Peter Glick, and Laurie A. Rudman, 278–92. Malden, MA: Blackwell, 2005.

Kirkwood, Neville A. *A Hospital Handbook on Multiculturalism and Religion*. Harrisburg, PA: Moorehouse, 1993.

Kluckhohn, Clyde, and Henry A. Murray, eds. *Personality in Nature, Society, and Culture*. New York: Alfred Knopf, 1948.

Knitter, Paul. *Introducing Theologies of Religion*. Mayknoll, NY: Orbis Books, 2002.

———. *One Earth, Many Religions: Multifaith Dialogue and Global Responsibillity*. Maryknoll, NY: Orbis Books, 1995.

Kogan, Michael S. "Bringing the Dialogue Home." In *Interfaith Dialogue at the Grass Roots*, edited by Rebecca Kratz Mays, 61–74. Philadelphia: Ecumenical Press, Temple University, 2008.

Kratz Mays, Rebecca, ed. *Interfaith Dialogue at the Grass Roots*. Philadelphia: Ecumenical Press, Temple University, 2008.

Küng, Hans, and Karl-Josef Kuschel. *A Global Ethic. The Declaration of the Parliament of the World Religions*. New York: Continuum, 1993.

Küng, Hans, and Helmut Schmidt. *A Global Ethic and Global Responsibilities: Two Declarations*. London: SCM Press, 1998.

LaCugna, Catherine Mowry. *God for Us: The Trinity and Christian Life*. New York: HaperCollins, 1991.

———. "God in Communion with Us: The Trinity." In *Freeing Theology: The Essentials of Theology in Feminist Perspective*, edited by Catherine Mowry LaCugna, 83–114. New York: HarperCollins, 1993.

Lahaj, Mary. "Making It Up as I Go Along: The Formation of a Muslim Chaplain." *Reflective Practice: Formation and Supervision in Ministry* 29 (2009) 148–53.

Lange, Ernst. *And Yet It Moves: Dream and Reality of the Ecumenical Movement*. Geneva: World Council of Churches; Belfast and Ottawa: Christian Journals, 1979.

Larsen, David J. "Supervising in an Interfaith Environment." *Journal of Supervision and Training in Ministry* 23 (2003) 54–59.

Lartey, Emmanuel Y. *In Living Color: An Intercultural Approach to Pastoral Care and Counseling*. 2nd ed. London: Jessica Kingsley, 2003.

———. "Pastoral Counseling in Multi-Cultural Contexts." In *International Perspectives on Pastoral Counseling*, edited by James Reaves Farris, 317–29. New York: Haworth Press, 2002.

Law, Eric H. F. *The Wolf Shall Dwell with the Lamb: A Spirituality for Leadership in a Multicultural Community*. St. Louis: Chalice Press, 1993.

Lee, Yueh-Ting, Clark McCauley, Fathali Moghaddam, and Stephen Worchel, eds. *The Psychology of Ethnic and Cultural Conflict*. Series: Psychological Dimensions of War and Peace. Westport, CT: Praeger, 2004.

Levine, S. E. Jihad. "Muslim Chaplains in America: Voices from the First Wave." *Reflective Practice: Formation and Supervision in Ministry* 29 (2009) 142–47.

Levy, Naomi. *Talking to God. Personal Prayers in Times of Joy, Sadness, Struggle, and Celebration*. New York: Doubleday, 2003.

Lindbeck, George. *The Nature of Doctrine: Religion and Theology in a Postliberal Age*. Philadelphia: Westminster Press, 1984.

Loller, Travis. "Far from Ground Zero, Opponents Fight New Mosques." Associated Press, 8/8/2010. ABC News, http://abcnews.go.com/US/wireStory?id=11353485, accessed 7/2/2011.

Mackie, Diane M., and David L. Hamilton, eds. *Affect, Cognition, and Stereotyping: Interactive Processes in Group Perception*. San Diego: Academic Press, 1993.

Marty, Martin E., and Scott Appleby, eds. *Religion, Ethnicity, and Self-Identity: Nations in Turmoil*. Hanover, NH: University Press of New England, 1997.

Maugans, Todd A. "The Spiritual History." *Archives of Family Medicine* 5 (1996) 11–16.

McCarthy, Kate. *Interfaith Encounters in America*. Piscataway, NJ: Rutgers University Press, 2007.

McCauley, Clark, Stephen Worchel, Fathali Moghaddam, and Yueh-Ting Lee. "Contact and Identity in Intergroup Relations. In *The Psychology of Ethnic and Cultural*

Conflict. Series: Psychological Dimensions of War and Peace, edited by Yueh-Ting Lee, Clark McCauley, Fathali Moghaddam, and Stephen Worchel, 309–26. Westport, CT: Praeger, 2004.

Miller, Norman, and Marilynn B. Brewer. "Categorization Effects on Ingroup and Outgroup Perception." In *Prejudice, Discrimination, and Racism*, edited by John F. Dovidio and Samuel Gaertner, 209–30. Orlando: Academic Press, 1986.

Miller, Norman, Lynn M. Urban, and Eric J. Vanman. "A Theoretical Analysis of Crossed Social Categorization Effects." In *Intergroup Cognition and Intergroup Behavior*, edited by Constantine Sedikides, John Schopler, and Chester A. Insko, 393–420. Mahwah, NJ: Lawrence Erlbaum, 1998.

Mills, Liston O. "Pastoral Care: History, Traditions, and Definitions." In *Dictionary of Pastoral Care and Counseling*, edited by Rodney Hunter, 836–44. Nashville: Abingdon Press, 1990.

Mitchell, Stephen A. *Relational Concepts in Psychoanalysis: An Integration.* Cambridge, MA: Harvard University Press, 1988.

Mollenkott, Virginia Ramey, ed. *Women of Faith in Dialogue.* New York: Crossroad, 1988.

Monnett, Mike M. "Developing a Buddhist Approach to Pastoral Care: A Peacemaker's View." *The Journal of Pastoral Care and Counseling* 59/1–2 (2005) 57–61.

Mueller, Paul S., David J. Plevak, and Theresa Rummans. "Religious Involvement, Spirituality, and Medicine: Implications for Clinical Practice." *Mayo Clinic Proc* (Mayo Clinic Proceedings) 76 (2001) 1232.

Nagda, Biren (Ratnesh), and Amelia Seraphia Derr. "Intergroup Dialogue: Embracing Difference and Conflict, Engendering Community." In *Education Programs for Improving Intergroup Relations: Theory, Research, and Practice*, edited by Walter G. Stephan and W. Paul Vogt, 133–51. Multicultural Education Series, edited by James A. Banks. New York: Teachers College Press, 2004.

The National Association of Jewish Chaplains. www.najc.org, accessed 07/05/09.

Nederveen Pieterse, Jan. *Globalzation and Culture: Global Melange.* Lanham: Rowman and Littlefield, 2004.

Niebuhr, Gustav. *Beyond Tolerance. Searching for Interfaith Understanding in America.* New York: Viking, 2008.

O'Neill, Maura. *Women Speaking, Women Listening: Women in Interreligious Dialogue.* Maryknoll, NY: Orbis Books, 1990.

Orr, John. "Religion and Multiethnicity in Los Angeles." Center for Religion and Civic Culture, University of Southern California, 1999, http://www.prolades.com/glama /CRCC%20demographics%20%20Los%20Angeles.htm, accessed 1/26/2011.

Oskamp, Stuart, ed. *Reducing Prejudice and Discrimination.* Mahwah, NJ: Lawrence Erlbaum, 2000.

Panikkar, Raimundo. "The Jordan, the Tiber, and the Ganges: Three Kairological Moments of Christic Self-Conciousness." In *The Myth of Christian Uniqueness: Toward a Pluralistic Theology of Religions*, edited by John Hick and Paul F. Ritter. Maryknoll, NY: Orbis Books, 1987.

Patel, Eboo. "Affirming Identity, Achieving Pluralism." In *Building the Interfaith Youth Movement: Beyond Dialogue to Action*, edited by Eboo Patel and Patrice Brodeur, 15–23. Lanham, MD: Rowman and Littlefield, 2006.

Patel, Eboo, and Patrice Brodeur, eds. *Building the Interfaith Youth Movement: Beyond Dialogue to Action.* Lanham, MD: Rowman and Littlefield, 2006.

Patel, Eboo, and Mariah Neuroth. "The Interfaith Youth Core." In *Building the Interfaith Youth Movement: Beyond Dialogue to Action*, edited by Eboo Patel and Patrice Brodeur, 169–180. Lanham, MD: Rowman and Littlefield, 2006.

Pettigrew, Thomas F. "Intergroup Contact Theory." *Annual Review of Psychology* 49 (1998) 65–84.

———. "The Intergroup Hypothesis Reconsidered." In *Contact and Conflict in Intergroup Encounters*, edited by Miles Hewstone and Rupert Brown, 169–95. Social Psychology and Society. Oxford: Basil Blackwell, 1986.

Pettigrew, Thomas F., and Linda R. Tropp. "Allport's Intergroup Contact Hypothesis: Its History and Influence." In *On the Nature of Prejudice: Fifty Years after Allport*, edited by John F. Dovidio, Peter Glick, and Laurie A. Rudman, 262–77. Malden, MA: Blackwell, 2005.

Poling, James. "Wahrnehmung kultureller Differenz und die Machtfrage: Drei Stufen kultureller Analyse." In *Handbuch Interkulturelle Seelsorge*, edited by Karl Federschmidt, Eberhard Hausschildt, Christoph Schneider-Harpprecht, Klaus Temme, and Helmut Weiß, 63–78. Neukirchen-Vluyn: Neukirchner Verlag, 2002.

Powers, Jeanne Audrey. "Women of Faith and This Volume." In *Women of Faith in Dialogue*, edited by Virginia Ramey Mollenkott, 3–6. New York: Crossroad, 1988.

Prentice, Deborah A., and Dale T. Miller. *Cultural Divides: Understanding and Overcoming Group Conflict*. New York: Russel Sage Foundation, 1999.

Prothero, Stephen. *God Is Not One: The Eight Rival Religions That Run The World—and Why Differences Matter*. New York: HarperOne, 2010.

Puchalski, Christina M., and Betty Ferrell, *Making Healthcare Whole: Integrating Spirituality into Patient Care*. West Conshohocken, PA: Templeton Press, 2010.

Puchalski , Christina, and Anna L. Romer. "Taking a Spiritual History Allows Clinicians to Understand Patients More Fully." *Journal of Palliative Medicine* 3/1 (Spring 2000) 129–37, www2.edc.org/lastacts/featureinn.asp, accessed 4/14/2000.

Religions for Peace. http://www.wcrp.org, accessed 1/22/2011.

Riedel-Pfäfflin, Ursula, and Julia Strecker. *Flügel Trotz Allem. Feministische Seelsorge und Beratung. Konzeption, Methoden, Biographien*. Gütersloh: Gütersloher Verlagshaus, 1999.

Ritzer, George. *The McDonaldization of Society*. 6th ed. Thousand Oaks, CA: Pine Forge Press/Sage Publications, 2011.

Roberts, Elizabeth, and Elias Amidon, eds. *Life Prayers from Around the World: 365 Prayers, Blessings, and Affirmations to Celebrate the Human Journey*. San Francisco: Harper Collins, 1996.

Roberts, Richard H. *Religions, Theology, and the Human Sciences*. Cambridge: Cambridge University Press, 2002.

Robertson, Roland. *Globalization: Social Theory and Global Culture*. London: Sage Publications, 1992.

Ruether, Rosemary Radford. *Integrating Ecofeminism, Globalization, and World Religions*. Lanham, MD: Rowman and Littlefield, 2005.

Samartha, Stanley J. *One Christ—Many Religions: Toward a Revised Christology*. Maryknoll, NY: Orbis Books, 1991.

Schipani, Daniel S., and Leah Dawn Bueckert, eds. *Interfaith Spiritual Care: Understandings and Practices*. Kitchener, ON: Pandora Press. In collaboration with the SIPCC, Society for Intercultural Pastoral Care and Counseling, Gesellschaft für interkulturelle Seelsorge und Beratung, Düsseldorf, Germany, 2009.

Schoem, David. "Teaching about Ethnic Identity and Intergroup Relations." In *Multicultural Teaching in the University*, edited by David Schoem, Linda Frankel, Ximena Zúñega, and Edith A. Lewis, 17–25. Westport, CT: Praeger, 1995.

Schoem, David, Linda Frankel, Ximena Zúñega, and Edith A. Lewis, eds. *Multicultural Teaching in the University*. Westport, CT: Praeger, 1995.

Schreiter, Robert J. *The New Catholicity: Theology between the Global and the Local*. Maryknoll, NY: Orbis Books, 1999.

Sedikides, Constantine, John Schopler, and Chester A. Insko, eds. *Intergroup Cognition and Intergroup Behavior*. Mahwah, NJ: Lawrence Erlbaum, 1998.

Sherif, Muzafer, O. J. Harvey, B. Jack White, William R. Hood, and Carolyn W. Sherif. *Intergroup Conflict and Cooperation: The Robber's Cave Experiment*. Norman, OK: University of Oklahoma, Institute of Group Relations, 1961.

Smith, Huston. *The World's Religions: Our Great Wisdom Traditions*. Revised and updated ed. of *The Religions of Man*, 1958. New York: Harper Collins, 1991.

Smith, Wilfred Cantwell. *Toward a World Theology: Faith and the Comparative History of Religion*. Philadelphia: Westminster Press, 1981.

Stephan, Walter G., and Krystina Finlay. "The Role of Empathy in Improving Intergroup Relations." *Journal of Social Issues* 55/4 (1999) 729–43.

Stephan, Walter G., and Cookie W. Stephan. "An Integrated Threat Theory of Prejudice." In *Reducing Prejudice and Discrimination*, edited by Stuart Oskamp, 23–45. Mahwah, NJ: Lawrence Erlbaum, 2000.

———. *Intergroup Relations*. Social Psychology Series. Madison, WI: Brown & Benchmark, 1996.

———. "Intergroup Relations Program Evaluation." In *On the Nature of Prejudice: Fifty Years after Allport*, edited by John F. Dovidio, , Peter Glick, and Laurie A. Rudman, 431–46. Malden, MA: Blackwell, 2005.

Stephan, Walter G., and W. Paul Vogt, eds. *Education Programs for Improving Intergroup Relations: Theory, Research, and Practice*. Multicultural Education Series. New York: Teachers College Press, 2004.

Stern Online. "Volksabstimmung in der Schweiz: Minarett-verbot schockiert Islamvertreter, http://www.stern.de/politik/ausland/volksabstimmung-in-der-schweiz-minarett -verbot-schockiert-islamvertreter-1525833.html, accessed 4/27/10.

Surin, Kenneth. "A 'Politics of Speech': Religious Pluralism in the Age of the McDonald's Hamburger." In *Christian Uniqueness Reconsidered: The Myth of a Pluralistic Theology of Religions*, edited by Gavin D'Costa, 192–212. Maryknoll, NY: Orbis Books, 1998.

Tajfel, Henri, and John C. Turner. "The Social Identity Theory of Intergroup Behavior." In *Psychology of Intergroup Relations*, 2nd ed., edited by Stephen Worchel and William G. Austin, 7–24. Chicago: Nelson-Hall, 1986.

Taylor, Bonita E., and David J. Zucker. "Nearly Everything We Wish Our Non-Jewish Supervisors Had Known about Us As Jewish Supervisees." *Journal of Pastoral Care and Counseling* 56/4 (2002) 327–40.

Taylor, Donald M., and Fathali M. Moghaddam. *Theories of Intergroup Relations: International Social Psychological Perspectives*. 2nd ed. Westport, CT: Praeger, 1994.

Tinker, George E. "On Not Requiring CPE for All Lutheran Students: A Letter." *Journal of Supervision and Training in Ministry* 14 (1992–1993) 175–79.

Toback, Phyllis Brooks. "A Theological Reflection on Baptism by a Jewish Chaplain. *Journal of Pastoral Care* 47/3 (1993) 315–17.

Tomlinson, John. *Globalization and Culture*. Chicago: University Press of Chicago, 1999.

Truitner, Ken and Nga. "Death and Dying in Buddhism." In *Ethnic Variations in Dying, Death, and Grief: Diversity in Universality*, edited by Donald P. Irish, Kathleen F. Lundquist, and Vivian Jenkins Nelson. Philadelphia: Taylor & Francis, 1993.

United Religions Initiative, www.uri.org, accessed 1/22/2011.

Vanman, Eric J., and Norman Miller. "Applications of Emotion Theory and Research on Stereotyping and Intergroup Relations." In *Affect, Cognition, and Stereotyping: Interactive Processes in Group Perception*, edited by Diane M. Mackie and David L. Hamilton, 213–37. San Diego: Academic Press, 1993.

Vatican. "Declaration on The Relation of the Church to Non-Christian Religions, *Nostra Aetate*, Proclaimed by His Holiness Pope Paul VI on October 28, 1965." http://www.vatican.va/archive/hist_councils/ii_vatican_council/documents/vat-ii_decl_19651028_nostra-aetate_en.html, accessed 1/27/2011.

Weintraub, Simkha Y. "Mi Sheberakh: May the One Who Blessed. The traditional Jewish prayer for the sick." http://www.myjewishlearning.com/texts/Liturgy_and _Prayers/Siddur_Prayer_Book/Torah_Service/Prayer_for_the_Sick.shtml, accessed 5/17/2011.

Weiß, Helmut. "Die Entdeckung interkultureller Seelsorge. Entwicklung interkultureller Kompetenz in Seelsorge und Beratung durch international Begegnungen." In *Handbuch Interkulturelle Seelsorge*, edited by Karl Federschmidt, Eberhard Hausschildt, Christoph Schneider-Harpprecht, Klaus Temme, and Helmut Weiß, 17–37. Neukirchen-Vluyn: Neukirchner Verlag, 2002.

———. "Seelsorgeausbildung. Begegnung in der Differenz. Einübung interkultureller Wahrnehmung für Seelsorge und Beratung." In *Handbuch Interkulturelle Seelsorge*, edited by Karl Federschmidt, Eberhard Hausschildt, Christoph Schneider-Harpprecht, Klaus Temme, and Helmut Weiß, 262–74. Neukirchen-Vluyn: Neukirchner Verlag, 2002.

Wilder, David A. "The Role of Anxiety in Facilitating Stereotypic Judgments of Outgroup Behavior." In *Affect, Cognition, and Stereotyping: Interactive Processes in Group Perception*, edited by. Diane M. Mackie and David L. Hamilton, 87–109. San Diego: Academic Press, 1993.

Wood, Karen. "Seminarians Interacting." In *Building the Interfaith Youth Movement: Beyond Dialogue to Action*, edited by Eboo Patel and Patrice Brodeur, 101–108. Lanham, MD: Rowman and Littlefield, 2006.

Worchel, Stephen. "The Role of Cooperation in Reducing Intergroup Conflict." In *Psychology of Intergroup Relations*, 2nd ed., edited by Stephen Worchel and William G. Austin , 288–304. Nelson-Hall Series in Psychology. Chicago: Nelson-Hall, 1986.

Worchel, Stephen, and William G. Austin. *Psychology of Intergroup Relations*. 2nd ed. Nelson-Hall Series in Psychology. Chicago: Nelson-Hall, 1986.

World Council of Churches, http://www.oikoumene.org/, accessed 1/22/2011.

World Council of Churches. *Guidelines on Dialogue with People of Living Faiths and Ideologies*. Geneva, Switzerland: WCC Publications, 1979.

World Council of Churches. *My Neighbour's Faith and Mine*. Geneva, Switzerland: WCC Publications, 1989.

Wuthnow, Robert. *America and the Challenges of Religious Diversity.* Princeton, NJ: Princeton University Press, 2005.

Yalom, Irvin D., with Molyn Leszcz. *The Theory and Practice of Group Psychotherapy.* 5th ed. New York: Basic Books, 2005.

Zeit Online. "Volksentscheid.Schweizer stimmen gegen Bau neuer Minarette."Online: http://www.zeit.de/politik/ausland/2009-11/schweiz-minarett-wahl, accessed 4/7/2010.

Zumach, Andreas. "Analyse des Schweizer Referendums. Frauen stimmten gegen Minarette." Die Tageszeitung Online. Taz.de, http://www.taz.de/1/politik/europa/artikel/1/frauen-gegen-minarette/, accessed 4/13/10.

Subject/Name Index